THE ART OF PHOTOGRAPHY
Image and Illusion

D1569820

GENE MARKOWSKI

University of Virginia

PRENTICE-HALL, INC., Englewood Cliffs, New Jersey 07632

Library of Congress Cataloging in Publication Data

Markowski, Gene (date)
 The art of photography.

 Bibliography: p. 222
 Includes index.
 1. Photography, Artistic. I. Title.
TR642.M36 1984   770   83-9703
ISBN 0-13-047705-2

This book is dedicated to the many students with whom I have been fortunate enough to be associated over the years I have been teaching, for it is they who have been my most accurate critics and most patient teachers.

Editorial/production supervision and interior design: Virginia Rubens
Page layout: Meryl Poweski
Cover design: Ben Santora
Manufacturing buyer: Harry Baisley

Printed in the United States of America

10 9 8 7 6 5 4 3 2 1

ISBN 0-13-047705-2

Prentice-Hall International, Inc., London
Prentice-Hall of Australia Pty. Limited, Sydney
Editora Prentice-Hall do Brasil, Ltda., Rio de Janeiro
Prentice-Hall Canada Inc., Toronto
Prentice-Hall of India Private Limited, New Delhi
Prentice-Hall of Japan, Inc., Tokyo
Prentice-Hall of Southeast Asia Pte. Ltd., Singapore
Whitehall Books Limited, Wellington, New Zealand

CONTENTS

PREFACE

Photography is the most influential art of our own period in history, depicting in vivid imagery the riches of daily experience, the defeats and triumphs of the human spirit.

In this book will be raised intellectual questions central to the photographic medium both through the example of individual photographs and through personal theories and observations. Photography will be discussed from the multiple standpoints of perception, aesthetics, the visual principles, the relationship of photography to the other arts, and the creative process as it relates to the photographer, rather than from a single, narrow point of view. Every effort has been made to let the photographs speak for themselves while directing attention to the various aspects of photography already mentioned. I have tried to strike a just balance between the art and science of photography. All aspects of photography covered, even briefly, have been focused in the theory that photography, like the other arts, is a human action, which reflects the psychological, physiological, intellectual, and emotional aspects of all humanity.

Photography, the truly new art of the nineteenth and twentieth centuries, can record rapidly life at its most terrifying, harsh, cruel, and destructive, and life in its most glorious moments. With the efficient tools of this medium, the photographer can express all aspects of existence. Through photography we may observe directly and without explanation the totality of human behavior, action, experience, and individual decisions. Whatever may determine or color the photographer's attitude toward life or that of his subjects can be observed in the image and made possible by the uninterpreting lens of the camera.

The aim of this book may best be stated in the form of a question: "What is photography?" This question implies another: "What does photography mean in the twentieth century?" The book is intended to suggest answers to these questions by examining some of photography's historical concerns, its visual principles, its content, some of its leading personalities, and its relationship to the other arts from a predominantly visual approach. It is my hope that, in a direct, straightforward way, this book will assist those who hold every shade of opinion about photography and bring them closer to the truth. And, for those who already embrace photography, this book may enhance their already firm belief.

Acknowledgments

I am indebted to the authors and publishers named in the following pages for permission to reproduce copyrighted material, and to the many photographers, collectors, museums, galleries, foundations, and historical societies who have kindly granted me permission to reproduce the photographs named in the captions. I am deeply grateful in particular to Marnie Gillett, assistant to the director of Light Gallery in New York, for her patience and cooperativeness with my many requests in organizing the illustrations for this book. Her intuitive understanding of my project when it was first proposed to her, and her endless efforts to work with the photographers of the Light Gallery in order to have their work represented here, have made this project a reality. I also wish to give special thanks to the photographers Helena Almeida, Heribert Burkert, Jill Gussow, Michael Northrup, Helmut and Gabriele Nothhelfer, Ron Talbott, Herbert Bayer, and Todd Webb for their generous contributions of their photographs.

I also thank the staff of the Museum of Modern Art and The International Museum of Photography at George Eastman House for their constant help over the many months of preparing the illustrations.

My warm thanks to Mr. George M. Craven, Professor of Photography at De Anza College, and to Mr. Stan Tatum for their criticisms and suggestions which have helped to make this book more useful. To my colleagues, Charles Abbey, James Cargile, Walter Korte, and David Weiss, warm thanks for their invaluable suggestions and assistance with technical information. To Virginia Rubens, who endured my inconsistent working procedures over many months and still managed to get the material for the book into production, I give thanks and gratitude. A special note of appreciation is due to Bud Therien for his confidence in me and in the idea for this book. His patience with my delays and changes in the material has been the mainstay of everyone's efforts in making the book a reality. To Janice Gurley, who struggled to type my manuscript with its many insertions and deletions, I am especially thankful.

Last and most important, I am grateful to G. P., who was my constant critic and support, and urged me on as I inched my way through the material forming the body of the book.

Gene Markowski

INTRODUCTION:
Photography and Us

Since its invention scarcely more than a century and half ago, photography has become not only a phenomenal technical means of communication and visual expression, but unquestionably the world's most powerful image-making system. Considering its brief history, the quick growth and global acceptance of photography have been astonishing. No one alive today, save perhaps in a handful of remote mountainous, oceanic, or jungle areas, can escape the media of illustrated publication and television, and thus photography has provided the form in which our view of the world and of ourselves is inevitably cast.

At first, aspiring artists used the new discovery as a convenient shortcut for the manual skills required by some of the older, established art disciplines, but these artists were soon to discover that the photograph could replace neither manual skills, vision, nor imagination. Surprisingly, photography has turned out to be an art form in itself, exercising a profound effect on every individual who has come in contact with it. Whether this effect has been consciously recognized is not the question. Photography has indeed changed us in ways sometimes subtle, sometimes dramatic, that the traditional arts have not.

Nonetheless many still find it difficult to accept photography as more than record-keeping, a visual equivalent of the computer's task of the impersonal storage and retrieval of information. Despite its permeation of every aspect of our daily lives, the photographic medium and its influence have not been given the serious study they deserve. It may perhaps be the quasi-scientific aspect of photography with its array of lenses, shutters, timers, films, papers, and chemicals, in which the photographer seems merely the operator of a machine, that has blinded art historians to the creative aspects of photography, and blocked the exploration of its principles and implications by art theorists. Central to this book is the contention that photography is an art, that it is today's art, and that its future, however unpredictable, promises to be a part of our lives for longer than anyone can foresee. It can moreover be seriously claimed that there is no single art form that has not been affected in some measure by photography, and that most have been radically transformed by the new vision of the photographic lens.

The past decade has even seen the other arts, in particular painting and drawing, turning directly to photography for technical and creative guidance. But more often than not, only the superficial aspects of photography have been given consideration, so that the result for painting and drawing was a demonstrably troubling, at times desperate, struggle, resulting in nothing more than painted copies of photographs. This was, however, a sign that the arts were growing closer and furthermore, that the traditional barriers between them were giving way to a new freedom, making possible a new artistic synthesis.

The emergence of photography as a modern, scientifically based medium was the most important modern bridge between science and art. Photography has steadily advanced both technologically and creatively in an unbroken flow of images in which human certainty has declared itself. But, as in the other visual arts, that certainty has not been unshakable, since behind the scientific equipment of the medium operate human error and fallibility. Nonetheless, as a medium characteristic of our time, it has served humanity in countless ways and will continue to do so in the future.

In my view, photography and those who practice it have established an aesthetic specific to the medium, but one that has also affected the other arts. The effects of photography's aesthetic have not yet been fully assessed, although there have been faint glimmers of such an understanding through what is now known as regional art, both in the 1930s and in the present. Just as philosophies generate philosophies, and ideas bring about more ideas, so photography's aesthetic will, I firmly believe, assist in the birth of a new aesthetic for some of the other arts. If we can understand ourselves more clearly by means of an awareness of the senses brought to us through photography, then we also can better understand our relationship to the environment and to each other. Photography cannot produce any quick, ready-made solutions or insights as to how we may best use our senses or perceptions, but it can offer points of entry leading to the center of each individual's awareness, where personal solutions may be reached. The rationalism inherent in the photographic process greatly assists us in the comprehension of the complex forces which produce our society, our culture, our science, and the total environment we live in.

Although no chapter in this book has been devoted to how to "read" a photograph, this subject is covered in detail throughout. In reading photographs it is important to be aware that they have relevance to themselves, not to painting, drawing, or graphic work of any sort. If we can recognize that relevance and let the photograph speak to us without intermediary we have touched the very core of what it means to be able to read photographs. Preconceived ideas of the nature of a photograph will inevitably prevent multi-readings from occurring and thus will become still another ossifying norm.

It takes time and effort to read any work of art. If we take the time and make the effort it is often surprising what the photograph will reveal as it unfolds and discloses the intangibles of meaning and mood. The spirit of the photographer, the integrity of technical performance, iconography, and style are but a few aspects which may be read from a sheet of printed photographic paper. Part of each photographic reading is the significance of the title. Titles are in a way images in themselves, whether or not they are coordinated with the visible image. They can be explicit, literary, paradoxical, unintelligible, or nonsensical. The significance of the title cannot be underrated in reading photographs, for it is as much an affirmation of the photographer as is the photograph itself.

Photographic reading is not a uniform experience then, but a pluriform phenomenon not limited to a methodology, a person, or a group of persons. It is at once personal and universal with the authority based in the photograph, which is an extension of the photographer. To look at a photograph is to enjoy it, but to look at it and read it is to discover its distinctions and multiplicity of functions, and above all else the creative endeavor of the human spirit.

From prehistoric cave paintings to the present day, image-making has been ultimately based on perception. A superstructure consisting of experience and instinctual and acquired motivations rests on this perceptual base. Added to this superstructure are the various environmental and social forces which help to shape perceptions and conceptions during the period when the work of art was created. It is from this combination of interacting factors that endlessly variable images and illusions are born.

When Spinoza said that "the mind can create sensations and ideas which are not of real things," he was speaking about conceptual attitudes, and of perceptual attitudes when he said, "For after having contrived some fiction and given it its assent, the mind can no longer conceive or fashion it in any other way. . . ."[1] Artistic creations born of perception and conception change or affirm the observer's own perceptions and conceptions. In the past before the invention of the camera, other artistic disciplines such as painting, sculpture, and drawing exerted a considerable influence over perception and conception. Today the artistic search for illusionism through still and moving photography has effected an even greater influence upon perception and conception.

The distinction between the illusion-image and reality will always remain as a dichotomy since one cannot become the other, nor can one replace the other. At best the relationship is temporal, ending with the completion of the work of art, at which time it becomes its own reality.

Artistic representations are images and illusions which result from external circumstance (perception) becoming internalized (conception) and eventually formalized into an object or image. The seemingly endless number of variables which shape both perception and conception within the artist, resulting in images and illusions, go beyond the scope of this book. Perhaps we can understand this subject better through our own observations of images and illusions which have stood the test of time. In them we may discover that the artist as an interpreter and image maker has brought together through his or her particular medium and vocabulary an illusion which reveals life's experience in a new and vital way.

Images and illusions are more than an affirmation of existence—the artist's and ours; they form a synthesis between physical being and the human spirit and a meeting ground for the sensory world and the metaphysical or symbolic divested of time, where mind and spirit are at once enclosed and disclosed.

Today, artists of exceptional talent, as many as possible of whom have been included in this book, expand our consciousness in unpredictable ways through internal and external vision, declaring the verities of photography and exploring its unpredictable future, without forgetting the foundations on which photography rests.

[1]Footnote references are found in "Notes to the Text" section on page 221.

There is no separate absolute identity for art and life; they are counterparts mirroring one another. To place limitations on either one takes the celebration out of both. The expression of the human spirit in art is possible only when that spirit is free to exist both within and outside the traditions of art and life.

We now come to what is perhaps the greatest achievement of photography as much as of any other art, a quality known as "transcendence"—the capacity to rise above the layers of ordinary experience into higher realms of feeling, thought, and meaning. In art as in life transcendence is a process taking place for the most part in the subconscious, and surfacing at times to consciousness through positive creation or through ordinary human actions and gestures. Through the work of art, which demonstrates the artist's transcendence, we may also better understand our own need for the same transcendence in everyday life.

On the other hand, not only does any inability of the artist to transcend human problems result in personality disorder, but the work of art becomes mannered and "strange" through the disruption of the creative process. That is not to say that works produced under such circumstances are necessarily inferior, but that they simply take on meanings different from those which demonstrate artistic and personal transcendence. Photographs, like all works of art, are signs either of the individual's capacity to transcend or of his inability to do so, and of course much more than this. But no matter which aspect of transcendence we may be observing in the work of art, the principal benefit is that the human spirit within the work may enrich our own emotional and intellectual life in one way or another, and that the artist's freedom to lay bare his inner life through the work of art should encourage us in a rediscovery of the self and of reality.

1 THE PHOTOGRAPH

For many people the photograph is something of a mystery. What is a photograph? This question will have as many answers as there are photographers. However, there will be, in all probability, an overlapping of ideas and definitions. Here are some of the answers given by eminent photographers.

Berenice Abbott:

> The photograph may be presented as finely and artistically as you will; but to merit serious consideration, must be directly connected with the world we live in. What we need is a return, on a mounting spiral of historic understanding, to the great tradition of realism. Since ultimately the photograph is a statement, a document of the now, a greater responsibility is put on us.

Ansel Adams:

> A photograph is not an accident—it is a concept. It exists at, or before the moment of exposure of the negative. From that moment on to the final print, the process is chiefly one of *craft;* the pre-visualized photograph is rendered in terms of the final print by a series of processes peculiar to the medium. But when a photograph has the "feel" of an etching or a lithograph, or any other graphic medium, it is questionable—just as questionable as a painting that is photographic in character.

Aaron Siskind:

> The business of making a photograph may be said in simple terms to consist of three elements: the objective world (whose permanent condition is change and disorder), the sheet of paper on which the picture will be realized, and the experience which brings them together.

Harry Callahan:

> The photographs that excite me are photographs that say something in a new manner; not for the sake of being different, but ones that are different because the individual is different and the individual expressed himself.

Minor White:

> When any photograph functions for a given person as an Equivalent we can say that at that moment and for that person the photograph acts as a symbol or plays the role of a metaphor for something that is beyond the subject photographed.

And last of all a quote from Edward Steichen, not just on what a photograph is, but on photography:

> As photography I would include color images directly projected on a screen by colored beams of light, even when made without the intervention of the camera.[1]

Each of these photographers has a very clear idea of what a photograph is, what it is not, and what it can be; but the central thought is that creativity, self-expression, and the individual experience are of the utmost importance to the photograph. The craft, or chemical-mechanical processes which are a part of the photograph, do not share equal footing with the more theoretical portions of the statements on the photograph.

A photograph may be said to have two aspects, factual and theoretical. Factually, the photograph is generally considered to be the result of a series of mechanical devices, such as the camera, enlarger, lenses, filters, and all of the other equipment in and out of the darkroom, as well as the chemical processes, developers, fixers, washes, and so on. But beyond this basic understanding of its elementary processes, what is it that makes photography different from the other visual arts, and yet so much a part of them? It is two-dimensional; however, there are efforts being made at three-dimensional photography, and it presents a suggestion of space that is uniquely its own. Photographic space is derived from the camera and enlarger lenses, which produce a monocular vision, compared to the binocular vision of the human eyes, and eliminate what is known as peripheral vision. The density and sense of weight of objects one may feel in a painting is absent from the photograph, which is the result of the lens. A time-space dimension, which is the central and inherent factor in filmmaking, is absent in the photograph. This dimension is frozen or in a state of suspended animation; it can neither telescope nor extend the time-space factor, even though there have been efforts to do so through sequential narrative photostories. Compared to the other arts, the photograph has its own special relationship between time and image. Beyond the obvious, literal images depicting movement in time in the work of such photographers and painters as Eadweard Muybridge and Thomas Eakins, as well as a great many photojournalistic photographs in which time is captured by the depiction of movement in an event, time as a subject and as an integral part of the photograph can be perceived and executed with greater imagination. In dealing with time, the photographer is at once in control and out of control of the photograph and the photographic process. While he may have power over the time element in relation to certain laboratory procedures and camera technicalities as well as decisions concerning time and object relationships, many other time elements completely escape the control of the photographer.

Time and light are the two fundamentals of photography and constitute its direct links with science, but it is the method by which these fundamentals are manipulated that joins photography with art. With the exception of filmmaking, no visual art form other than photography includes time as a crucial, demanding, elemental part of the medium. Photographers who understand time beyond the basic level have at their disposal the possibility for greater creative efforts.

Time is the measurement and controller of all activity, of life itself. Time is often divided simply into past, present, and future. These divisions may be clearly understood if we imagine a matrix consisting of an endless vertical line intersected by an endless horizontal line, with the present represented by the point where the two lines intersect one another, the past below the intersection and the future above it. The lateral space beyond the intersection of the point of now is everywhere else in time. Imagine the point of now being able to move upward along the vertical line, and we have the present moving into the future and future events, but the point always remains in the present regardless of the distance covered into the future.

When a photographer releases the shutter on the camera to record an image, that action is performed in the present and instantly becomes part of the past. But it is quite possible that the action itself may have been predetermined, or even a kind of accidental stumbling into the event. If we think of this action taking place along the vertical time line of the time matrix which may hold other events as well, the matrix may then become a time-space matrix. The latent image, when developed, and the print itself in this context, then, are past actions produced in the present when they are actually realized in the photographic lab, the result being the isolation of a moment of time. It is as if a single frame from an endless moving picture had been lifted from the film and allowed to exist outside of the film's total time span and meaning. "Freezing" a momentary event isolates it from its relationship to other times, actions, events, and meanings, and brings it into a new situation, automatically giving it another significance.

This single action by the photographer tripping the shutter of the camera has a number of important ramifications in relation to time and the photograph. Cartier-Bresson's term "the decisive moment" tells us that in the passage of time, the physical world, the seen and unseen, are in constant change as the present moves into the future, and that the photographer must in an instant of time decide when and how to freeze that moment. In that instant of time the photographer concentrates from his conscious and subconscious mind all his creative energies to a single point. The image he creates will ultimately reflect that moment, and all the qualities, both inner and outer, of the object will be revealed in the photograph for others to perceive. Of particular significance is that when a photographer understands the time elements and object qualities in this respect, avoiding mere physical likenesses, the photograph becomes more than an exclusive expression of the originator's personality; rather, it reaches other levels of significance for those who see the image as well. In this light, it cuts a path through one-, two-, and three-dimensional concepts of time and space, into the fourth dimension.

The photograph, unlike other works of art, such as music, which has a predetermined duration of listening time to grasp total meaning, does not place time requirements upon the perceiver. Further, unlike a narrative, the photograph can present its entirety to the perceiver's eyes at once. Whatever additional time is spent in front of the photograph is entirely determined by the perceiver. But one must also remember that those who perceive the image will view that isolated moment according to their own understanding of time and their own relationship to reality.

Photographers such as Paul Caponigro, Aaron Siskind, and Minor White have produced photographs that seek out those inner qualities of objects which free them of time and space. These photographers do not concern themselves with literal representation, but move toward abstract expression, and thus align themselves with time concepts found in most nonvocal music, the supreme art form, which cuts directly into the fourth dimension, free of visual images and common, general time concepts.

General perceptions of physical reality, time, and space are based primarily on physiological responses feeding the information to the mind, and these are generally superficial perceptions which do not allow deeper perceptions to occur when limited to physical external appearances alone. Those mysterious regions of the mind, when allowed to respond to the past and future realities, can lend greater meaning to isolated moments of time held within the context of the photograph. Whatever time-leaps or time-distances the photographer wishes to cover, he can do chiefly by internal time configurations of the imagination expressed through the photograph. But as Einstein said, "Time and motion are relative concepts," and one need only compare the work of such photographers as Henri Cartier-Bresson, Robert Capa, Anne Noggle, or Wynn Bullock (see Figure 3-4, page 79) to understand the truth of Einstein's statement. For each of these photographers, time is an internal voyage of the mind specific to his own personality. Events which anticipate or depict change are evident in each of these images and link them together as experience in time.

Throughout the history of photography, the photograph has served as a document of the human life span in all its positive and negative aspects, and reminds us each in its own way of our own humanity. The photograph, which has depicted changing cultures, societies, and customs, reminds us that all human efforts are regulated by time, as are the lives of those whose efforts are depicted. The photograph, not exempt from time as a regulator, is the perfect contemporary time capsule in which the time of human existence is documented, affirmed, and preserved.

The photograph can be reproduced indefinitely through the repeated use of the negative, and it is here that the graphic medium and the photograph may have a common ground, as etching, silkscreen, woodcut, and so on may also be reproduced many times. The photographic image may also be manipulated so that new and varied images can be devised by the simple manipulation of the negative, as well as by the use of a variety of other techniques, such as the Sabattier effect, toners, various photographic papers, chemicals, and filters.

Fred Endsley's solarized print *Fred and Ivan* (Figure 1-1) is an outstanding example of the sort of photomanipulation that creates exciting images outside the mainstream of the "straight photograph" or the unmanipulated negative or print. Endsley's photograph and many others in this category keep photography growing as a changing and vital art form. These photographers are in many respects the lifeline and the hope for the future of photography.

Factual visual information that cannot be seen by the unaided human eye can be recorded by the photograph, such as the clouds of gas and dust four thousand light years away, photographed with a 200-inch lens in red light (Figure 1-2), or the photograph taken with a bentograph at 50 fathoms (293 feet) of sea whips, sea urchins, and worm tubes on the ocean floor at Jewfish Point, Santa Catalina Island, California (Figure 1-3). Although these images are scientific, they are images that artists and art photographers have been finding a stimulus for their own work.

Figure 1-1   FRED ENDSLEY, *Fred and Ivan* (solarized print—multiple solarization) (Courtesy of the photographer)

Figure 1-2   HALE OBSERVATORIES,
Cone Nebula (Courtesy of
Palomar Observatory, California
Institute of Technology)

Figure 1-3   *Sea Whips* (Courtesy of Allan Hancock Foundation, University of Southern California)

Photographs produced to give us documents and records of places, events, objects, and information are often seen and accepted as works of art. Consider the photograph of the astronaut Colonel Edwin E. Aldrin, taken on the moon during the Apollo 11 mission, July 16, 1969 (Figure 1-4). This exciting and stunning event in the history of American technology was documented by astronaut Neil Armstrong. Photojournalistic images such as WeeGee's biting and satirical photograph *The Critic*, 1943 (Figure 1-5) not only give visual factual information, but make a social statement. Hector Rondin's photograph *Aid from the Padre* (Figure 1-6) shows us Father Luis Manuel Padilla, a Venezuelan navy chaplain, holding up a government soldier in a street after the soldier was wounded during an uprising in 1962. Rondin's photograph not only documents a horrifying event but speaks of compassion photographed and compassion expressed by the photographer.

Figure 1-4   NEIL ARMSTRONG, *Apollo 11 Mission* (Courtesy of NASA Lyndon B. Johnson Space Center)

Figure 1-5 WEEGEE, *The Critic* (Collection of The Art Institute of Chicago)

FIGURE 1-6   HECTOR RONDIN, *Aid
from the Padre* (Wide World Photos)

A photograph and a photographer can show intense emotion, and both can plumb the depths of the human condition and reveal to us facets of human existence of which we may not have been aware. It is another sort of factual information that often is explored by the fine art photographer as well as by the photojournalist, and those photographs are intended as documents. Diane Arbus's *Puerto Rican Woman with a Beauty Mark* (Figure 1-7), photographed in New York City in 1965, shows us human dignity and interior life revealed through an easily intelligible photograph of great psychological insight. This photograph goes beyond visual information; deeper and more significant revelations are made not by what we see but by what we do not see. It is this which gives this type of photograph its dynamic and shattering power. *Death Comes to the Old Lady*, by Duane Michals (Figure 1-8), is a photostory composed of sequential photographs, which speaks of the spiritual world, the photographer's and ours. We tend to accept the action in this series, not because of what we see—the photograph is the truth—but because of what we know it to be, a depiction of an unseen reality that each of us will experience. We recognize this event, the invisible and the visible interacting, the inevitable that each of us experiences, in this photographic narrative that tends to enclose the coherence of time. *Poet's*

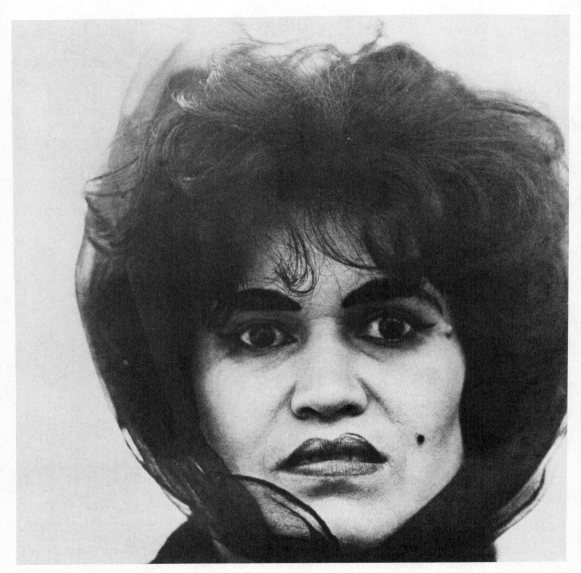

FIGURE 1-7 DIANE ARBUS, *Puerto Rican Woman with a Beauty Mark,* N.Y.C. 1965 (Copyright © 1965 The Estate of Diane Arbus)

(1)

(2)

(3)

(4)

(5)

Figure 1-8 DUANE MICHALS, *Death Comes to the Old Lady* (Duane Michals Inc.)

House (Figure 1-9), by Jerry Uelsmann, like the photograph by Michals, reveals the inner life of the photographer, but *Poet's House* arises from the subconscious inner life, with a resulting image that does not rely only upon the external physical world for image results. While the photograph refers to external stimuli, it is carefully manipulated through photographic procedures so that the end result is a highly developed imaginative image which allows us to participate in a complete world of fantasy, not reliant upon external stimuli, but motivated by internal vision. It is a dream world of a certain complexity, filled with symbolism, allowing and encouraging reflections on our own dream world.

In 1936 Kodachrome film and Agfacolor (invented at about the same time in Germany) made available to still photography what had earlier been available only to motion pictures—the color photograph. In 1950 the reversal film Ektachrome became available to photographers, allowing them to do their own color processing. This film was invented by Leopold Mannes and Leopold Godowsky in cooperation with the staff at the research laboratories of the Eastman Kodak Company. In 1963 Edwin H. Land released his Polacolor material through Polaroid. These inventions in color photography opened an entire new world of color to the public, with an immense impact upon advertising as well as upon science, and made the world of art available to everyone through color reproduction. Professions that existed only in germ before the inventions of photography were fully realized with its aid, while others were born as the direct result of the photograph. The profession of art history, until about 1860 largely the province of archivists and antiquarians, became transfigured by the photograph, and much later by the color photograph. For the first time, works of art could be documented and presented to large audiences within the context of their historical and creative development by the use of the photograph and lantern slide. For nearly a century, the black-and-white photograph dominated as a teaching aid in the history of art. The photograph, with its ability to bring detailed information of a work of art, made the study of works of art an easier process for the scholars within art history. Stained glass windows or sculpture in hard-to-reach places, which were impossible to reproduce fully by such means as drawings and engravings, were now within easy reach through the photograph. Within a short period of time, the work of the art historian could be published with fully illustrated photographs in the form of books and periodicals, bringing the study and appreciation of art to the general public and the specialist as well. University and college art departments and art schools accepted the new possibilities opened up by the photograph and were soon offering an array of classes in the history of art as well as a number of degrees for various special areas within the field.

As André Malraux's thesis, *The Museum Without Walls*, postulates, the average person's knowledge and understanding of art is for the most part based on photographs of art, in color and black-and-white, reproduced in the huge number of art books published today. Many of the publishing houses specialize in the "artist monograph," a single book or series of books composed of superb photographs of one artist's production, which also serves as a means for the art historian to present investigations, discoveries, and theories about the artist and his or her work. The photograph has been of invaluable service to the art historian,

Figure 1-9 JERRY UELSMANN, *Poet's House* (Courtesy of the photographer)

often revealing certain aspects of an artist's work that had, until seen in the photograph, gone totally unnoticed. Malraux's concept of the museum without walls has not only been of great service to the public, but has become the museum where we may observe the growing knowledge of art through photographs and the written word of the scholar.

One of the most inventive and original uses of color and black-and-white Polaroid material in art has been the work of the painter-sculptor-photographer Lucas Samaras. His use of this medium has released through the photograph all the psychological and emotional forces of color available to him (Figure 1-10). He explores aspects of autoeroticism-narcissism and turns his own body into a living work of art. In Samaras's self-portrait, extraordinary honesty and openness of spirit confront the observer by means of the Polaroid photograph. Here is highly personal color, invented and actual, combined in a kaleidoscopic color structure of the highest order.

Imagine the world without photographs. How different would our opinions, ideas, concepts, and desires be from what they are now? Through such photographic specialties as documentations, photojournalism, and advertising photography, many of our concepts and ideas about the world and ourselves have been shaped and continue to change on a daily basis. Politically, economically, and socially, our lives are shifting and changing through continual exposure to this powerful medium. The deliberately subliminal photograph that reaches us through television, through publications, as well as through a variety of other media, can often be a seductive force operating on the subconscious of the observer. Without our fully realizing why certain of our wants and desires change, they are transformed by the reality of this type of photograph, within the meshed complex of the media and advertising. An enormous industry has

Figure 1-10   LUCAS SAMARAS,
Phototransformations #6469
(Collection, The Museum of
Modern Art, New York. Gift of the
American Art Foundation)

been built upon the simple snapshot. While this little personal photograph has generally been taken for granted by the amateur as entertainment or hobby, it must be remembered that from the days of the Brownie box-camera to its present sophisticated incarnation, it has played an extensive role in our lives. It has been an important factor in the social life of the family unit, peer groups, and the economy. The ubiquitous snapshot has finally found itself elevated to museum, gallery, and collector status as an accepted art form practiced by professionals.

While this consideration of the photograph has pointed out some of the more obvious factual aspects, it by no means covers all that might be said. Its social, economic, artistic, and scientific roles, as well as its role as a transmitter of ideas and information, have been only lightly touched upon as a means of introducing the photograph.

From a theoretical point of view, the photograph becomes more controversial. Relatively speaking, the photograph is the youngest child in the family of the visual arts, yet within a short period of time, its presence has been considered informative, disintegrative, authoritative, revolutionary, and problematic in its aesthetic. Yet this child of the arts stays with us, astonishing and disappointing in its growth alongside the other visual arts. It has established itself within this brief period as a powerful phenomenon, to be accepted as an authentic expressive artistic medium in our most recent history of the arts. In its short evolutionary period, the photograph has had a far-reaching formative influence upon our understanding of the general aesthetic of the arts, and has led to a deepening of our own comprehension of human visual perception. It is the individual visual, emotional, and intellectual experience, united with the immediacy of the medium, that places the photograph in a unique position relative to the other visual arts. This important and fundamental position is central to the photograph; beyond this spirit of the photograph lies mere craft. It is this aspect of the photograph that places it in a remarkable role which painting, for example, is unable to fill. Whether the form the photograph assumes is documentary, photojournalistic, advertising, or artistic, the vitality, energy, and spirit spring from the inexhaustible variety of the internal and external human experience. Through photographs, ideas of great fertility and complexity are made apparent by means of images recording the multiform consecutive or simultaneous experiences of the individual. The stream of consciousness, a process usually relegated to the psychiatrist's office, is often operational and compatible with the effective recording speed of the camera. The interaction and flow of ideas, thoughts, and emotions, unifying with and guiding the camera, allow the photographer not only to record and to form equivalents, but to have the opportunity to select material that in turn becomes the photograph. The process may reveal hidden experience, bring forth images long forgotten or half remembered, and serve as an information source. A result could be the catalyst which sets in motion conscious or subconscious investigations, resulting in a photograph or photographs of highly charged image and content for the photographer.

In a direct reference to drawing, one may find that throughout the recorded history of art, artists have maintained sketchbooks of one sort or another, filled with conscious and subconscious drawings, sketches, doodles, and studies.

These ideas and thoughts were often developed later into major works of art. But the sketchbook has also remained as a document to the stream of consciousness for many. The camera as a sketchbook-tool, in which the stream of consciousness is recorded, documented, and later utilized in photographic production, is not unusual for many photographers. Even though the stream-of-consciousness procedure appears as an operation to itself, its roots remain within the individual experience. It is the variety within the individual experience that guides the instrument to record the reality which may reflect the experience. Photographs that appear to be nothing more than decorative efforts, or that seem to use the craft as the reason for their own being, may also be reflections of individual experience. That experience may be very limited or it may be one in which a universal is recognized. The broad spectrum of experience conveyed to each photograph by the observer brings to full life the photograph that, until that interaction took place, said nothing. What goes on between observer and photograph may not be at all what was intended by the photographer, for each person may see what he wants to see. The photograph may function on many levels at once, engaging all or part of the senses while bringing the observer into a state of remembrance or projection which may or may not be directly associated with the photographic image or content.

At the beginning of this chapter we read attempts by various photographers to define the photograph. The last quotation was by Edward Steichen: "As photography I would include color images directly projected on a screen by colored beams of light, even when made without the intervention of the camera." Clearly Steichen did not restrict himself as to what photography or the photograph is; he left his statement open-ended. For each person the meaning of a photograph is varied and will continue to be so. This is true for the other visual arts as well. If we examine the history of art, we will find that little progress is made during those periods when strict guidelines and definitions are formulated and enforced. Steichen's statement is clear—the photograph can be what it wants to be, according to its creator and those who see it, utilizing or rejecting the traditionally accepted tools and materials. The photograph is a beautiful, universally produced art form that fulfills a multitude of desires, with both commercial and noncommercial practitioners. Its tradition, though brief compared to those of the other visual arts, is rich and astonishing, free from some of the encumbrances that have plagued a number of the arts.

Finally, the photograph is not an excuse for a better or inferior painting, nor is it in the same context an extension of a silkscreen print or etching. It is itself, with its own reality, which can be created without the intervention of the photographer. It is this aspect of the photograph that is the motivation behind the strongly held belief that the photograph cannot be, itself, a creative form. An early Kodak slogan, "You push the button, it does the rest," still lingers in the minds of many to support this conviction that the photograph can never be the embodiment of creativity. Those who decide that they would like to become photographers and produce works of art instantly are quickly disappointed when they find that when they push the button, the camera does not do the rest. Any instrument of creativity—brushes, pencils, chisels, camera—can be only as creative as the person using it.

   The reality of the photographic image is quite different from that of the other visual arts in that it is not the reality of the object itself, but an image or likeness of the object. Painting or sculpture, on the other hand, is a mental configuration or concept of the object, which is tempered by clusters of other factors inherent in the character of its creator, such as levels of experience, knowledge, and often the coordination of mental process with manual ability, which in turn produces a semblance of the object. The photograph is the witness to a physical reality, but the painting or sculpture is an affirmation of an indirect reality that speaks directly of its creator, the artist.

   Photography has found its place alongside the other arts, not because it has continued the tradition of the specific reality of likeness, of objectness, but because it has used this reality in conjunction with disciplines inherent in the process of the photograph and used them as foundations that have been expanded upon. Just as painting, sculpture, all of the visual arts, along with science, have enhanced and enriched our society, so has photography. It continues to reach towards new realms of expression as it matures and redefines itself.

2 PERCEPTION

"The soul never thinks without an image."

ARISTOTLE

The statement above, while poetic, suggests questions that remain unsolved. Do we have images during the thought processes? Is it possible to solve problems without images? And if such images exist, are they formed only during the active, conscious times of thinking? The Greek philosophers believed that the processes of perceiving and reasoning formed a dichotomy and that the senses were not to be trusted; however, they believed that vision was nonetheless a source of wisdom.

Perception, images, and image making have been a mark of the human species since before recorded history. From the caves of Altamira in Spain and Lascaux in France we have some of the earliest examples of images and of image making, spanning a time period of some 35,000 years. These realistic representations depict animals in a variety of positions; often overlapping, they are life-like in movement and physical characteristics. They are never shown in perspective, but always from a side view, which may have been simply the easiest way of drawing and describing them. However, these images not only speak about the cave dwellers' powers of perception, but also of their extraordinary visual retention. The image of the wounded bison from the cave at Altamira (Figure 2-1) describes the animal near death, or perhaps already dead, with legs folded under the body and the tail over the haunches. This image captures the likeness of the animal, but also graphically delivers the impact of death. Since the cave

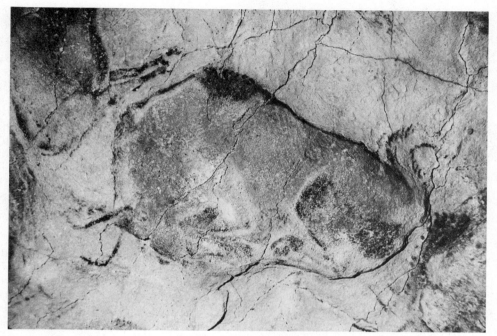

Figure 2-1   JEAN VERTUT, *Wounded Bison* c. 15,000–10,000 B.C., Altamira, Spain
(Courtesy of the photographer)

dwellers did not have the wounded animal as a model to copy from and record upon the walls of the cave, they had to remember the animal and the details of the situation. What this gives in a rather small way is an example of primitive people's ability to deal with constants and inconstants on a visual level within their environment. Further, these depictions of the animals are shown free from any sort of environment, such as trees, rocks, or ground formations. They are painted and drawn as figure-field relationships, a process common to primitive cultures and to children when they begin to draw and paint. The first appearance of a drawn or painted image must have been an astonishing event, the first method of communicating other than through auditory methods.

Eratosthenes, the Greek philosopher (275–195 B.C.) especially noted as an astronomer and credited with having measured the circumference and tilt of the earth and the size and distance of the sun and moon, used visual perception as a basic tool in his calculations. His simple observations of the elongation and contraction of cast shadows from a vertical object thrust into the earth were instrumental in his calculations of the circumference of the earth as well as its rotation and tilt from the sun. It all appears so simple today, but it was Eratosthenes' basic perceptions which triggered the investigations that he pursued. Wherever we look, in art, science, economics, sociology, or politics, we find that perception, passive and active, is so much a part of our lives that most of us never take time to think about the role it plays. A better knowledge of perception cannot but help to promote a higher understanding of ourselves as individuals and of the world in which we function. Perception is an awareness of external and internal phenomena through the senses, an immediate or intuitive cognition through direct experience. Maturation of perception is dependent on genetic and environmental factors and on experience. Our concerns here are primarily with visual perceptions, and specifically those of the photographer.

The photographer's visual perception is distinctly different from that of other artists, and this difference is the result of the tools used for image making, the camera and other mechanical devices. The senses, when considered as perceptual systems, are made evident in photographic images. Touch, smell, taste, hearing, orientation, and vision, whether observed and recorded or extensions of the photographer, may be experienced in photographic images. The information and stimulus given to the sense receptors can often be a major consideration, consciously or subconsciously, in the act of creation. Feeling does not exclude perception, and perception does not exclude feeling. Rather, they enhance each other. For the photographer, recording the evidence of the senses may be incidental, since it is a part of everyday human existence, or it may be a conscious effort intended to preserve such evidence as the subject.

Two authors who have made great contributions to understanding the physiology and psychology of perception are Rudolf Arnheim and James J. Gibson. Their work remains fundamental and, to date, unsurpassed. The work of these two men brings into focus the relation of perception to art. What remains to be answered, if it ever can be, is the question of the relation of creativity to perception. Arnheim suggests an answer in the conclusion of his book, *Visual Thinking:*

> Art works best when it remains unacknowledged. It observes that shapes and objects and events, by displaying their own nature, can evoke those deeper and simpler powers in which man recognizes himself. It is one of the rewards we earn for thinking by what we see.[1]

James Gibson defines perception as "the process by which an individual becomes aware of what exists and what goes on around him."[2] And Arnheim says:

> Visual perception, I tried to show, is not a passive recording of stimulus material but an active concern of the mind. The sense of sight operates selectively. The perception of shape consists in the application of form categories, which can be called visual concepts because of their simplicity and generality. Perception involves problem solving.[3]

In his book *The Senses Considered as Perceptual Systems,* Gibson states,

> Physical optics makes a distinction between "real" and "virtual" images. In optics, what I have called a screen image (the picture made by projecting shadows on a surface, the structuring of an array by artificial variations of illumination) is called a "real" image, and so it is. What I call an optic array (the structured stimulus for an eye, chambered or compound) when it comes from a mirror or a lens is said to produce a "virtual image." It is virtual, a virtual object, but not an image in my terminology. The apparent face in the mirror and the apparently near thing in the

field of a telescope are objects in effect, not in fact, but they are not pictures or sculptures or screen images. The "virtual" image of optics is nothing more than a consequence of the fact that perception is caused by stimulation and depends on stimulus information.[4]

Stimulus information and the selective sense of sight are key concepts when we consider the photographer's perception as distinct. The photographer emphasizes visual selectivity each time he operates his camera. The physical make-up of the camera forces the photographer to frame, and framing introduces selective vision. Is stimulus information perceived in a slightly different manner by the photographer as compared to the painter? And is this difference due to the instruments of the discipline alone? And if perception is partly a learning process, does the photographer eventually learn to perceive in a specialized way according to the dictates and limitations of the instruments?

The visual perception and actual physical processes involved in creation for the photographer are in fact quite different from those of the painter. For the photographer these processes are those of immediacy and selectivity through framing and fixed vision. The painter may visually scan and assemble the parts into a whole at will through the process of building by addition and subtraction. The painter's tools and materials do not inhibit this process; they in fact support it. If we place a photographer and a painter in front of a landscape, each will respond to the stimulus of the landscape in a different way, through knowledge of the advantages and limitations of the tools and materials. Furthermore, each will respond to the landscape according to his own associations with the objects before him. Each form and texture will have its own associative relationship with each individual artist. The painter may be very selective about the objects he decides to use in his work. He may manipulate the forms, textures, light, space relationships, and proportions as he wishes. He may guide the observer through a composition designed to bring the observer's attention to a certain segment of his work. Surface texture may be built by the addition of greater amounts of pigment, and offer another visual stimulus to the observer. These concepts may even be clearly defined for the painter before he begins his work. He may decide to leave the level of maximum generality and refine those segments of the landscape which compel his personal interest. On the other hand, he may bring a reductive attitude to his subject and to the work as a whole. For the photographer some of these approaches to image making are unavailable.

Often in discussions on the relationship of photography to painting, the name of the Impressionist painter Claude Monet is cited, in particular his series depicting Rouen Cathedral (Figure 2-2). The relationship of photography to painting in terms of visual perception appears to be pinpointed on the word "immediacy." The immediacy of the camera's ability to record quickly and the immediacy of the Rouen Cathedral series are, however, not identical. While Monet was concerned with the changing qualities of light observed at different periods during the day as it interacted with the cathedral, he represented this interaction as a field. His paintings are fields which require reading over the entire pictorial field. As for the cathedral, the treatment of it was reductive. The cathedral is free of its environment. No other forms are shown around it; the ground plane has been removed, allowing the cathedral to function as a

Figure 2-2 CLAUDE MONET, *Rouen Cathedral at Sunset* 1894 (Courtesy Museum of Fine Arts, Boston. Juliana Cheney Edwards Collection, 36.671)

flattened screen with no anchor. Most of the forms of the cathedral are given nearly equal projection, which allows for an easy reading of light and color. The paintings are studies of color and light, not investigations of a cathedral. Monet says, "I seek 'instantaneity', especially the 'envelope', the same light spreading everywhere."[5]

We cannot be sure just how Monet meant the word "instantaneity" in reference to these paintings. He painted a series composed of twenty views of the cathedral, eighteen of which were frontal. He began the series from the window above M. Edouard Mauquin's shop, Au Caprice, on the Rue du Grand Pont, opposite the facade of the cathedral. These basic studies were accomplished in 1892–93, but he continued to work on the canvases in his studio. His interest resided not in the cathedral itself, but in the transient effects of light and atmosphere, which he depicted at various times of the day, from early morning to sunset. Each study in the series is therefore a composite, worked on day after day as the right moment occurred, and this clearly demonstrates the painter's concern with the variants of the cathedral as it interacts with light, and not with the constants. The cathedral itself is only a screen on which he hangs light and color, and this is his true subject.

Monet's compositional method of extracting the cathedral from its environment is opposed to the compositional effects achieved through framing with the camera. Monet's composition was intended simply to bring attention to light and color, a method of reducing the cathedral as cathedral. The surfaces of the paintings are heavily built up with pigment so that they become textured and tactile. This surface contains no references to stone and mortar, but simply acts as a further device in psychologically removing the observer from associations with the cathedral. Nor is the scale of the brushwork and richly pigmented surface in alignment with the scale of the facade. Even the brush movements are independent of the form and formal relationships of the cathedral. The textured surface functions as an assertion of the picture plane. Monet's series treats the cathedral as a shimmering screen of low projections to exemplify his concern for changing atmosphere, color, and light. Photography later proved Monet's observations to be accurate, that the key to color is in the changing light and atmosphere, and not in the inanimate object. Monet separates the natural physical reality of light, color, and atmosphere from the physical reality of man-made objects, and brings forth a painting that allows the observer to follow his intended perception in a coherent way. When Monet stated, "I seek 'instantaneity,' especially the 'envelope,' the same light spreading everywhere," he meant exactly what we see in the Rouen series, that is, the instantaneousness of the eye, not the camera. He was concerned with light, not to suggest form and volume, but to reveal color. The Rouen Cathedral series is one painter's directed visual perception of the problem of light and color interpreted through color. Each element in the painting is selected to focus upon the observer Monet's creative use of the information received from the stimulus of light and color.

Would the photographer's perception of the Rouen Cathedral be different from Monet's? And would the image be significantly different? Since the photographer's art is largely based on visual selectivity and framing, these direct his visual perceptions and image making. As knowledge about the essentials of photographic creation is extended, the photographer moves away from the early response of figure-field relationships to more complex arrangements. Beginning photographers tend to place the subject in the center of the field when framing while ignoring the surrounding material. The field is often out of focus while the subject is focused. Arnheim states:

> There is considerable evidence to indicate that the graspability of shapes and colors varies, depending on the species, the cultural group, the amount of training of the observer. What is rational for one group, will be irrational for another, i.e., it cannot be grasped, understood, compared, or remembered.[6]

It is the photographer's cognition of the limitations and advantages of his instruments that eventually changes and develops his perceptions for photographic image making. Even when the photographer is not actively working with his camera and framing, the process of visual framing continues through his conscious visual experiences. These visual experiences are continually related to the camera's framing device. For certain photographers the process of framing without the camera is intentional, a kind of visual exercise in which new and inventive arrangements are made within the imagined frame. For both the photographer and painter, visual perception involves problem solving on an external-internal level. For the painter the process is complex in relation to the building of images through addition and subtraction. The more complex the shape or shapes, the more difficult the perceptual task of extricating it, especially with consideration to environmental factors. For the photographer the process is somewhat easier as the camera may record his perceptions quickly. However, the photographer cannot comprehend both the substance and variability of material things in his images, nor can the camera record the flux of constant modification in material things.

Arnold Newman's photograph *Haile Selassie I, Emperor of Ethiopia,* 1958 (Figure 2-3), shows us a wealth of material things; it is fixed in time for as long as

Figure 2-3   ARNOLD NEWMAN, *Haile Selassie I, Emperor of Ethiopia,* Addis Ababa, 1958 (© Arnold Newman)

we have the photograph. But Newman appears to have made a conscious effort to depict permanence, with nothing in flux. This is an official portrait of the emperor, intended to project a certain perception for those who know him. Substance and power are intended; the opulent interior with elaborate decoration, rich fabrics, and crystal speak of them. The emperor is seated on a gilded throne in the foreground, dressed in a splendid uniform, his chest covered with decorations. His unsmiling face is turned toward the observer; his eyes are fixed in a gaze revealing calm control, implying power and position. There is no break between what is seen and what is known about the individual presented amid the material things which surround him. But if an object completely out of context with the image had been introduced, or if some unknown factor had been suggested, our perception of this situation and person would be altered.

Every object in this image is fixed, but in reality these objects continued to change after the picture was taken. Newman exercised selectivity and control within the situation. Were the photographer's own perceptions of the represented things preconditioned? If they had not been, these objects could not have been assembled to produce the message of the image. His perceptions were so arranged to convey not only his own feelings, but those of the subject. This photograph functions as a symbol of those who are acquainted with the things represented, signifying power, position, perhaps intelligence and taste as well. But what if the same photograph were shown to a person from another culture, with no understanding of the material things or the person represented? To such an observer the image would simply represent a man sitting. Perception is not only physiological but cognitive as well. If perception were just a matter of physiology everyone would see things alike. Cognition and the process of cognition are the result of the cultural and environmental situation. They are not only a part of perception but affect perception.

Photographic images can also function as signs, as Todd Webb's photograph *First Spiritual Psychic Science Church, Harlem* demonstrates (Figure 2-4). But a sign can also be a symbol. The cross situated at the apex of the sign in the window of the storefront church is a visual symbol for Christ and his crucifixion, but is also a sign for a place of worship, a church. The lettered sign which announces the kind of church also has the traditional shape of a church, including stained glass windows and what could be a bell tower, topped with a cross, painted on the door. As a sign, this image could be perceived in two different ways, according to whether or not the observer is associated with the church. If he is, he will perceive the entire image as a church, since his associations with the building and the functions that take place inside tell him it is a church. If not, the building is not a church to him since his perceptions of a church have been conditioned in another visual and intellectual way. He has learned through individual experience that a church has a very distinct architectural style, which may include elegant spires, arched windows, and stained glass. But Webb's photographic image is clever, since he presents a sign within a sign. If the building is not perceived as a church at first, it will become clear after slight investigation that it is truly a church, because the lettered sign in the window proclaims it to be one. Todd Webb's own cognitive perceptions of church architecture find their way into his photograph. He divides the picture plane into thirds, a traditional compositional method. But it is interesting to note of the total image of a church

Figure 2-4 TODD WEBB, *First Spiritual Psychic Science Church, Harlem* 1946 (Courtesy of the photographer)

the division into thirds directly relates to the flat, painted image of a church in the window of the storefront. Moreover, churches are often divided into thirds—nave and side aisles. Once this image is recognized as a church, it can then aid in reversing our preconceived ideas, determined by architectural association of what a church is. We may then be allowed to perceive new forms, shapes, and spatial relationships within the image.

Webb has photographed the storefront church so that it is free of its environment, even a ground plane, and frontally so as to emphasize flatness. This device has produced an image that is now a floating collage of shape, textures, and tone moving around the central idea, the lettered word as a sign for church, in a composition of rectilinear elements. The observer is now led to accept the image for the object. How much of what we see is the result of Webb's idea of a church and how much is due to picture taking cannot be said with certainty. But he has also used language, the word church, as an additional perceptual medium.

Can an image function solely as a picture without content, without statement? Can it ever be free of association with signs and symbols? Is it possible for a photographer to produce images without allowing preconceived and stored images and experiences to affect the finished product? And if the photographer's art is largely one of selectivity and the framing of material imposed by the camera, is it possible to move through the photographic processes without previsualization or any intellectual participation? Contemporary artists have occasionally attempted to prove that it is possible to produce totally unorganized works of art, free of any association with mental processes, conscious or unconscious. It is generally concluded that they have not succeeded. But the interesting aspect of this experiment was the reaction to the works of art by the audience. The viewers perceived organization, structure, composition, and personal statement by the artist. One must then ask if the perceptual process is one in which the human need for organization and meaning coexist with perception? If we examine the work of Aaron Siskind we may find answers to some of these questions.

Siskind won recognition as a documentary photographer, and after a long period of work in that vein he said, "I found I wasn't saying anything. Special meaning was not in the pictures but in the subject. I began to feel reality was something that existed only in our minds and feelings."[7] He then moved on to a "new reality," which he found in abstract images. These images were often fragments of larger constructions—walls with peeling paint, chalk and spray-painted areas on sidewalks, graffiti by children, abandoned trash—used as sources for extraordinary photographs.

Although Siskind did this work during the period of the American Abstractionists, when such painters as Franz Kline, James Brooks, Willem de Kooning and others were at the apex of their work, it would be a mistake to say that he considered himself an Abstract Expressionist. His concerns with his images were quite different from those of the artists working in that mode. Siskind was intensely interested in the human activity represented by graffiti, scribblings, and partly decayed structures. It was from these often incoherent traces of human activity that he sought out organization and brought into existence, by converting and transforming the visual stimuli, the meaning and expression of his own vision.

Paint on Brick Wall, Chicago, 1948 (Figure 2-5), is an example of a photographic image brought about through Siskind's selectivity, perception, and creative organization. The splattering and swirling free-form movements of paint over a systematic organization of pattern formed by the old brick that supports the thick paint functions as an exciting visual foil. Even though this image has the look of an accident, made without the engagement of the thought processes, it is complex in form and content. It must be remembered that the source of the images is the photographer's own experiences and perceptions, which is the true meaning of the photograph. There is no doubt that we may enjoy photographs for their pure "pictureness," but that quality springs from the inner workings of the perceptual-experiential relationship.

Scrambled Fence, Harlan, Kentucky, 1951 (Figure 2-6), not only combines the remains of human activity displayed upon rough-textured wood planks and the photographer's selectiveness through framing, but also moves into the simple optics of negative-positive reversals. Can the recognition of an optic principle be present in this image by accident? The role that the negative-positive reversal plays is of such significance that it is difficult to imagine that it was not a major consideration during the framing process. Siskind's nonrepresentational, unmanipulated images are fragments of larger objects, but his use of repetitious complementary forms, tones, and textures are complete perceptions of reality beyond something that exists only in mind and feeling. They are affirmations of human existence in relationship to the environment.

The examination of photographic images as symbols, signs, and as pictures along with statements concerning the photographer's perception has shown that while the photographer does have a distinct perceptual approach, it is conditioned by his instruments. Information from our world, our environment, is

Figure 2-6 AARON SISKIND, *Scrambled Fence* Harlan, Kentucky, 1951
(Courtesy of Light Gallery, New York)

dealt with daily by everyone through the senses, actively and passively. Our adaptation and survival depend largely upon how we use the senses, independently and in coordination with one another. We will be examining how the senses are used as perceptual systems and how they provide information for the photographer, as well as how that information is transmitted to the photographic image. We will also examine depictions of the senses as the subject itself, or as a subject within the photographic image. This material will be examined and discussed from the position of the senses used and depicted for aesthetic creative reasons in photographic images, and not from a standpoint of physiology or psychophysics. The senses of general orientation—hearing, touch, smell, taste, and sight—will be discussed through the use of photographic images that depict them individually or in combination.

Two photographers who have used the senses in their work in an interesting manner are Man Ray and Lucas Samaras. They appear to have made a conscious and deliberate effort to work with the senses not only as statements about themselves, but about all humanity. Man Ray says of his photographs:

It is in the spirit of an experience and not of experiment that the following autobiographical images are presented. Seized in moments of visual detachment during periods of emotional contact, these images are oxidized residues, fixed by light and chemical elements, of living organisms. No plastic expression can ever be more than a residue of an experience, recalling the event more or less clearly, like the undisturbed ashes of an object consumed by flames, the recognition of this object so little representative and so fragile, and its simple identification on the part of the spectator with a similar personal experience, precludes all psycho-analytical classification or assimilation into the arbitrary decorative.[8]

Of particular note here is the reference to the observer's identification with a similar personal experience. Although Man Ray does not state it precisely, we can take his words "personal experience" either from the position of direct perceptual experience or indirect perceptual experience. Further, he states that the images were seized in a state of visual detachment during moments of emotional contact. He appears to make a distinction between the visual aspect of perception and the other perceptual systems; it was the emotional or other systems that were given consideration in forming his photographic images. However, can visual detachment or visual passivity exist in the visual arts, especially in the production of photographic images? One may seek to achieve this effect in an image, but striving for that end means that it is no longer passive or detached.

Orientation

Basic orientation, the interaction of the vestibular apparatus and the other perceptual systems and organs in our bodies, functions automatically as we constantly maneuver in our environment. Our orientation to the direction of gravity provides the upright posture, equilibrium, and balance which are made possible by the vestibular apparatus itself.[9] Most animals possess simple orientation, that is, orientation to what is up or down, and to the ground plane, as well as the possibility of locomotion. Oriented locomotion may be a response to light, sound, or sight which depends upon the senses of sight, touch, smell, and sound as well as a more complex oriented locomotion to a goal in which certain distances are to be covered. The perception of the permanent structure of the environment on which other perceptions depend allows the perception of space or of the permanence of things. Directed locomotion is governed by what Gibson calls "symmetrical stimulation," in which an individual directs locomotion by balancing stimulation and then maximizing or minimizing certain features of it.[10]

All of the senses, in cooperation with one another, contribute information in various combinations, which in turn govern orientation and locomotion. Orientation as a perceptual system is represented in the images of many photographers through a variety of means, either consciously or subconsciously. For certain photographers, a specific aspect of the complex perceptual system of orientation will be of particular interest; others will concentrate on the interaction of the systems depicting orientation or locomotion.

The father of the motion picture, and the one photographer to systematically study locomotion through photographic images, was E. J. Muybridge. He left his native England in 1852 for America, where he photographed landscapes of Yosemite, later published in the first guidebook to that site. In 1872 he became interested in photographing motion when asked by ex-governor Leland

Stanford to photograph his trotting horse. Stanford had made a bet with a friend that a race horse had all four feet off the ground at one time during a running gait. Muybridge proved this to be true through a series of twelve sequential shutter trips set off by the horse as it passed through them. The University of Pennsylvania gave him a grant for the study of animal and human locomotion. From 1872 to 1885 he produced more than 100,000 photographs, mainly of the nude human form in hundreds of different poses. In 1887 eleven volumes of his work were published by the University of Pennsylvania under the heading, *Animal Locomotion: Electro Photographic Investigations of Consecutive Phases of Animal Movements.* His photographs of human locomotion were not concerned with motion alone, but were intended to be compiled as an atlas of poses for artists to use in substitution for live models. *Figure Hopping* (Figure 2-7) depicts a

Figure 2-7   EADWEARD MUYBRIDGE, *Figure Hopping* (Animal Locomotion Plate 185)

Figure 2-8 HARRY CALLAHAN, *Chicago 1961* (Courtesy of Light Gallery, New York)

woman hopping or running from side, back, and three-quarter views, to be read from left to right horizontally, and in sequence. The sequence of eight stages of movement were simultaneously photographed by cameras situated at three different positions as the figure moved through the stages of oriented active locomotion. These studies of human locomotion are the first intentionally related sequential photographic images and paved the way for other photographers such as Duane Michals, who used the sequential image format in his photostories. The work of Muybridge and others interested in the problem of locomotion was to have an enormous effect upon painters and sculptors as well as on other photographers.

Oriented active locomotion is dramatically depicted by Harry Callahan in his photograph *Chicago*, 1961 (Figure 2-8), which shows six female figures perceiving external space within the dimensions of the constructed verticals and horizontals of the third dimension, judging distance and receiving information from the senses as they pursue their way in directed locomotion. In the middle ground two erect figures look down to the ground plane, their eyes focused to the ground plane to establish equilibrium and assist in balancing with the changing ground-plane relationships. Two foreground figures with heads in opposed directions appear to be responding to an environmental stimulus, perhaps sound or some visual attraction, as they move with the other figures through terrestrial space guided by external information.

Callahan photographs this scene from a low position that emphasizes verticality of the surrounding structures, giving a strong sense of up-down and gravitational pull by a slight tilt of the camera. The figure in the foreground is at a slightly opposing angle to the other verticals in the composition, emphasizing its movement and balance even though the ground plane is not visible in this part of the image. Other manufactured objects function as symbols for the auditory-visual stimulus in purposive locomotion. Streetlights of various sorts occupy the left-hand side of the composition, and a clock is seen in perspective in the upper right-hand portion of the photograph. While these objects regulate human locomotion—when to stop, when to go—and activate the auditory and visual systems in determining the movement of the figures in directed locomotion, they also operate as symbols of intelligent beings who have regulated their movements within a time-space factor. Callahan's photograph has demonstrated how human orientation to the constants of the earth over millions of years has moved into what appear to be the constants of the modern world.

Hearing

The ear is the sense organ for hearing; nonetheless perception of sounds requires listening as well as hearing, and listening involves two ears along with the muscles for orientation to the source of the sound. Perception of sound, its location and identification, requires turning the head in the direction of the sound or the source of the vibration. This may also be accomplished by either half of the binaural system independently of the other. Sound may often trigger recall of past experiences or anticipation of those that are to come, as well as activating the other senses—touch, smell, taste—but through association. The reciprocal action of the perceptual systems may often be accompanied by images of actual experience or images of fantasy. Sometimes no image is cooperative with the activated sense. All kinds of sound received—such as natural sounds, wind, air-friction, water, thunder, solids breaking and colliding—have a beginning and an end. So do human and mechanical sounds and the noises of animals. All sounds may interact with the receiver in a number of ways: emotional, intellectual, and muscular responses to sound are achieved by what Gibson calls the wave front, a concentric sphere of vibration in the air.

> The wave front is specific to the direction of the source. The train of waves is specific to the kind of mechanical disturbance at the source. The former affords orientation and localization. The latter affords discrimination and identification.[11]

Alfred Eisenstaedt's *Nurses Attending Lecture, Roosevelt Hospital,* 1937 (Figure 2-9), depicts a group of nurses seated in a tiered lecture hall. Their bodies are directed toward the source of activity, the lecture. Heads and ears are adjusted to the source of the sound, faces reflect the particular type of sound they hear, human, with its own intended inflections projected into the speech according to the specific material being delivered. In this extraordinary photograph Eisenstaedt has captured the sound of human speech. The source is not shown but the direction from which it emanates is indicated by the position of the nurses. He has shown us the response to the lecture through the concentrated expressions on the faces of the nurses. From these expressions we may assume

Figure 2-9   ALFRED EISENSTAEDT, *Roosevelt Hospital Nurses Attending Lecture* 1937 (Life Magazine © 1943 Time Inc.)

that the lecture is technical and delivered in an unemotional manner. This photographic image depicts quite clearly overt listening, adjusting of the head and ears to a source. Every element within the composition is seized and composed to support the sense of listening and of sound.

Internal listening, covert listening, and the ability to select one sound from many concurrent sounds is shown in Brassai's photograph *Le Bal Nègre in the Rue Blomet,* 1930 (Figure 2-10). A nightclub is filled with dancers engaged in conversation or concerned with the sound of the music as they dance. A couple in the foreground is in animated conversation, and in the background, part of the band may be seen. This image conveys the many types of sound one might hear in such an environment—music, human speech, shuffling of feet on the floor, clatter of china, all intermingling at different pitches and volumes. Each may be clearly identified and its source located. In such a situation one may adjust to the overall sound which may be a general buzz, or select any one of the identifiable sounds while generally excluding the others. Selective listening and oriented locomotion are clearly seen in the couple dancing in the middle ground of the

Figure 2-10   BRASSAI, *Le Bal Nègre in the Rue Blomet (At the Cabane Cubaine in Montmartre)* c. 1932 (Editions Gallimard)

photograph. They direct their movement toward the couple seated at the table in the foreground—the source of sound they have selected from all others.

The man and woman dancing have their heads tilted and turned so that they synchronize binaural reception for the sounds they select, while tuning out the others. So while Brassai's photograph speaks of many sounds blending in the nightclub, he is also pulling out a specific sound from the mix. He directs our attention to the couple in the foreground who are overtly listening, and includes an example of covert listening. The camera is focused for the foreground. The focused forms are pulled out from the others so that our attention is placed upon them and the social interaction of the two couples, made possible by human speech and the auditory system.

A perception of sounds heard inside the head, such as breathing, eating, or one's own voice, is another kind of auditory perception or listening. If you put your hands over your ears and press so that other sounds are excluded and then speak or hum, you will hear your voice inside your head. This effect does not depend upon binaural balance or head movement. It is an effect which takes place continuously and goes unnoticed unless one pays particular attention to it. The auditory system then is capable of proprioception and exteroception as well (internal as well as external hearing).

Fritz Goro, a sculptor who turned to photography, is an inventive, science-minded photographer. He found a method of photographing a gas-laser hologram and has sought new ways of producing photographs for science and technology. His disturbing photograph *Aborigines of Australia* (Figure 2-11) is shot from above the action on the ground. The observer is in a position of looking over the shoulder of the men performing the circumcision ritual and becomes part of the activity. Two pubescent boys are being held horizontally on the ground while the circumcision is performed by older men. Goro allows the

Figure 2-11   FRITZ GORO, *Aborigines of Australia* 1955 (Life Magazine © 1955 Time Inc.)

viewer to see the actual incision being made into the boys' penises, as their heads are turned upward and sideways, screaming in pain. The men's arms and legs are used as line elements directing our attention to the screaming heads and the operation. Sound is produced here by a stimulus, pain, and the sound is identifiable as that of pubescent boys. That sound has its own characteristic pitch and volume as well as its own emotional meaning.

One does not need to understand the culture depicted in this image, the language, the ritual, or anything else about these South Sea islanders to understand the sound produced as a scream resulting from pain. Nor is it necessary to understand the meaning of the individual screams and the motives that produced the situation in order to perceive the sound. In the upper middle area of the image one boy has his head held in position by a hand placed over his ear, while the other ear is pressed against his shoulder, blocking off external sound so that his scream is heard in his head. The other boy, with his head tilted backward, lets his scream issue from his mouth, his face contorted by pain. Goro's photojournalistic image does not just document an event of social and emotional significance for a certain culture, but also overcomes cultural differences by portraying a common human response of sound to pain. But more specifically, the sound is determined by the vocal range of the boys.

The natural sounds of the environment, of wind and water let us say, are romantically depicted in Edouard Boubat's photograph *Brittany,* 1946 (Figure 2-12). Wind rushing through a woman's hair and flapping her garments speaks

Figure 2-12   EDOUARD BOUBAT, *Brittany* 1946 (Rapho Agence de Presse)

of two different types of sound. The fluttering garments produce a characteristic sound, as does her hair softly flowing over her ears. In the background, ocean waves break upon the shore in an irregular repeated sound. All these sounds will produce their pitches and volumes according to the velocity of the wind as well as its direction. Not only is the figure the receiver of the sounds, but she also acts as a foil for them as she faces into the wind.

Goro's *Aborigines of Australia* depicted variables of sound according to source, and so in another way does Boubat's *Brittany*—sounds identifiable as water and wind in interaction. A subclass of sound not depicted but implied is the sound of water as it seeps into the sand and the sound of the sand as it is lifted and scattered. All the sounds implied in this image can be perceived only by association and by a cognitive experience related to this particular landscape situation. As the woman faces into the wind, her form is revealed by the force of the wind as it presses her garments to her. Boubat appears to be making an association between the natural elements of wind, water, and air and romantic femininity.

Sounds produced by musical instruments are in a way an extension of the human voice, and perhaps not unlike the articulation of the human voice itself. These sounds can be expressive, emotional, resonant, patterned, paced, pitched, and modulated according to the individual behind the instrument. Some of the distinguishing characteristics of the human voice may be heard through musical instruments, which also carry the meaning of the musical score and the interpretation of the music according to the performer. But each instrument will have its individual, characteristic sounds, even though they may be intentionally modified by the musician for expressive reasons or according to the specific music being played. Since audition is proprioceptive and exteroceptive, the sounds heard by those not producing them may be interpreted quite differently from the interpretation desired by the musician. Recognition and definition of those sounds will vary according to the individual physical, intellectual, and emotional differences and levels of experience with musical instrumentation.

Robert Frank's *Political Rally, Chicago*, 1958 (Figure 2-13), is an image that may first be read as a political message. That message could be a political joke or a true protest. As the small sign pinned on the right side of the musician playing the sousaphone indicates, the rally is for Adlai Stevenson. Since the figures are depicted as faceless, our attention is directed to symbols—the American flag and musical instruments, especially the sousaphone placed in the lower center of the composition and parallel to the picture plane. If the observer is acquainted with the sousaphone, his first response is recognition of the characteristic sound this instrument produces. But that imagined sound is detached from other possibilities for this instrument until one notices that the musician's fingers are placed on the keys, when one begins to imagine a succession of sounds rather than a single note, which can be interpreted as having a political message, the more so since the American flag appears to be attached to the top of the sousaphone or to be emerging from it. Just as Frank has left the question open as to whether his political meaning is sarcasm or serious protest, the sounds may be left open to interpretation as satire or a variety of musical patriotism. No matter which way one interprets them, we are certain to connect the imagined sounds

Figure 2-13 ROBERT FRANK,
Political Rally, Chicago 1958
(Collection of The Art Institute of
Chicago)

with the political symbols clearly intended by Frank, therefore leaving little room
for other possibilities.

Implied sounds, rather than images of their actual source, are depicted in
Man Ray's photograph *Le Violon d'Ingres*, created in 1924 (Figure 2-14). His
model, the celebrated Kiki de Montparnasse, is placed so as to resemble a violin.
She is seated nude with her back to the camera, and her head, with a turban and
earrings, is turned to the left. Sound holes, painted on or cut from paper, appear
on her back. Man Ray's photograph has a double meaning, clever and amusing.
As the title indicates, Ray is referring to the fact that Ingres played the violin as a
hobby and was by all accounts very good. The sound holes transform Kiki's
curvaceous form into the more tense curves of the violin. The patterned turban

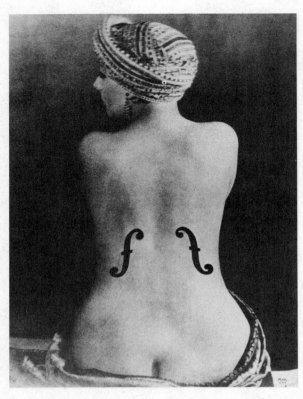

Figure 2-14   MAN RAY, *Le Violon d'Ingres* 1924 (Courtesy of Juliet Man Ray)

she wears derives from one in Ingres' early painting *The Turkish Bather,* and in a later painting, *Turkish Bath,* the same pose reappears among other female bathers. Kiki, whose real name was Alice Prim, came from a very poor family and was known as Kiki in the free life that she led in Montparnasse. Her relationship to Man Ray lasted for six tempestuous years during which she often posed for him. The image not only refers to the paintings and violin of Ingres, but also to the fact that Kiki was Man Ray's violin. All the sensuousness of her torso is brought out in this image, and the reference to the violin so often connected with romance is intended to be read along with her person.

The sounds we are to imagine are left open to interpretation, but within the context of romantic involvement between two people. They might be a violin, the voice of Kiki, or the actual voice of Kiki emanating from the sound holes. Imagined perception of sound, instrument or human voice, comes not from a visual or auditory response to an instrument, but from associations with that instrument through a visual symbol. The symbol of a violin in this image is simply the sound holes. Removing them from the back of the model removes any connection between the torso and a violin and all that remains is a female torso seen from the back. The title of the photograph is an aid to our imagined sound. *Le Violon d'Ingres* is essential to a full intellectual and emotional perceptual response to the photograph. A visual response is the primary phase, but the other senses may be activated once the title is read and understood. This image is not just a picture, but an intentional symbol for a partly private, partly public message.

Touch

Of all the senses, with the possible exception of vision, touch has been depicted most often by photographers. The haptic or tactile apparatus co-functions with receptors which appear to be distributed all over the human body, therefore providing the photographer with endless opportunities to record the sense of touch. When the word "touch" comes to mind, the first impression is that of the fingers extended to touch something. In many ways the haptic system is parallel with that of vision. It is a powerful system if one considers the manner in which a blind individual may perceive information and sensation through the appendages of the body as well as through the skin. The sorts of information that may be received through the haptic system from a single object are weight, size, shape, texture, sharpness, dullness, softness, hardness, consistency, temperature. While touch may be passive or active, it can and often does produce haptic-experiential associations with the past or a projected future. Gibson has tentatively classified the subsystems of the haptic system as cutaneous touch, haptic touch, dynamic touching, touch-temperature, and touch-pain. Oriented touch, he says, is the combination of haptic information with the unceasing input of the vestibular information.

In cutaneous touch, the skin and deeper tissue can be stimulated without movement of the joints or muscles. The exploratory members of the body, such as the fingers, toes, lips, and tongue, develop the highest degree of cutaneous differentiation. David Seymour, who was born in Poland and later became an American citizen, is known for his photographs of war, but especially for his compassionate photographs of children as victims of war. His deep concern for them is expressed in his photograph *Handless Blind Boy Reading Braille with His Lips*, photographed in Italy in 1948 (Figure 2-15). Seymour positioned himself

Figure 2-15   DAVID SEYMOUR,
Handless Blind Boy Reading Braille with His Lips Italy 1948
(Magnum Photos Inc.)

slightly above his subject in order to observe the boy, shown from the shoulders up, and the full page of braille. His head is gently bent down to allow his lips to touch and lightly move over the raised and depressed sections of the page. His lips actively explore and respond to the forms and their relationships as he converts these forms into words and images. The information received through the cutaneous touch, as it is tenderly shown in this image with the lips acting as the perceiver, allows the boy to read through a system of touch. Seymour's photograph shows us how one perceptual system, that of vision, may be effectively replaced by another and allow an individual to function intellectually and socially within his environment. Furthermore, we are reminded by this image that systems are often considered as performing certain functions while excluding others. Instead, Seymour's photograph reminds us and shows us that the systems are adaptable and flexible when required to be. This photograph convincingly points to human persistence, will, determination, and adaptability.

If the skin and the deeper tissue are stimulated together with movement of the joints, this would give perceptions of haptic touch. The appendages of the body are sense-exploratory as well as performing motor organs, such as arms, legs, toes, and fingers, and are capable of changing the environment in addition to sensing or feeling it. In Cartier-Bresson's *Children Playing in Ruins, Spain* (Figure 2-16) we observe, through a huge hole in a wall, a group of children playing outdoors. They touch one another in various childish attitudes of play,

Figure 2-16   HENRI CARTIER-BRESSON, *Children Playing in Ruins,* Spain 1933 (Magnum Photos Inc.)

while in the foreground one child is walking toward the opening with the aid of crutches, which function as an extension of his touch, as "feelers," through which he may receive information. For a blind person, crutches could partially replace sight. Like the antennae of arthropods, crutches would allow one to feel and judge ground-plane relationships, textures, degree of angle, forms, and space relationships. But in the Cartier-Bresson photograph the child's vision is a co-functioner with the crutches, which are essentially operating as a replacement for the legs in a motor performance. Haptic perception allows him to feel his crutches as crutches and at the same time allows sensations from the ground plane to reach the skeletal structure, muscles, and skin of his arms in haptic touch. In spite of the physical handicap of the boy and the squalor of the ruins, Cartier-Bresson's photograph shows us the happy, carefree attitude of children in their world of play in which touch takes on a variety of meanings.

Inhabited Drawing, by Helena Almeida (Figure 2-17) depicts two hands holding a pen and what appears to be a section of wire between the thumb and forefinger. The image allows one to consider what Katz terms objective and subjective touch. One may direct one's attention to the object one holds so as to be aware of its characteristics, or shift attention to the impression the object leaves on the skin. This photograph offers the opportunity to imagine two distinct polarities, the pressure applied by the fingers on the pen making its hardness, roundness, and thickness felt, or the impression the pen leaves in the

Figure 2-17 HELENA ALMEIDA, *Inhabited Drawing* 1976 (Courtesy of the photographer)

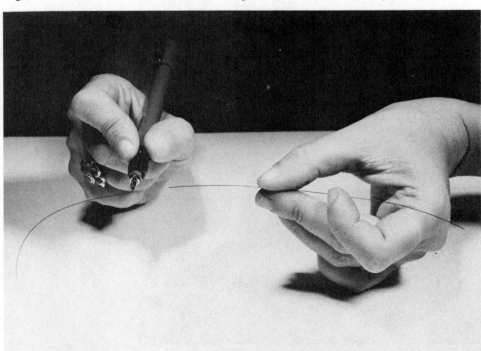

skin. Almeida's photograph is concerned essentially with representations of space and artistic imprints. But it also is a clear example of objective and subjective touch focused on the hands as exploratory sense organs as well as performing motor organs. These meanings are stated in a photographic image of cool simplicity, unencumbered by superfluous objects and patterns.

Richard Owen's photograph *Hand and Wire Ball* (Figure 2-18) treats objective and subjective touch in a more straightforward manner than does Almeida's image. The hand is brought close to the picture plane, and the impression upon the thumb with considerable pressure by the wire ball is clearly demonstrated. However, Owen turns this image into an interesting play of textural opposites becoming a visual game. The hardness of the wire and softness of the cloth and human flesh, the geometric rectilinear design of the sleeve, and the curvilinear design of the wire ball, as well as various textures are in juxtaposition to one another. Both Almeida and Owen use touch as the springboard for their photographs. These photographs do not remain just medical illustrations of the sense of touch but become personal statements about individual perceptions of reality and fantasy within the framework of the art photograph.

Heribert Burkert's *The View into Pictures*, a photograph of personal fantasy and physical reality, shows us an arm reaching down to the earth to lift up a small section of sod (Figure 2-19). Beneath this arrangement an actual cut has been made into the photograph at an angle echoing that of the sod. Burkert says, "A picture is reality with a false bottom composed of psychological, physiological, sociological or technical presuppositions. The purpose of my work is to investigate the phenomenon 'Picture' with reference to these aspects."[12] *The View into Pictures* does just that and also illustrates what Gibson calls dynamic touching. The skin and joints stimulated together, in combination with muscular exertion as the hand and arm work together to lift the section of sod from the earth, isolate graphically dynamic touching. The hand is centered to attract attention

Figure 2-18   RICHARD OWEN, *Hand and Wire Ball* (Courtesy of the photographer)

Figure 2-19 HERIBERT BURKERT,
The View Into Pictures 1977
(Courtesy of the photographer)

while emphasizing the sensation of exertion. As the fingers of the hand curl to lift the sod, the muscles of the forearm are in a position of exertion indicating weight and mass. As exertion operates, the fingers may read texture, firmness, temperature, and elasticity. The section of photograph beneath the hand and sod curls upward, allowing one to see into another layer beneath the surface, but also assists in the sensation of lifting. Burkert's photograph achieves a certain psychological impact by depiction of the physiological activity of dynamic touching. His image brings this to us with some force through his straightforward manner in approaching his subject. His visual field becomes our visual field by means of his selectivity and close-up range to his material.

Gibson states, "The combination of skin stimulation along with vasodilation or vasoconstriction might possibly give perceptions of touch-temperature."[13] To touch for temperature is part of the haptic system, while medium response is the body's temperature-regulating system and partakes of motivation as well as perception. If someone is chilled by the air, for example, he will be motivated to correct the temperature change by adding more clothing until his body has achieved a comfortable level of temperature, preventing heat loss. The reverse may be said of heat.

The French photographer Lucien Clergue became known for his use of nude female models placed in cold sea water (Figure 2-20) to provoke "gooseflesh." Often the uneven smoothness of the skin as it reacted to the cold water and air was used as a textured surface to be played off against different shades of coarse sands so as to achieve strong tactile associations. The soft, smooth, sensuous forms of the models, low light, and foaming, splashing sea water on the sand combined to form some of the most erotic photographic female nude images of the twentieth century. *Nude in the Sea,* an image abstract in concept, shimmers and sparkles with light, water, and the gooulefleshed skin of the nude female torso. This image precisely points to touch-temperature and the media of air and water. The reaction of these media upon the body's temperature-regulating system brings forth the gooseflesh along with shivering. Clergue's knowledge of the body's reaction to touch-temperature (the media of water and air) has greatly assisted him in his famous "Nus de la Mer" series, which began in 1956, a series that has allowed him to express his love for the sculptured forms of the female nude bathed in impressionistic light and tactile sensations achieved

Figure 2-20   LUCIEN CLERGUE, *Nude in the Sea 1964* (© by Lucien Clergue, 1965. Courtesy of the photographer)

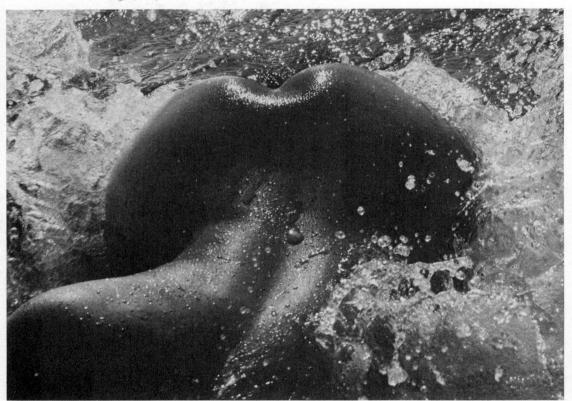

through water, sand, and air. This is a contemporary parallel to the lofty position to which the ancient Greek sculptors elevated the female nude.

The effect of heat on the body's temperature-regulating system is depicted in Margaret Bourke-White's photograph *South African Gold Miners*, taken in Johannesburg in 1950 (Figure 2-21). Two black miners are photographed in what appears to be an area of the mine, facing the picture plane from the waist up, safety helmets pushed back upon their heads. Their shirts have been removed to allow body heat to escape so that the regulating systems may function within the apparently high temperature of the mine. Streams of perspiration flow down their well-developed muscular torsos and faces, indicating thermal reception upon the skin. The image speaks eloquently about black miners and their response to their working environment as it is reflected in their faces and perspiring bodies. Bourke-White's journalistic photograph isolates an instant of time and relates a complete story full of visual insights. Not only has she effectively captured the physical reality of the mine, the miners, heat, emotions, and probable laboring conditions, but she states these realities with empathy. She believes that good photography is an editing process, one in which the photographer must be discriminating in selection. *South African Gold Miners* stands as a supreme example of what she believes in. Her concept of the mine is pruned and fastidious, cleared of extraneous material so that her story is clearly read and

Figure 2-21 MARGARET BOURKE-WHITE, *South African Gold Miners* 1950 (Life Magazine © 1950 Time Inc.)

understood. It is forcefully stated through velvet blacks, pure whites, and descriptive greys. The image depicts the skin as a receptor of temperature, heat in this case resulting in sweating, with unusual straightforwardness and clarity of intent. It remains a memorable image, beautiful in its stark simplicity.

Oriented touch combines the messages from the vestibular receptors, (skeletal structure of the human form) joints, and skin in relation to the ground and to gravity. Oriented touch appears often in photographic images, and is especially clear in Barbara Morgan's photograph of Martha Graham, entitled *Letter to the World* (Figure 2-22). The dancer is frozen in a sculpturesque stance, vertically and horizontally oriented to the ground plane as her dress flows out into space, enhancing the lines of the pose. Her arms and legs create and define new space and forms as they shift direction and position in haptic response to visual perceptions. The controlled motor skill or oriented touch of the dancer has been brought into geometrical patterns in an unusual image of articulated form relationships. Precise articulation of the hands, arms, and legs, mastery of skeletal movement and space perception comprise the dancer's art clearly depicted in *Letter to the World*. While many photographers blur their images of dancers for a greater sense of movement, Morgan has stopped the action so as to exploit fully

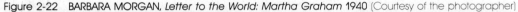

Figure 2-22   BARBARA MORGAN, *Letter to the World: Martha Graham* 1940 (Courtesy of the photographer)

the geometry of the dancer. The synchroflash technique that Morgan prefers to use has helped in defining the dancer's joints and projecting her forms. Strong blacks and whites sharpen the contours of the figure, accentuating the balance and orientation of the pose within the uncluttered field on which the dancer moves. Morgan's understanding of the physical aspects and the art of the dance and dancers reflects her own deep interest in this art form. Her use of artificial illumination and the stop-action does not give us a mere record but an interpretation of the dance through light, an interpretation of form, movement, and orientation related to space as the dancer redefines it. Her perception and interpretation of these elements are centered to bring out the human qualities of the dancer as well, with great warmth and sensitivity.

Pain and painful touch can require action. Also, motion is essentially an activity in which stimulus information about the environment is received. It can be combined with visual perceptions in which the negative values of certain things may be obtained. As an example, touching a source of heat—a stove, a burning match, the flame of a candle—or pricking the skin with a sharp point will not only give information about the object but may require action. The sight of certain things such as fire or sharp objects inspires caution based on experience. Images of potential sources of pain can often motivate emotional-physical reaction as effectively as the actual interaction with the source itself. The producers of horror films exploit the emotional-physical responses of their audiences by merely dwelling on a threatening instrument, anticipating its use. Journalistic and documentary photographs have used pain as their subject for social and political reasons as well as for instruction. Children discover their environment through touch and probing, to find out whether it will hurt or not, and make their discovery through pain.

Lucas Samaras explores pain and painful touch in several photographs in his *Samaras Album*. Painful pricking is shown in four separate Polaroids of his foot, seen from above as it presses upon a bed of nails (Figure 2-23). These four photographs are identical except for changes of illumination, as each depicts a different intensity of light which may be read as degrees of sensation. Since the sole of the foot also responds to pleasure, and tickling it often produces laughter, Samaras mixes the sensations of pain and pleasure. None of the images shows the foot actually being pricked, so that one is required to imagine the contact which may not be really painful. And since one can tell nothing about the emotional-physical reaction of the owner of the foot, which remains motionless, that reaction too is left to interpretation. The observer may perceive a visual stimulus as he desires.

Since Samaras has assembled four photographs, each with a different illumination, each foot may be a different foot or a different degree of pain-pleasure. Each field of nails changes from photograph to photograph according to the degree of illumination and angle of the light source. These changes accentuate or diminish their characteristics as nails and their overall texture as a support for the foot. Although these photographs are a part of the *Samaras Album*, an intense physical, emotional, and intellectual self-portrait, one may still identify with many aspects of the senses he depicts. For example, four painted photographs refer to touch-pain through two images of a lit candle supported on a spoon and two supported by an inserted fork (Figure 2-24). In each photo-

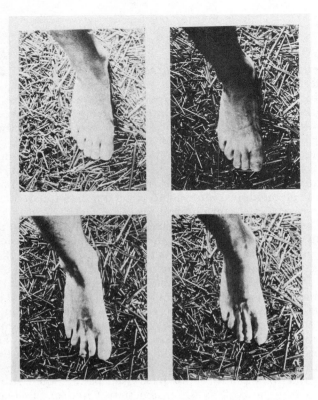

Figure 2-23   LUCAS SAMARAS, *Four Feet* (Courtesy of the Pace Gallery, New York)

Figure 2-24   LUCAS SAMARAS, *Four Torsos with a Candle* (Courtesy of the Pace Gallery, New York)

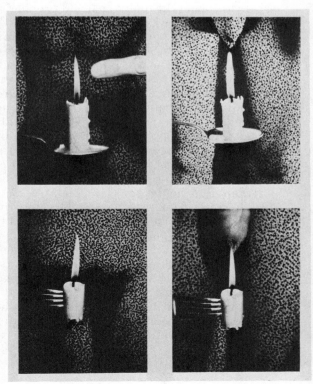

graph the candle is placed differently in relation to the body, indicating that the entire body surface may function as a receptor to touch-pain-pleasure. Samaras appears to be relating pain visually to sexual pleasure. Three photographs are in color and one in black-and-white. In all four the support for the candle is left unpainted, as well as the finger in the upper left photograph and the penis in the lower right. Each presents a different spatial relationship of candle to torso that may refer to anticipation of pain-pleasure. Through the Polaroid photographs Samaras explores his body and the senses in an intensely graphic and personal manner.

Social touch is so much a part of our lives that we seldom take the time to examine its important role. This type of touching has its emotional-physical satisfying aspects as well as its symbolic meanings, and can be active as well as passive. A simple handshake may symbolize friendship, welcome, trust. These feelings may be a true extension of the individual, or the handshake may simply be a physical performance without meaning. Social touching appears in photographs more than any of the other aspects of the haptic touch. Early social touching between mother and child is an important building block in social interaction, which may determine later social touching as an adult. Tina Modotti's photograph *Mother and Child from Tehuantepec, Oaxaca, Mexico* (Figure 2-25)

Figure 2-25   TINA MODOTTI, *Mother and Child from Tehuantepec, Oaxaca, Mexico* c. 1929 (Collection, The Museum of Modern Art, New York)

shows a nude child grasping his mother around the shoulder while his legs hold
onto her at the waist. His body is pressed to his mother as she holds and supports
him with her arm around his waist and under his arm. As the child responds to
the warmth, comfort, and security he finds in the soft forms of the mother, the
mother in turn is provided stimulation by the child. The social touching depicted
here is a passive touch in which emotional-physical stimulus is supplied by each
individual in a reciprocal social situation that may later prove to be an important
factor in the child's emotional stability. Modotti's photograph appears to be so
offhand, so unconscious and natural in presence that its attitude supports the
content of the image.

For each member of the sexual pair depicted in Brassaï's untitled photograph (Figure 2-26) we may find similarities to the social touch depicted in
Modotti's *Mother and Child*. But in this image touch is active, directed. Brassaï's
photograph of a couple making love reflected in a mirror shows each member of
the pair responding to touch with touch. Each is shaped to the other as comfort
and pleasure are sought through a particular type of social touching. It is in a
way an extension of the social touching depicted by Modotti. Each member of
the pair provides the physical emotional stimulation for the other, and each
responds to that stimulus which permits and controls their social interaction.

Figure 2-26 BRASSAÏ, *Untitled: Houses of Illusion* (Editions Gallimard)

Brassai has photographed this intimate scene from the space in which it takes place, but we see the space and the social interaction of the two by a reflection of that space and activity in the mirror. The geometrical format provides an unusual stage for an image of quiet social touching.

A kiss and touch of the hand in Cartier-Bresson's *Cardinal Pacelli* (Figure 2-27) depicts another sort of kiss, very different from that depicted by Brassai. It is a social touch with direction and intent in psychological-physical desires. One individual seeks the touch of another, but here one gives the touch, the other receives it. Each receives comfort and assurance from the other, but these aspects of social touch are given and received on different levels secured by position and social-cultural custom. In both the Brassai and Cartier-Bresson photographs, the social touching is depicted as a kiss and touch of the hand, but each has a different meaning. Both photographs depict social touching as a means of bringing people together in physical-emotional contact with one another. Visual perception and haptic touch are evident in each photograph. Brassai does not show us the full faces of his sexual pair, so we may only guess at their possible visual responses as they register in expression. Cartier-Bresson on the other hand directs our attention to the visual responses of the man and woman looking into the cardinal's face as the man kisses his hand. Internal desires and motivations are evident on the faces of the man and woman through their expressions as a social touch is performed. The camera lens is focused on the two

Figure 2-27 HENRI CARTIER-BRESSON, *Cardinal Pacelli* 1948 (Magnum Photos Inc.)

figures facing the cardinal so that most of the remainder of the image is in soft focus, offering a kind of peripheral vision. Our attention is fixed to this segment of the composition by the focus technique. Brassai photographs his couple with a certain physical-psychological distance, through a reflection in a mirror, so that the scene has an ethereal, dreamlike quality. Cartier-Bresson moves in close to his subject, allowing little space between the three central figures and the observer. These distance relationships add an enhanced coloring to the social touching depicted.

Finally, self-touch, which may be considered a type of social touching, is depicted in Man Ray's *Figure* (Figure 2-28). Self-touching has a variety of possible meanings and can be passive as well as active. Meaning through self-touch may be intended for another individual to read, as a method of nonverbal communication as well as a method of communicating with oneself. *Figure* shows us a woman touching her lips with two fingertips pressed lightly to the lower lip. This action may be sensual touch, rubbing the fingers lightly over the lips, or may indicate oral desire as well as a pensive mood. The art of mime is partly concerned with self-touch in which a story is told by expression of the body through touching of imagined and actual objects as well as the self. It is in its own way an international nonverbal form of communication in which certain movements and touchings are standardized and visually interpreted. Man Ray's photograph concentrates on the sensitive areas of the lips and fingertips in which the rougher area of the back of

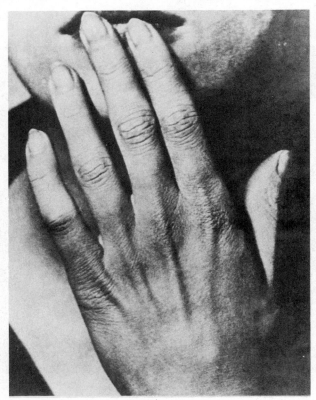

Figure 2-28   MAN RAY, *Figure* c. 1928 (Courtesy of Juliet Man Ray)

the hand is juxtaposed to the smoothness of the fingertips and lips. This juxtaposition tends to bring our attention back to the touching of the lips with the fingers. While this touch is subjective, one may still note the fingers applying the pressure, or the lips, or the interaction of the two duplicating a sensation received by the lips and fingertips. While Man Ray's photograph poetically depicts self-touch, it also examines clearly the human characteristic of body language, and from this perspective the photograph offers multiple readings.

Taste and Smell

The senses of taste and smell do not appear very often in art photography, but they do in commercial advertising. Those photographic images that do depict taste and smell are often obvious and contrived looking. Smell is seen much less than taste, probably because it is somewhat more difficult to photograph. Taste and smell are closely allied so that smelling can often involve the sense of tasting a substance as well. Taste and smell interact with and enhance each other. Smell is not only produced by odors drifting in the air, such as the scent of flowers or apples, but by a substance in the mouth whose aroma rises to the nostrils from within. The taste of the apple comes partly from solutions in the apple and partly from its aroma, which intensifies the taste.

Visual stimulus can activate the senses of taste and smell. Often colors activate the senses of smell or taste through association of color with foods, such as red with apples or orange with oranges. It is not uncommon for the olfactory and taste receptors to function by recall-experience. In addition to tasting, the mouth can determine the shape and size of an object, its consistency, texture, temperature, and solid or liquid state. Tasting also consists of identification, such as sweet, bitter, sour. But the primary functions of the mouth are chewing, eating, and speaking, while the sense of smell is limited to identification, such as fruity, flowery, sour, putrid.

American Soldiers, American Folk Festival, Berlin, 1974, by Helmut and Gabriele Nothhelfer (Figure 2-29), depicts two American soldiers out of uniform eating what one would expect to find at an American celebration—ice cream and cotton candy. Eating is the visual element which ties the photograph together in composition and content. Each soldier's face registers a blank expression as the sweet food acts as a pacifier. These expressions appear at odds with the festival surrounding them. Surprisingly enough, it is the food that draws our attention, not the soldiers. The rivulet of ice cream about to touch the finger of the left figure brings about not only associations with taste and temperature, but also the sticky quality of dried ice cream. The other figure, consuming the cotton candy, part of which hangs down from his mouth, brings our attention to the quality of the thinly spun texture of the candy, its sweetness, and swift solubility. The title aids us in fuller enjoyment, for it is impossible to discern that the American soldiers are in fact attending a festival. Two soldiers eating sweets form the subject; taste is projected through associations. Nothhelfer's visual response to this scene is the true marvel of this photograph.

Figure 2-29   HELMUT AND GABRIELE NOTHHELFER, *American Soldiers, American Folk Festival,* Berlin 1974
(Courtesy of the photographers)

Figure 2-30   MAN RAY, *Transatlantic*
(Courtesy of Juliet Man Ray)

Man Ray's *Transatlantic* (Figure 2-30) depicts cigar butts, cigarette butts, ashes, and partly burned matchsticks with scraps of paper in a discarded heap upon the ground, photographed from above. We look down upon this mass of abandoned material with some puzzlement until the objects are identified, resulting in associations of a characteristic rank smell which permeates the image. But associations with the material can also bring about a sense of smell related to its previous states. The sweet spicy scent may be recalled as a reverse response to Ray's image, or we may recall the distinct scent of burning tobacco. It is the smell rather than the activity of smoking that Man Ray brings out in his image. He shows us the discards and remains of that activity and not the activity itself, which can only be imagined. Man Ray's title and image co-function, conveying not only smell but transition—of material objects, time, people and their activities.

Smoke, either thick, black, and combined with steam, or light and grey, clouds and chokes out the skyline and buildings as it rises from the factory chimneys in Eugene Smith's photograph *Smoky City* (Figure 2-31). His journalistic photograph of Pittsburgh in 1955 is black with soot and smoke so that our vision is partly blocked by it. So convincing is Smith's photograph of smoke-

Figure 2-31   W. EUGENE SMITH, *Smoky City* (© 1955 W. Eugene Smith)

polluted air that the sense of smell is activated by associations with sulfur from coal smoke; acid and rancid chemical smells seem to fill the very air we breathe. Although Smith's photograph of this polluted city has been criticized as too emotional and dramatic to be considered a true photojournalistic effort, the message is clear and remains as a lasting statement of Smith's personal convictions. The visual-olfactory responses to this image are, in their way, confirmations of the power of his message.

Almost in complete contrast to Smith's photograph *Smoky City*, Mario Giacomelli's *Paesaggio Scanno* no. 230, 1959 (Figure 2-32) depicts a mountainside village as soft mists drift over the rooftops of a cluster of small houses clinging to one another. The absence of any visible human form generates a mood of stillness about the image. Giacomelli's photograph celebrates the light and air of the mountains. The small structures are secondary to his primary concern, which he gently asks the observer to experience by means of the image. *Landscape Scanno* abolishes the restrictions of time and space through the multiplicity of shifting lights and mists, which begin to dissolve the tangible reality of the village.

Visual-olfactory responses to this photograph emerge slowly, nearly undetected at first, and then become a mental reality as the spirit of this photograph stirs the imagination and instinctual responses. Perishable physical reality is superseded by Giacomelli's power to suggest effectively the invisible, the intangible—past experience retained only in memory and perhaps half forgotten.

Figure 2-32   MARIO GIACOMELLI, *Paesaggio Scanno*, 1959 (Bristol Workshops in Photography, Bristol, Rhode Island)

This image is sharply distinguished from other landscape photographs because of its dynamistic spiritual aura. The magical, mysterious character is its substance.

The extraordinary phenomena of creativity based on the fulfillment of personal convictions can lead one to a comprehension of what the melding of the human spirit, expressing itself through the contemporary medium of photography, and strongly held personal belief, may accomplish.

There can be no misunderstanding about the intention of this photograph, as it springs from the photographer's personal being, and was not produced by accident, but by an intentional personal force inseparable from man and spirit. If a photograph can remind us of our physical and spiritual selves as Giacomelli's does, can we not then recognize through the same vehicle that it is as much an affirmation of our being as it is of the photographer's?

Belle Haleine by Man Ray (Figure 2-33) uses a photograph of Marcel Duchamp in female clothing as part of a photographic image that not only speaks of scent, Eau de Violette, but is also full of double meanings, all tongue-in-cheek. And while it is a humorous assemblage it is also quite serious. Sexual ambiguity is often found in the work of Marcel Duchamp and Man Ray, who were close friends. Their work often merged and overlapped in image and meaning. The oval photograph, which has a certain funereal quality about it, may indicate the death of the real identity of the man. Ray's script beneath the bottle ("*par Procuration*—Man Ray") underlines the ambiguity of Duchamp as well as the

Figure 2-33 MAN RAY, *Belle Haleine* (Courtesy of Juliet Man Ray)

image. *Belle Haleine* may be read as Belle Hélène, or beautiful breath, may also refer to the famous dessert consisting of a cooked pear with chocolate sauce, and may even refer to Helen of Troy. The label is in the shape of a pear, which is often considered feminine. "Eau de Voilette" may identify the scent, violet; with the o and i transposed it also becomes the definition or word for the antimacassar, but it also refers to a woman's name and is translated as "water of little veil." This may be another way of speaking of the metamorphosis from male to female. But above all one must keep in mind that this photograph is in the spirit of the Dada movement, and is a linguistic joke. However, Ray has assembled the parts of this image into the shape of a bottle intended to contain a scent associated with women. The association and identification of scent are left open to interpretation, just like the rest of this Dada photograph.

Jean-Paul Merzagora worked as a photographer for just three years, before which he was a fashion model. His suicide brought to an end what promised to be a most unusual photographic career. His work depicts a fantastic, almost Baroque world of opulence in which visual symbols are used to speak of a transitory sensual life. In an untitled photograph (Figure 2-34) a female model is

Figure 2-34   JEAN-PAUL MERZAGORA, *Untitled*

seated inside what appears to be either a plaster egg or a fungus, partly cut away to reveal the interior. She is surrounded with fruit, vegetables, earth, rocks and leaves. Her hair is fashioned in a fantastic coiffure incorporating vegetables and leaves. Merzagora makes reference to taste–smell by his use of the dark, ripe grapes draped about the model's neck, and the mushrooms, earth and other organic material on her lap. Her hands are hidden beneath her garments so that all we see of her is her face. She gazes out at us from a cornucopia world of earthly products with dark eyes that question and invite us. Strong textural differences are depicted and played off against each other: the smooth gleaming grapes, the fleshiness of mushrooms, the reticulated surfaces of the vegetables, leaves and rocks. The earthy scent of mushrooms, whose sweetness is mixed with the musky scent of the grapes, the fresh scent of vegetables and the earth itself all refer to the gustatory and olfactory senses. The transitory pleasures of eating and tasting are associated with the voluptuous female figure surrounded by the bounty of the earth as she becomes part of them. Physical sensations have a beginning and an end, and Merzagora may be indicating this by his use of the egg shape from which all these pleasures emerge. Merzagora's own work as a model is strongly felt in this image. The fashion world with its seasonal changes, models often with extreme poses and makeup, and photographic style are underlying elements in this photograph. Merzagora mixes his knowledge of the technical side of fashion photography with his own feelings about life. It is an image that plays upon our senses and emotions as an *ersatz* for our own reality.

Sight

Vision, often considered the major perceptual system for obtaining information, may be active as well as passive. Orientation may be the primary function of vision and offers information at all levels of activity. When entering an unknown environment, one's visual attention is given to signs and markers as a method of finding one's way. After the necessary information has been obtained, maneuverability then may take place on a subconscious level while vision or attention may be directed in other ways. The eyes, whose position in the head is fixed, may rotate along with the rotation of the head and movement of the entire body, or may move separately, in relation to the ground plane, and obtain information through light which surrounds and illuminates the environment. Self-guided vision allows for locomotion, and locomotion makes orientation to the environment possible. The information-gathering process through vision is basic to almost all animals. It can be selective, directed, and stimulated through a number of methods. In man, beyond this first level of vision, higher levels of visual maturation allow for visual attention, selection, retention, and visual exploration. For each individual the perceptual system of vision has its own typical mode. It is these individual differences in vision made manifest in photographs or any work of art that bring them to our visual attention. Certain perceptual systems are developed and utilized more than others according to the artistic discipline which engages them; for the musician, touch, hearing, and vision; for the photographer, vision and perhaps touch. The photographer's awareness of his dependence on the visual is constantly revealed through the photograph. His visual awareness is affirmed each time he produces a photograph. The photograph is his vision. It is his individual mode of vision, and that vision may often be his subject.

The ancient aphorism, "The eye is the window of the soul," is exemplified by Man Ray's photograph *Eye with Tears* (Figure 2-35). Not only does the eye see and gather information, but it can give information. It may speak of inner states of happiness, depression, stress, grief, and well-being. Tears may be a physical response to an inner emotional state as well as to rapid blinking of the lid and quick eye movement or rotation. Ray shows us an eye close up, with a heavy beaded eyelash makeup and two artificial tears nearby. The eye looks out of the picture but not to the observer, so that we may contemplate its structure, moistness, transparency, and depth. It is presented as that part of the human anatomy which is often associated with sensuality, to be admired and contemplated as an object of beauty. But the eye may also contemplate as well as being contemplated, read as well as being read, see and be seen. From the photograph it cannot be determined if the eye is that of a female or a male. This gender ambiguity is often found in the work of Ray as well as Marcel Duchamp. The two artificial tears are also a play upon the theme of ambiguity. Originally the photograph was larger and depicted a female dancer, but Ray cropped it until he reduced it to what he thought was its most intense portion. Before cropping, the eyes of the dancer were shedding real and false tears. For Ray the false tears must have been a greater reality than the real ones. *Eye with Tears* not only speaks of seeing and of looking, but of the eye as a symbol for intense human emotions and relations.

Giuseppe Penone, in a self-portrait, wears contact mirrors, which reflect what he would otherwise be seeing (Figure 2-36). *Eyes Turned Around Backwards* is a direct statement about vision. The photographer's sight is blocked by the

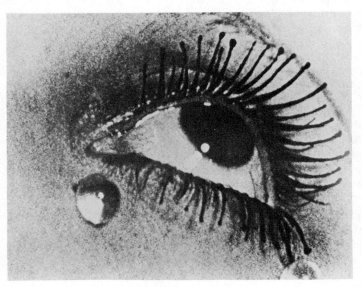

Figure 2-35 MAN RAY, *Eye with Tears* (Courtesy of Juliet Man Ray)

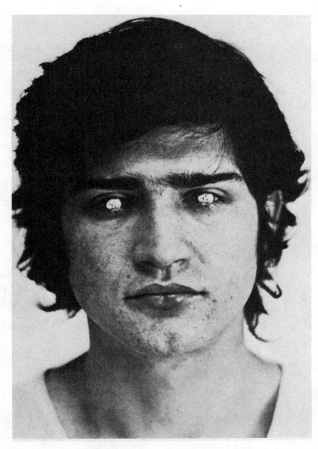

Figure 2-36 GIUSEPPE PENONE,
Eyes Turned Around Backwards
(Courtesy of the photographer)

reflecting lenses so that the images he would be receiving through the medium of light are reflected outward again while he relies upon memory for images of the past. Our present becomes his past, for the images we experience while he wears the lenses are lost to him. His image tells us of an inner vision, an outward vision, and of images stored and recalled. Penone speaks of a higher level of image transmission. We are in a sense directly behind his eyes and see what he should be seeing. Penone short-circuits the entire process of making photographs in order to tell us what he sees and feels by wearing contact mirrors. And if his concept eliminates the photograph, it also sweeps away the collecting of recorded images. All the cumbersome stages of art vanish, and we enjoy his selective vision in direct communication with him. It is a firsthand sharing of vision and experience with a creator. *Eyes Turned Around Backwards* transmits a unique idea about seeing, seeing delayed, future seeing. But it also speaks of the inadequacy of the photographic process to relate vision and experience, and proposes that in the future that process will perhaps be eliminated entirely.

Fixed, directed vision reflected in a mirror is the subject of Russell Lee's *Southeast Missouri Farm, Son of Sharecropper Combing Hair* (Figure 2-37). As the child stands in front of the mirror combing his hair, his gaze is fixed and directed toward his reflection in the broken mirror. We see the child from the back as he looks into the mirror at his own eyes, which return his gaze. His

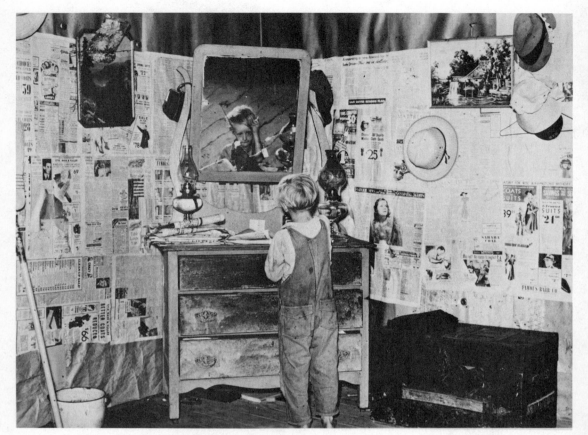

Figure 2-37   RUSSELL LEE, *Southeast Missouri Farm, Son of Sharecropper Combing Hair* 1938
(Reproduced from the collections of the Library of Congress)

grooming in front of the mirror is an activity which needs no explanation. But the environment which surrounds him sets that activity apart from ours, speaks of a specific socioeconomic level which may not be ours, and certainly depicts a specific moment in American history. The interior walls are covered with sheets of newspaper on which we may see other photographs and print, suggesting the further visual activity of reading. These two visual processes are played against one another compassionately by placing the boy in the center of the composition, surrounded by the newspapered walls. Flanked by the reality of poverty, the child is encompassed by visual symbols of an outside world.

Visual scanning, in which the eyes are shifted from area to area not to form a single image but to see changing images and impressions, is offered in Robert Doisneau's *Creatures of Fantasy* (Figure 2-38). Smoking a cigarette while lying upon a cast-iron bed, a male figure rests his capped head upon a pillow. He guides his vision through a series of tacked-up photographs and reproductions of paintings of females in various states of undress, all in provocative poses.

Figure 2-38   ROBERT DOISNEAU,
Creatures of Fantasy (Rapho
Agence de Presse)

While each image is different from the next, together they form a whole, the seminude female. Vision shifts from part to part of this collage of images, receiving a succession of information and stimulation. These feed the man's fantasy as he rests one tattooed arm over his chest and allows a puff of smoke to issue from his mouth with some force. In Doisneau's depiction visual scanning and sexual fantasy are cleverly and amusingly combined. While we may speculate about the man's fantasies, we find our own generated by the images he gleefully savors. Even though the image has a certain dated quality, there is a timelessness about it. Sexual fantasy stimulated by stereotyped depictions of women is common to most men and spans all time periods. Doisneau's intentions in *Creatures of Fantasy* are well put together and his invitation to participate easily accepted.

The visual field and the visual world of sensation and perception are brought together in Nicholas Nixon's photograph *South Boston* (Figure 2-39). Nixon stages the reality of the fantasy; Doisneau represented a semblance of that reality. *South Boston* shows us two young men in bathing suits, their bodies oriented so that their gaze may be followed to the source of their visual stimulation, a female in a bathing suit stretched beneath them. We respond by following the line of the two men's gaze, but then return to their faces to read their response to the visual stimulation. We search their eyes for possible expressive meaning.

Figure 2-39   NICHOLAS NIXON, *South Boston, Massachusetts,* 1978 (Courtesy of the photographer)

Since one man wears sunglasses, our attention shifts to the other. Following his line of gaze, we wonder what part of the girl's anatomy he may be staring at. Nixon allows us to fantasize on our own as we observe the faces and facial expressions of the men. Doisneau offers the profile of his male figure so that reading of the facial expression is difficult. Nixon's photograph is highly charged with male sexual aggressiveness. Doisneau on the other hand presents a private sexual fantasy with an ingredient of humor, more internal than Nixon's dark and predatory undercurrent. Each one speaks of sexual attitudes of the period. And each achieves a certain mood according to the environment, one interior, the other exterior. It is the difference between erotic daydreaming and sheer animality. But it is the act of vision that unites them, as well as male sexual fantasy. Each speaks of the same subject in different languages and from different times.

Visual perception can be hindered by blurring caused by fog, smoke, haze or by a physiological deficiency. Artists and photographers have quite often used blurring successfully for artistic reasons. In cases where visual perception has been blurred by atmospheric conditions, photographers have been quick to

Figure 2-40 ALFRED STIEGLITZ,
Spring Showers c. 1900
(Collection, The Museum of
Modern Art, New York. Gift of
Georgia O'Keeffe)

record what is generally known as aerial perspective. Definition of form and textural aspects is lost with increasing distance from the eye or camera lens. *Spring Showers* by Alfred Stieglitz depicts the blurring of structure and form through aerial perspective (Figure 2-40). To a degree certain camera lenses or filters may give the impression of aerial perspective, but this is a mechanical device and not a perceptual problem confronting the photographer. Stieglitz's romantic picture plays the sharp contours of a thin sapling in the foreground off the increasingly diffused forms and shapes in the middle ground and background for spatial effect. A streetcleaner with a huge brush-broom repeats the slight angle to the right of the tree as their reflections shimmer in the wet pavement. Atmospheric conditions in nature have been artistic challenges for photographers almost from the birth of the camera as we know it. In painting perceptual blurring reached its peak during the Impressionist period. Stieglitz's blurring emphasizes the verticality of the skyscrapers as they vanish into the mists and rain.

Lonely Inhabitant of a Big City (Figure 2-41) is a photomontage by Herbert Bayer in which two eyes, one light and one dark, are superimposed upon the palms of a pair of hands; proportionally larger than the windows of the building on which they cast their shadows, the hands reach upward with their palms facing the picture plane. Bayer fuses the senses of sight and touch in a surreal

Figure 2-41   HERBERT BAYER,
Lonely Inhabitant of a Big City
(Courtesy of the photographer)

image. The form of a face floating in front of a gloomy facade is created by the hands and eyes. Bayer places equivocal information before us from which we may read ambiguous figure and ground relationships interacting to form a face at one time and hands at another. Alternative perceptions from the same elements (the so-called "double image") have long been of interest to artists and psychologists. Bayer mixes his own psychological state with the technique of photographic montage to form a memorable image. If we fix our vision upon the space between the hands, the hands become a face, part of the facade between the hands functioning as a nose and mouth, and if we concentrate upon the fingers, the form returns to hands. It is an image whose conflicting information, deriving from alternating sets of stimuli, is cleverly put together with an understanding of and affinity with surrealism. The title of this photomontage puts emphasis upon the quality of aloneness. The expression in the eyes, the empty-looking building with dark holes for windows, bring Bayer's intended meaning across with a certain chill.

Perception in general, and in particular for artists, has been thought of as a process in which one perceives by vision alone. But the senses functioning together aid and assist us in perceiving our environment and ourselves. Perception through the senses is a complex process not yet fully understood, but there can be no doubt that the senses are perceivers that have made themselves evident in works of art and in photography. Perception, feeling, experience, ideas, and problem solving are all linked with one another and are part of the creative process. Just how this interaction takes place within the creative process remains a mystery, and perhaps it should continue to. For the photographer recognition and an active use of the senses in forming new images can be of great value in relating his feelings and experiences. Perceptual maturation can bring richer experiences and material for image building that may lead the photographer to higher levels of creative productivity. Moreover, it can bring him to a deeper understanding of himself and his environment. Inadequate as photographs are in relating feeling and experience, they nonetheless stand as a form of visual language made possible by the senses. If we approach these faint reflections of human experience with the knowledge that they are such, we may find that we learn through perception, and perceive through learning. E. H. Gombrich suggests that painters paint what they have been taught or have learned to paint.[14] If this is true, or even partly true, then we might also say that photographers photograph as they have learned to see and compose through the viewfinder. Then perception and learning are interchangeable processes that coexist within the complex makeup of the human personality. Nonetheless, new developments and original achievements in both painting and photography can take place only when individual perception is strong enough to overcome the limiting framework imposed by the learning process.

3 THE VISUAL ELEMENTS: Light

Since before recorded history, light has been the object of mysticism, worshiped, glorified, and adored by humanity, used as a regulator of human life, studied, analyzed, written about poetically and scientifically, depicted in countless works of art as spiritual, natural, and unnatural, tapped as a source of energy to serve humanity in its struggling existence on the planet earth. Our physical and psychological balance revolves around light. The stream of life and all that it means is supported by light. The interconnectedness and continuity of life as seen and felt through countless works of art and, in particular, the photograph, which not only depicts light but must use it physically in creation, may confer on each second of our existence the character of mystery. Light is the medium that forms the photograph, which is an ideal extension of individual consciousness to light as it relates to all observers. Light which makes reality possible, manageable, and transparent may be seen through the photograph, in which we recognize ourselves inhabiting our self-constructed modern environment. Photographs are free-standing objects of matter, reflecting our history, past and present, and are made possible by a single source—light.

Light, natural and artificial, a completely fluid element, is everywhere; it surrounds us and satisfies both our physical and psychological needs. Natural light, our strongest source of illumination, comes to us from the sun. The psychological and physiological effects it continues to have upon all humanity are immeasurable. Our planet's sun is a completely self-contained energy source, having all the visible colors, and without a doubt gives itself instantaneously, copiously, to every level of expression from our earliest recorded existence to the present. We measure distance, time, and space by the standard of light the sun has provided for us. For the present, light has placed a limit on speed, that is, nothing can travel faster than the speed of light. Sound and light are both vibrations, yet light has far greater space-time dimensions than sound.

As a great source of energy and light, the sun is less of a mystery today than it was in our distant past, and yet, just as our ancestors did, we equate light with the most highly esteemed qualities of spirituality, virtue, and intellectual clarity. Literature from every nation makes reference to light in one way or another. The Bible places the creation of light at the beginning of all things. In the first chapter of Genesis we read, "In the beginning God created the heaven and the earth. And the earth was without form, and void; and darkness was upon the face of the deep. And the spirit of God moved upon the face of the waters. And God said, Let there be light: and there was light."

John Milton equated light with the power and divinity of the Creator:

Hail holy light, offspring of Heav'n first-born
Or of the Eternal Coeternal beam
May I express thee unblam'd? Since God is light,
And never but in unapproached light
Dwelt from Eternitie, dwelt then in thee,
Bright effluence of bright essence increate...

Fountain of Light, thyself invisible
Amidst the glorious brightness where thou sit'st
Thron'd inaccessible, but when thou shad'st
The full blaze of thy beams, and through a cloud
Drawn round about thee like a radiant Shrine,
Dark with excessive bright thy skirts appear,
Yet dazzle Heav'n that brightest Seraphim
Approach not, but with both wings veil their eyes...

Look downward on that Globe whose hither side
With light from hence, though but reflected, shines;
That place is Earth the seat of Man, that light
His day...

These passages from Book III of *Paradise Lost* show us Milton at the very height of his power as a poet, and his use of light both metaphorically and literally to form word-images in which the poet reveals the complete plasticity of his medium. But he also uses light as a vehicle signifying deep psychological, spiritual expression, luminous, transparent, through which his multileveled meanings are as light itself filling the pages of his epic of human destiny.

Leonardo da Vinci wrote extensively about light in his notebooks, for example: "No substance can be comprehended without light and shade; light and shade are caused by light. Light is the expeller of darkness. Shadow is the suppression of light."[1] Leonardo's statement appears to be more than just a comment about light as it may relate to the various technical problems associated with painting and drawing. It is Leonardo's own perception of light, but is also a distinctive aspect of the artist himself. In his statement we can recognize that he not only perceives but projects himself with great freedom into and beyond the existence of things and phenomenalistic occurrences. Through these he recognizes his own existence in the midst of the world, of other beings, and in particular of the natural environment which he was consistently probing through his studies and drawings.

Milton and Leonardo, painters, sculptors, and photographers, indeed all creative minds which have as an intrinsic part of their makeup *l'esprit de géométrie, l'esprit de finesse,* whether expressed through the qualities of light or shape, have the clarity, exactitude, objectivity and freedom to express the total person in all his dimensions as a human being. Through such imaginative endeavors we may observe the complexity and the unity of reality, even though we know from the outset that reality itself is a multidimensional stratification.

Some of the earliest known representations of light survive from the art of ancient Egypt. From the Eighteenth Dynasty, about 1355 B.C., in a sculptural fragment showing King Akhenaten with his family presenting gifts to the sun god Aten (Figure 3-1), Aten is depicted with ideological clarity. According to Akhenaten's religion, the sun was symbolized by a disk with beams of light ending in hands that reach for the offerings presented by the family, and at the same time bestow vital forces on the king and his family. These forces, represented by the hieroglyph for "life," are held to the noses of the king and his wife, Queen Nofretete, for them to breathe in.

Figure 3-1 *King Akhenaten with Family* 18th Dynasty c. 1355 B.C.
(The Egyptian Museum, Cairo)

Throughout history light is treated in a multitude of ways, in painting, drawing, sculpture, architecture, and, most recently, photography. In most traditional sculpture, light which ultimately becomes part of the sculpture is considered by the sculptor as an essentially physical element to be manipulated in order to reveal form, texture, and plane relationships. By manipulating light in this manner, the sculptor is able to bring to life spatial relationships within the sculpture as well as surrounding spatial relationships. Perhaps light is perceived and even thought of by the sculptor in an entirely different way than by the painter and photographer. Since sculpture does not deal in illusions, at least the kind of illusions that painting does, it is not difficult to see that the painter and sculptor could think of light differently.

Traditional two-dimensional painting is based on illusion, an illusion of the physical reality of the third dimension. Sculpture, on the other hand, is in itself a three-dimensional reality, which, when completed, exists in the physical space of ordinary perception. Light in a painting, a Monet landscape for instance, is not manipulated by the painter as it might be by a sculptor; instead, it is perceived and represented by the manipulation of the painter's pigments through adjustments of hue, color, chroma, tone, tint, and value on a two-dimensional surface. It is on this surface that the illusion of light is executed. The painting is an interpretation of light, never the light itself.

Painting and sculpture concern themselves with external, surface qualities of light as it relates to art, while architecture internalizes light as well, fusing light and space into nearly inseparable elements. In architecture, space, light, and function inevitably become dominant factors, intertwined and superseding, for the most part, aesthetic modes. Architecture differs in this way from painting, sculpture, and photography on the most fundamental level.

One need only examine such architectural masterpieces as the Pantheon, the Gothic cathedrals, and the Baroque churches by Bernini or Borromini, or Le Corbusier's church of Notre-Dame-du-Haut at Ronchamp to understand fully light as it is manipulated by the architect. In each of these examples, light is used as more than mere illumination for a variety of internal spaces. It is the architect's personal expression through light, but is also intended as a supreme extension of the ideology, philosophy, or theology of a particular institution within the period of the architectural concept.

Such elements as the rose window, lancet window, deep and sometimes angled embrasures, tracery, clerestory, and above all stained glass, are more than structural or design concerns; they are complex and extremely effective methods of light control. Light may be filtered, refracted, reflected, fractured, focused, and diffused in a number of ways by combining, adjusting, and placing these architectural elements in and out of alignment with one another to achieve dramatic or soaring effects with light. The interaction of the various light-controlling architectural elements and light itself helps to shape and define the internal spaces.

Often light within these structures was manipulated in such a way as to exclude external natural light associations. Instead, it was intended to give an aura of light from sources other than the physical surroundings. The result was to be a spiritual light entering through a variety of apertures throughout the structure, and intended to lead the visitor into mystical states of being, into meditation, and into a sense of separation from the physical world. Within this environment, the individual was to feel as if this were a safe, protected, otherworldly place suspended in time, where the spirit could seek an understanding of God and find its relationship to God through reflection. In these spaces, light represented God on a very grand scale. Today, when we experience these spaces and light through our modern understanding of God, whatever it may be, the gulf between us and the period in which these structures were constructed closes. It is not difficult to realize that the psychological and physical effects intended by these architects through such light manipulations is still extremely effective.

Today, the architect has far greater latitude in working with light, since modern heating and cooling systems are effective, complex installations which allow for larger apertures and expanses of glass, permitting light to enter the internal spaces as never before. Philip Johnson's Glass House or Minoru Yamasaki's World Trade Center would be impossibilities without the technological advances in materials and systems. These advances have without a doubt changed the contemporary architect's approach to the entire question of light, both natural and artificial. If one merely compares the chapel at the United States Air Force Academy in Colorado, which is nearly all glass, to any Victorian Gothic church, it becomes evident that interior climate control is of such importance that design concepts are completely circumscribed by it.

However, in more recent times, the influences of these disciplines upon one another have had dramatic effects upon each, allowing for greater crossover between disciplines, with light exerting a greater psychological effect upon the observer and inhabitant than ever before.

For a short period of time in the history of painting, artists concerned themselves with luminary qualities which further extended ordinary concepts of light and optics. The Impressionist painters explored and crystallized their own perceptions of light, aided by what they had learned about light in the recently published scientific discoveries concerning light and color. For some of these painters, the photograph became an additional aid in their pursuit of light, color, and optics. At the same time, (1870–1880), in America, a group of painters known as the Luminists were making efforts towards studies of light largely through landscape paintings. This group was not interested in the more logical, scientifically based information concerning light as were the Impressionists. Few of the Luminist painters, if any, ever reached the heights of accomplishment and originality of the Impressionists. Unlike their American counterparts, the French Impressionist painters made free use of other disciplines for their work, including photography, which is and was the first conceptual art to represent the triumph of idea over object. In the final analysis, the Luminists simply gave the illusion of light in the most superficial, literal, and unconvincing manner.

If differences between the perceptions of light by the painter and sculptor exist, then does the photographer perceive light in a way that is exclusively his? Is there a difference in the way a photographer perceives light to produce color photographs? And what of those photographers who work with light in what is termed "photographic installations" rather than the so-called straight photographic method? It would appear that in all cases the photographer sees light in accordance with the photographic medium, since it is dependent on light. Manipulations of light in the darkroom are understood easily enough since there it is procedure-oriented. But what of the photographer's general perceptions of both natural and artificial sources of light? Psychological and physiological perceptions of light are complex, fissured realities for the photographer which affect his expressions of light, made evident in the photograph.

Unlike the painter and sculptor, the photographer cannot change the largely fixed intrinsic qualities of natural light, and there is a clearly defined limitation on just how much it can be manipulated. This understood restriction placed on the photographer by the mechanical equipment results in an image which is a resemblance of light, never the illusion of light which the painter achieves. This distinction, it would seem, gives the photographer a concentrated approach to light. His perceptions would have less to do with light as the element which reveals texture, shape, volume, spatial relationships, and coloristic aspects of an object which may be manipulated at will, but instead with light understood as a source which continually changes both the outer and inner characteristics of the object. In a sense, light for the photographer is the creator of objects and their characteristics, which are again manipulated and changed by light. If light is perceived in this manner, that is, as the source of continual change, it places the photographer in a position of perceiving light entirely differently from other artists. He becomes in a way the co-creator, since he decides when to stop the changing action of light in the environment through his camera. If the interaction of light and object is perceived in this respect, the environment becomes a kaleidoscope of changing, interacting elements propelled by light. When the photographer consciously involves himself in this interaction of light and environment, he and his perceptions become an integral part of unexplicated absolute reciprocity of light, time, and space.

Simultaneously, the latent image contains the individual experience of light perception, precisely extracted from the flow of change, free of expressionistic interpretations, and encapsuled for further creative manipulations if so desired by the photographer. The latent image in the darkroom becomes for the photographer, when made visible, the recollection of consciousness in light, which was both an inward and outward reaching of mind and spirit. It is connected with references to the world of light, and to the absolute self of consciousness and subconsciousness which refers to those perceptions of light both experienced and imagined.

In the black-and-white photograph, one has a greater sense of light simply because the whites are read as light itself, and all the blacks and some greys as the absence of light. If this is true, then the photographer may develop a strong feeling for those dark-light relationships as he perceives them in the environment. Admittedly, there could be confusion between those dark-light objects and light itself. However, these tendencies to confuse values, or zones of tone, with light are eventually eliminated, and light perceptions transcend tone perceptions.

In at least two respects, color photography is problematic in comparison to black-and-white and the perception of color. First, the emotional responses to color are extremely powerful, which could prejudice the photographer's perceptions of light. And second, the physics of color, as well as the technical-psychological understanding of local, optical, pigment, and light-color, are complexities which require separate perceptions.

Once the photographer understands the theory of color and can distinguish the differences between the quality of light or brightness present in hues and colors and light itself, he has without a question a most powerful tool to work with. The complexities of color and color photography as it relates to light are far too extensive to be dealt with in this book, which is essentially a consideration of black-and-white photography. However, for our purposes, the question of light perceptions in color photography can be answered directly and simply. The continual change of natural light in the environment, which constantly recreates all objects, is also visually recreating all apparent hues and colors. It is the perception of these changing hues and colors as an independent phenomenon, as well as those intrinsic qualities of light itself, that distinguishes the perceptions of the color photographer from those of the photographer in black-and-white.

In the creative, perceptual process, natural light is to artificial light as water is to ice cubes. The element is the same, yet different. Artificial light may be manipulated, shaped, and changed, redirected at will. Light in this respect begins to parallel light as it is manipulated in internal architectural spaces.

With the great variety of artificial lighting equipment available today to the photographer, his choices for light effects are only as limited as his imagination. Whether dealing with traditional studio, flash, or stroboscopic lighting for action events outside the studio, the photographer has never had as much freedom with the manipulation of light as he does today through artificial methods. Continuous artificial light, the most common, is perhaps the one which offers the most predictable photographic results. Intermittent artificial light is somewhat less predictable, and has effects that are clearly different from continuous. The photographer's intellectual understanding of the electrical light source helps to shape his perceptions of light from these sources. The substantial differences between perceptions of natural and artificial light directs the photographer toward other creative approaches than those he would use with natural outdoor lighting in seeking solutions to intuitive or preplanned efforts.

Whether light is used as a source of reflection or as an aid to transparencies in photographic installations or other related photographic efforts, perceptions and manipulations of light in such cases are quite different from those instances mentioned already. The controlling action of the photographer can create another world in which the reality of light becomes the object. In such instances he understands the affinity light has for the object, the environment, and the forces that transform all it touches. Artificial light is perceived as the element of transformation with or without demarcations, entirely within the photographer's comprehensive and absolute control. In a sense, light is liberated from the commonplace literal perceptions related to the spaces of the physical world when it is redirected by the photographer. In this respect, light is a tangible, tactile medium which can be shaped in rationalistic or intuitive modes of action as a living substance. The synthesis of the concept of light as a tangible substance, which can be manipulated as an acute natural mental reality by the photographer, and the empirical sciences within photography, results in a vital reconstruction of our own ideas and perceptions of light when observed in photographic installations and other light-manipulated photographic efforts.

There are no systems or analytical procedures to be followed if we wish to broaden our own perceptions of light. The various categories and terminologies for light are meaningless unless we determinedly avoid preconceptions. Minds preoccupied with dogmatic procedures have ceased to perceive light. Photographs are expressions of light, and they may serve as reasonable visual stimuli in significantly reawakening our concepts and perceptions of light.

It would be a mistake to leave the topic of light without some mention of associations of light as an expression manifested in photographs. In viewing photographs, the general approach is to understand the image through object representation, or if nonobjective, through shape. Consideration of light is often a kind of mental footnote, if it is given much attention at all. Often it is the quality of light that tells more about what the photographer, or painter, wishes to convey, than any of the other aspects of the photograph or painting.

In certain of Van Gogh's paintings, light and the light sources, both natural and artificial, are the telling factors in understanding the psychological makeup or attitude of the artist. *Starry Night,* 1889 (Figure 3-2) is a landscape with illusions of natural light, represented as coming from the moon and stars, and the painting *The Night Café,* 1888 (Figure 3-3) an interior illuminated by artificial light, depicts light coming from hanging lamps. In both paintings, the light is shown something like sound waves, moving outward from their central sources. The light moves outward with great force and energy; however, the interior of

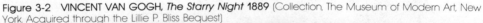

Figure 3-2   VINCENT VAN GOGH, *The Starry Night* 1889 (Collection, The Museum of Modern Art, New York. Acquired through the Lillie P. Bliss Bequest)

Figure 3-3 VINCENT VAN GOGH, *The Night Café* 1888 (Yale University Art Gallery. Bequest of Stephen Carlton Clark, B.A. 1903)

the café is filled with illumination, while the landscape is not, the light being concentrated in the heavens. Each painting is a different psychological expression through light, one of religiosity (light in the heavens), the other with a downward crushing light (perhaps of depression). In both paintings, light is the dominant force. Light, the artist's true issue in these paintings, may be read perhaps somewhat more clearly if object orientation is put aside for a moment.

Wynn Bullock's *The Stark Tree*, 1956 (Figure 3-4) and Diane Arbus's *A Castle in Disneyland, California*, 1962 (Figure 3-5) are both expressions of an inner reality through light. Bullock's use of natural light is an overpowering image of an interaction between light and land mists, where light is diffused by the mists, and mists given life by light. The physical world of objects is used in an abstract manner, rather than a literal one. The physical reality of the landscape is obscured by light and mists, dissolving into space. Bullock uses light to express the mysterious. As he states: "I think everything is mysterious. It's just a matter of your power to perceive it . . . The photograph of the tree is not the tree . . ."[2] The deep psychological, emotional attachment he has had with nature since his childhood is clearly perceived through his use of light, which expresses the mysterious power within the natural environment.

Figure 3-4   WYNN BULLOCK, *The Stark Tree* 1956 (Wynn and Edna Bullock Trust)

Figure 3-5   DIANE ARBUS, *A Castle in Disneyland, California* 1962 (Copyright © 1972 The Estate of Diane Arbus)

Arbus's photograph of artificial light seen coming through various apertures in the castle and reflected in the water that surrounds it is the most striking
aspect of her image. Other artificial light sources illuminate the castle from
hidden places, giving the whole an eerie sensation. This castle, which is a delight-
ful structure during the light of day, has become, through Arbus's use of artificial illumination at night, an expression with threatening, ominous overtones.
Light in this image appears to hold the frightening unknown.

Both of these expressions through light are clearly not concerned with the
resemblances of light in the ordinary sense, but light as extensions of the psyche,
the conscious and subconscious. The substance of light is a vehicle for a personal,
psychological expression, which reveals the innermost emotions, feelings, and
visceral responses of the individual to his condition, both real and imagined,
from the past and present.

Mid-nineteenth-century photography, essentially concerned with portraiture, in which the photographer arranged the lighting, pose, and props, stands
out in sharp contrast to the stroboscopic lighting developed in the early 1930s by
Harold Edgerton. Stroboscopic lighting allowed photographers to produce clear
exposures in as little as one-millionth of a second. Exposures produced under
such lighting conditions rendered visible events that moved too quickly for the
unaided eye to see. When a fast-moving event was "stopped" by a strobe light
and recorded on film, as in Edgerton's *Girl Skipping Rope*, c. 1950 (Figure 3-6),
the result was an image which illustrated superbly how the action really looked.

Figure 3-6   DR. HAROLD EDGERTON, *Girl Skipping Rope* c. 1950 (Courtesy Daniel Wolf, Inc. New York)

Although this lighting was primarily used for scientific photographs, it quickly became part of the art photography vocabulary. It is not just that *Girl Skipping Rope* clearly outlines all the movement of the event that makes the photograph a delight to look at, but that in a limited way it manipulates space and time. Without a doubt, there are the abstract elements in this image that one may enjoy as well, the overlapping figure creating new shapes and movements, the linear rhythms of the rope as it moves through space, and the sense of transparency. These effects can be seen in the work of the Cubists and the Futurists, as well as the photographs of Thomas Eakins, such as his *Pole Vaulter,* a wet-plate photograph of 1884 (Figure 3-7). However, it is Edgerton's stroboscopic lighting that makes the distinct difference between *Girl Skipping Rope* and *Pole Vaulter.* Edgerton's photograph offers greater detail, clarity, and greater latitude for multiple overlapping images compared to the earlier efforts of Eakins. John Szarkowski, director of the Department of Photography at the Museum of Modern Art, says of such photographs as *Girl Skipping Rope,* "They have hung on our museum's walls almost as consistently as Picasso's paintings have" and "must be as familiar to many of our visitors as the Guernica."[3]

In the past, such visual elements as texture, light, color, volume, and space functioned as vehicles for the artist's ideas, while representation of objects was the primary concern. In contemporary art, the visual elements often play a more important role for the artist, becoming the leading object of his concern, if not the very subject.

Light, the primary consideration for any photographer, is a crucial ele-

Figure 3-7 THOMAS EAKINS, *Pole Vaulter* 1884 (The Metropolitan Museum of Art, gift of Charles Bregler, 1941)

ment, for without natural or artificial light the photographic image would not exist. Photography depends on light. The word "photography" is derived from two Greek words meaning "light" and "writing." Light reveals our environment, illuminating what we see, allowing us to gather information so that we may function within that environment as well as enjoy the aesthetic qualities of natural and manmade objects. In looking at photographs, one may merely gather information or experience emotional responses activated, at least in part, by the quality of light. Qualities we attribute to light, such as ominous, peaceful, soft, romantic, spiritual, and a host of others, may be limited only by the photographer's sensitivity to the variations available to him. All light has fundamental qualities, whether it comes from natural or artificial sources, and these qualities are subject to the photographer's ability to bring them out as they react with his subject. It is not the light source that should be of any real concern, whether from the sun, photo-flood, flash, or other sources, but how the light interacts with the subject to produce the desired results for aesthetic or informational reasons.

Shaping, revealing, and altering subject matter or creating moods may be accomplished by manipulation of light or careful adjustments of the subject to the available light. Direct light from a single source, natural or artificial, has alternating qualities depending upon the size of the light source and its distance from the subject. The smaller the size of the source and the farther it is from the subject, the stronger the contrasts, the sharper the edges, and the less the detail in shadow areas. Bringing the light source closer to the subject and increasing its size will reverse some of these effects. In both cases, the light must be directed at the subject to produce these qualities; however, the source may be directed toward another surface and allowed to reflect the subject, producing a slightly different effect. In this case, a softening of form results from the bending of the light rays. When the light rays are parallel, or at least nearly so, dramatic effects are created by distance and size.

Judy Dater's *Twinkla* (Figure 3-8) depicts natural light as a direct source streaming through the leaves and lighting the photographer's figure, the contours of which are etched against a dark, rich background of leaves and tree trunk. The quality of light is soft, mysterious, and inviting. There are no sharp shadows or cast shadows, so that all the forms are gently modeled, revealing textures in low relief so that they appear graceful, flowing, shimmering, and sympathetic to the subject. Light is shown as fragile, elusive, yet warm and unconditionally life-giving. The thin, revealing, provocative frock the photographer wears absorbs and reflects light to and from its gauzelike surface, enhancing the mood of the forest creature discovered and surprised by an intruder in its secret place and ready to spring away in fright. Points of light reflect from the large, dark, orblike eyes, which become the focal point of the image, almost hypnotic in their steady gaze directed at the observer. Although the image plays upon fantasy, there remains something profoundly, essentially true about that dominion, plausible and without pretext. It is as if the light which occupies and illuminates the space gently radiated outward with personal assurance to those who observe the magical embellishments revealed in that environment by the warm light. The figure appears as the embodiment of femininity through the costume, pose and facial expression, as she crouches wrapped in gossamer veils

Figure 3-8   JUDY DATER, *Twinkla*
(Courtesy of the photographer)

of light in a dark thicket, a mythological figure out of *A Midsummer Night's Dream*. Dater's photograph builds with convincing deftness a hidden world of the imagination temporarily revealed in light, constructed by means of light, characterized through light. The inward freedom of this photographer is characterized by the superiority of her exalted ability of perception, infinite imagination, and uniquely vivid dramatic, environment-conditioned interpretations, proclaimed in psychological transformations directly expressed in the photograph.

Diffused light coming from a specific source creates distinct shadows with edges somewhat softer than those caused by direct light. This effect is caused by some of the light rays being diffused or scattered at various angles. The areas to light are gradual rather than sharply defined. Diffused light entering through windows or doors may be reflected from the outside into a room, giving a sense of light direction. Floodlights may give the same effect when the source is directed at a reflecting surface. Outdoor bright sunlight can give the same results when it is diffused and reflected from another surface to the subject. A moderately overcast day can produce the same result. In the next photograph, the sky is the main source of light and acts as the reflector. William van der Weyde's *Man in the Electric Chair,* c. 1900 (Figure 3-9), is a chilling depiction of a gruesome affair—the arrangements for an execution. Light enters the room through a window or door, direct and diffused. The floor acts as a reflector so that the light rays are scattered and bounce into the shadow areas, filling them with soft light, revealing textures and details. Light entering the room picks up and accentuates certain elements, such as leather, wood, cloth, and flesh, lending a greater sense of reality to the approaching event. The expression of the man in the electric chair is one of quiet resignation, as the five men surrounding him go about their tasks in a rather cold, detached manner, completely oblivious to the human occupying the chair. Their faces register nothing concerning the end of a man's life, just polite attendance to the adjustments of the equipment used in carrying out the punishment. The light, casting long, low shadows and softly diffused, is strangely in harmony with the condemned man. Perhaps it is his light-toned and light-reflecting clothing that joins him with the direct-diffused light filling the room. Light and subject are fused in an uncanny manner, forming a composition and image not easily forgotten.

Light that is fully diffused shows no source or direction and is uniformly

Figure 3-9   WILLIAM VAN DER WEYDE, *Man in the Electric Chair* c. 1900 (International Museum of Photography at George Eastman House, Rochester, New York)

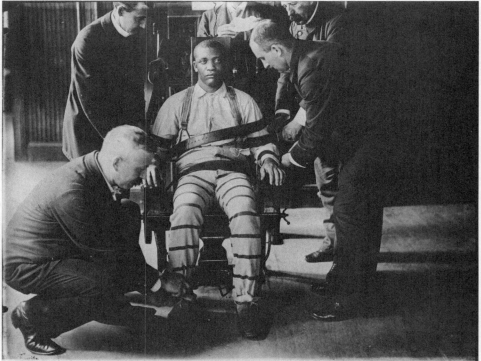

scattered over the subject. The edges of shadows become indistinct, and the subject matter appears surrounded by light. On an overcast day, the sky becomes the main source of light, as the sun's rays are completely scattered. Indoors, a fully diffused light would require an extremely large source, close to the subject, with reflectors or fill-lights to open up shadows if one wanted to approximate the fully diffused light found outdoors. Adam Clark Vroman's *Navajo Man—"Coyote"*, 1901 (Figure 3-10), photographed in fully diffused light, shows no strong or cast shadows; however, a light direction from above is indicated by the softly lit cheekbones, nose, and chin. His eyes reflect the sky, which is the major source of light, since the sun's rays have been scattered by the cloud overlay. If a specific source of light had been used, a small point of light would be seen in the eyes. Forms are strongly projected even though the light is diffused and soft. Yet the light has allowed textural aspects to emerge, particularly the skin, which functions as a counterpoint to the textured background. Vroman's use of light for his subject works very well in creating a mood of introspection held lightly in a moment of time.

To create a silhouette effect, the subject must be in shadow or underexposed aginst a brightly lighted background. Ralph Eugene Meatyard's untitled photograph of 1960 beautifully illustrates this silhouette effect (Figure 3-11). A child is standing between two doors reflecting strong light and is in the shadow of one door. Her complete silhouette, except for one sock with two stripes

Figure 3-10 ADAM CLARK VROMAN, *Navaho Man—Coyote* 1901 (Courtesy of Southwest Museum, Los Angeles)

Figure 3-11   RALPH EUGENE
MEATYARD, *Untitled* 1960
(Courtesy of Madelyn O.
Meatyard)

repeating the horizontal line or motive of the doors, at first glance appears to be a negative shape, almost a cut-out section of the door. It is only when one discovers the one striped sock that the impression of a negative shape is reversed to a positive one. If the aperture of his camera had been opened perhaps three or four stops more, the exposure would have produced a recognizable portrait of the child, but then the image would have become something entirely different, perhaps not as mysterious as it is now; certainly the play of negative-positive shape would have been lost. Meatyard's sensitivity to light, in this case a forceful, single source from a low angle reflecting upward on the doors from the floor, has allowed him to assemble a haunting image of dark overtones, transporting us back into our own shadowy childhood existence of innocent fantasy.

During the formative years of photography, lighting with a flash was problematic, but today, with the variety of flash units, strobes, flash-cubes and bulbs, different shutter types, synchronizations of shutter speed, and other technical advances, it need not be. Generally, flash photographs show a flatness of modeling and lack of texture, with thin shadows giving little suggestion of any volume. Often with flash photography, the inverse-square law is apparent; that is, the farther the object is from the source of light, the less light will fall upon it, with the effect that the background goes black and lacks detail while the foreground is often brightly lit.

Aaron Siskind's *Savoy Dancers,* 1936 (Figure 3-12) from *The Harlem Document,* clearly illustrates the inverse-square law in which shapes and forms in the middle and background are in darkness while the foreground depicting the two

Figure 3-12 AARON SISKIND, *Savoy Dancers* 1936 (Courtesy of Light Gallery, New York)

dancers is brightly lit. For some photographers, Aaron Siskind for example, the lighting effects produced by the inverse-square law are desirable for aesthetic or technical reasons. The two wildly dancing figures show very few areas of shadow as they move in the darkened space behind them. Certain segments of their clothing are lacking in detail, and texture is nearly eliminated while the volume of the subject appears to be diminished. Yet for all these seeming "problem areas," the flash, as it was used in *Savoy Dancers,* is in keeping with the subject; the illumination accentuates it, brassy, sharp-edged, and fast. The light gives the impression of pulsation, a beat that moves with the music and the dance pattern of feet as the couple quickly moves over the uneven wooden floor of the dance area. Siskind has used light that brings together the quality of the sound the figures dance to, and has sealed in time a period of pre–World War II American history that now looks distant, innocent, and nostalgic.

Light normally travels in straight lines, but it can be bent, absorbed, transmitted, refracted, diffused, defracted, or dispersed when coming in contact with a variety of materials and surfaces. Outdoor light is constantly changing from moment to moment; shadows shift, elongate, and contract, and what looked one way a fleeting second ago can suddenly appear quite different the next, as atmospheric changes occur and the sun moves across the heavens. As the seasons and the earth's distance from the sun change, so do the qualities of light, offering an endless variety of opportunities for the individual who takes enough time to look, study, contemplate, and perceive their ever-changing characteristics. The direction light takes on a clear day or an overcast day can transform an ordinary, recognizable situation or object into the unknown. What once looked flat and uninteresting can, with a shift in light-angle, undergo a complete metamorphosis of volume, texture, shape, size; what was transparent becomes opaque; what was opaque becomes transparent. Shapes, scale, and proportions can change from the clear, hard light of early morning to the softly glowing light of late afternoon. Humid and rainy climate conditions that diffuse and scatter light rays may effectively turn the least interesting landscape into a surreal or romantic one. At night, outdoor artificial light can turn the ordinary into the extraordinary.

Natural light, entering an interior through doors, windows, or other openings, and artificial light have special qualities distinctly different from outdoor light. Artificially lit areas from a single source that quickly fade off into blackness offer dramatic light effects, but when surrounding surfaces reflect that light, the mood may shift, offering new opportunities. In an interior, many fluorescent lighting fixtures can produce a flat greyness, diffused and cold, which may be appropriate for certain effects and moods. Natural light entering an interior directly or indirectly by reflection may turn the ugly into the beautiful or turn it around so that the beautiful becomes unattractive.

In Harry Callahan's *Eleanor,* 1948 (Figure 3-13), light reveals and in-

Figure 3-13 HARRY CALLAHAN, *Eleanor* 1948 (Courtesy of Light Gallery, New York)

terprets the nude woman seated in the corner of an austere room. She is softly modeled by the diffused reflected light entering the room through two windows on either side of her. The diffused light reflects upon the various surfaces softly, gently, creating an atmosphere of quietness and peacefulness that one associates with the woman, whose face is turned away so that she becomes every woman. It is a daydream that evokes longing, wistfulness for time past, a dream spun of light, perceived, understood, and deeply felt by Callahan. The image is no greater than the photographer's sensitivity to recognizing in the substance called light a method of speaking directly about a woman. The woman becomes the light; they are interchangeable within the space defined by the light.

Light as a subject may be found in many photographs; the form that it takes is limited only by the imagination and inventiveness of the photographer. Minor White's *Grand Tetons* depicts light as apocalyptic, breaking through dark clouds over the Grand Tetons in radiating beams. Ansel Adams's *Moonrise, Hernandez, New Mexico* shows us clear, cool, white moonlight over an eerie bank of clouds, and Wynn Bullock's *Let There Be Light* speaks of light as mystical, softly diffused over a dark seascape. *Dawn* by Dennis Stock depicts the early morning light refracting through thousands of droplets of moisture clinging to, and running down, a window pane, creating an abstraction of light, water, and movement. Alvin Langdon Coburn's *Vortograph*, 1917 (Figure 3-14) depicts light as a universal. The light of the enlarger becomes the subject, crystallizing it,

Figure 3-14   ALVIN LANGDON COBURN, *Vortograph Number 1* 1917 (Collection, The Museum of Modern Art, New York. Gift of Alvin Langdon Coburn)

turning it into many-faceted prisms refracting and sparkling, dazzling the eye with its gemlike quality. His abstraction, undimmed by time, radiating light, is a reminder that it is light, and light alone, that is the photographer's medium.

Fluorescent light, wire, cut and torn paper suspended from overhead in huge sheets, or smaller pieces of paper strewn about on the studio floor are the current tools that David Haxton uses to create his installations, which he later photographs. His carefully assembled combinations of brightly colored papers and syncopated lighting effects have something of the stage set about them, but this first impression is not entirely accurate. They are far more complex in their graceful references to the landscape architecture of the Orient, or to landscape itself. In some of the installations the fluorescent lighting tubes have been smashed on the floor, their shattered pieces echoing the tips and jagged tears in the suspended sheets of paper. These residues of violence refer to destructive forces and energies just beneath the surface in all of nature. Haxton's installations share the duality of nature, the visual poetry of brilliant or subdued colors interacting with one another through light, and the unsuspecting terror of its force disguised by these elements. But his work reveals these two aspects at once through materials at once delicate and humble.

Once the exposure has been made for one of Haxton's installations, he never adjusts the image in the darkness in any way, nor does he crop the image later for whatever reason. His experience as a filmmaker exerts itself through the elements he employs and the way he works with them. Electrical wires and cables are randomly scattered about the floor and direct the eye to the light sources by the black lines they create as they cross over the multicolored papers. The choice of materials suggests impermanence; it is as if the entire installation is about to disintegrate, never to reappear in just the same arrangement.

Haxton's *Torn Orange Front and Rear* (Figure 3-15) has two light sources,

Figure 3-15   DAVID HAXTON,
Torn Orange Front and Rear
(Courtesy of the photographer)

one hidden behind the torn and slashed dark red-orange paper, and the other positioned on the right side of the composition in front of a lighter orange ripped and curling section of paper. These lighting effects remind one of the dramatic lighting effects in the paintings of Georges de La Tour, in which the light source is partly or entirely hidden by a human hand, head, or some other object. But Haxton's concerns with light move beyond La Tour's painterly devices in which the light shield was generally a translucent material. Artificial light is used in an extremely poetic manner by Haxton to create a number of visual effects, and to bring the observer effectively to the *via regia*, which leads into the photographer's realm of the conscious and unconscious, as the interpreter of the creator's dreams.

Paper in these installations is used as an architect would use more durable materials to create external and internal spaces for a structure. Walls, screens, dividers or partitions with openings suggesting windows allow light to enter larger spaces created by the vertical planes of paper. By placing other sheets of paper of a different color behind these openings, the apertures create shapes which appear to float in space and set up movements and countermovements throughout the entire installation. Their spatial relationship to the light source activates them so that they often become negative-positive equivocating shapes. The equivocating shapes assist in establishing elusive, deceptive spatial relationships throughout the installation. Shadows and cast shadows form mysterious, dreamlike shapes, poised as though ready for flight. Light passing through the various openings echoes those openings on adjacent uneven planes of colored paper, transforming the simple vertical planes into willing receptors on which the light-shapes gently float and undulate.

Haxton's *Magenta Shadows on White and Violet* (Figure 3-16) is fragile, delicate—the first flowers of spring emerging through the cool white snow. Broken

Figure 3-16   DAVID HAXTON,
Magenta Shadows on White and Violet (Courtesy of the photographer)

transparent glass and a shattered opaque lighting tube in this installation refer to the transparency of light, but also light as an opaque substance of milky white coloration. Light entering the installation from the upper left and extending the range of values in the magenta and violet colors as they interact with white, comes from an unseen light source. The cool colors, broken glass, and light that is delineated as soft, diffused, and sharp-edged are combined to disclose an undisguised dream fulfilled and laid bare.

The structures and dynamisms at work in these installations present the photographer's motivations, which are uniquely his. These evocative images, which spring from his mental stratum, are the interplay and transformation of the energies and forces within him. Light, which he directs to reveal his dreams and wish fulfillments via the installation, depicts illusory shifting spatial relationships, order and disorder, violences, and tranquillity. They are light-filled spaces of the imagination in which we may hear the lyrical and dark unsung music of the natural environment, echoing through the hollow empty chambers of Haxton's architectural fantasies. These are unpeopled places inhabited by light and shadow, without specific place or time. Yet in the deeper recesses of our own half-forgotten memories, we recognize them as personal, timeless events which push beyond the limits of rational experience, beyond *a priori* concepts, to metaphysical needs held deep within the psyche. These images do not satisfy reason alone, for the limits are clearly set by a lack of visible systematic unity, consequently they press on toward universal ideas feeding the psyche. Haxton's images are ideal, pure, visual statements in which our own deeply rooted needs and longings are met.

For Eliot Porter, light is the essential aesthetic consideration, existing alongside color, which is ultimately the same. Mysterious, poetic, glorious light drifts into his images, revealing the natural environment of the landscape with tender caresses melting into unimagined color. *Glen Canyon* (Figure 3-17) is flushed with soft rose, slate blue, mauve, salmon pink, and rich browns laced with gold. The cross-light focused on a central form in the composition picks out the contours of the rock as sharp-edged against the dark browns of the other rocks behind it, while the interior mass becomes soft, flowing, sensual undulations, as if breathing with life. Rock stratifications are picked out in detail by the soft light, and form a composition of a few strong diagonal lines encompassing the highly textured rock surfaces, which are played off the other surfaces worn smooth by wind and rain.

There is a stillness about the entire image which seems to be manifested in the quality of light and air, and is set in contrast to the power and might of the rock masses as a giant asleep. At once beautiful and majestic, tranquil and violent, *Glen Canyon* is a masterpiece of landscape photography created by Porter's complete understanding of those forces within nature that were dormant as he recorded them. His photographic image is clearly the reflection of a man who loves and respects his subject. But more than this, Porter makes no attempt to transform the majesty of the landscape into something else; it remains itself, revealing just one of its changing aspects for the moment, then moving on to another. Porter understands extremely well landscape metamorphosis as part of the totality of metamorphic unity of the planet earth. His understanding and respect for this aspect of life is revealed to us through the formality of his work.

Figure 3-17   ELIOT PORTER, *Glen Canyon* August 29, 1961 (Courtesy Daniel Wolf, Inc. New York)

Glen Canyon, like Porter's other landscape photographs, does not attempt to suggest that we are helpless in the face of nature's terrible and wonderful aspects, but that we are simply part of it, an inevitable coexistence accepted peacefully and gracefully. His unpeopled images affirm his position to his subject directly and without sentiment or dramatics. Light as the revealer of change, and subject to change itself, is documented through Porter's love and understanding of color and light, sealed in the photographic image. His color photographs are made into fine prints from color transparencies, and thus allow him to control the final statement. For Porter color is the ultimate expression in photography, but within the tradition of straight photography. All the subtle nuances and shadings of color harmonies in *Glen Canyon* are in their naturalistic setting, but the psychological and emotional forces of color and light come to life and are released by his perception and his camera. The exciting new insights revealed through color and light in his work are partly due to Porter's control over the image, which becomes in the final analysis expressive and deeply moving, pervaded by his concerns as a preservationist. Color and light are for Porter the fabric of his work, seamless in their revelations of the landscape. As John Szarkowski says of Porter, "In the late fifties and early sixties, Helen Levitt and Eliot Porter made photographs which demonstrated that color, like other aspects of pictorial form, was not necessarily a distinct issue but could be seen as organic part of meaning."[4]

As a colorist Porter brings to photography what the Impressionist painters and Rembrandt did—the interaction of light and color as an expression of the deeper self, as well as color and light understood as a physical chemical process. Porter's perception and expression of color and light through the photographic image have left a legacy to photography, to art, which other photographers and artists recognize as indispensable if one is to attempt to understand color and light. But Porter's work, for those interested in landscape, the environment, and birds, has also left a legacy of inspiration and creativity drawn from the natural environment as a tribute to it.

Photographs that demonstrate these unusual perceptions and manipulations of light stand as living proofs of the photographer's personal empirical reality. These relationships of the photographer to light are not merely superficial, dualistic expressions of the self and the outer realities, but are brilliant examples of a synthesis—of technique, stupendous knowledge of the visual physical reality, and a co-realization, whether admitted or not by the photographer, of the self as rational and irrational. It is impossible to speculate about how such photographers possess such personal characteristics which are clearly the driving force in their work. But that we have such original dialectical minds, fearless of expressing the deeper self, is reason enough to accept them and spare the all-too-trivial objections. The self-movement of spirit and consciousness through expressions in light are consequently, in the photograph, ideal and tangibly real representations of predominantly individual triads (self, expression, liberation). If we as observers can gain some recognition of the photographer through our own intellectual-speculative selves via the photograph, we have not only progressed with our own reinterpretations of the known and unknown, but have also become less prisoners to our notions concerning ourselves.

The continous challenge of self-discovery through light for the photographer is presented by Minor White in his statement:

> . . . I can point out that light seems to come from inside (a) photograph, which is certainly not at all like the condition which my reason tells me prevailed at the time, though exactly like what I saw in a moment of highly charged vision. I can also say this symbolizes the emotion felt while making it, and know only how little of this vision the picture must cause in others. Feeling and photographing what causes feeling is no assurance that others will feel. But after once discovering what one wants to arouse in other people, the knowledge that one may frequently fumble in trying is only a challenge.[5]

Even though Minor White expresses here uncertainty that the photographic image can always convey the moment of exposure and his personal meaning as well, he has the conviction that emotion is symbolized by the image. But more important is "discovering what one wants to arouse in other people." In the beginning of his statement he points out that light seems to come from inside the photograph. Light in his photographs functions as an equivalent for the reaction he wants to arouse in other people. For White, as for all photographers, photography has the status of a language by means of which each may discuss, preach, exhort, confess, understand, and be understood. The complex significance of this language of photography is made possible by light and through light offers itself as an orthodox individual-psychological approach to expression of the variety of impulses inherent in human character, but specifically the character of the photographer. Through the language of the photograph (which may be understood as light) we may recognize the numerous intellectual and emotional impulses, problems, and queries, repressed or admitted, made visible by the photographer.

The question of whether the photographer should discover or understand those deeper impulses within himself that he wishes to arouse in others is open to debate. Freud believed that a person should become aware of himself by learning to control his instincts, to bear the burden of his history and master the problem of his sense of guilt. However, there are examples which may be pointed to in which the self-awareness of which Freud speaks did not produce positive results in an artist, either through any of the psychoanalytic approaches professionally conducted or by self-motivation (Diane Arbus, Jackson Pollock, Van Gogh). Without a doubt there are artists who have been and are still greatly assisted in their work and as individuals through these means, but it would seem that certain limitations must be understood from the outset in order to preserve the innate creative urge, whatever it may be, within the personality if the object is the container of, and expression of, that syndrome or psychosis.

The environmental, experimental, and innate disposition of the photographer-artist combined constitute the unique individual expressions of the photographer, and proceed to a final visual form manifested in the photograph through the language of photography. When these factors are integrated and assimilated into the structure of the personality, the continual formation of consciousness and unconsciousness, they become major factors superseding the physiologically programmed instincts, which are the foundations on which the photographer's creative energies rest. Human needs, love, friendship, acceptance, compassion, and understanding are in the final analysis the dynamic aspects of the personality structure, either in conflict with instinctual motivations or in harmony with them, that determine such processes as feeling, thinking, and acting. Action within a given medium, such as photography, brings to light artistic expressions which encapsule these human characteristics, or as Minor White stated, "symbolize the emotion."

There are in the final analysis no irreconcilable oppositions between light, environment, the photographer (who is the embodiment of consciousness and unconsciousness and the experiential receptor), and the symbolic language of photography. What may be said is that they form a kind of ritualistic interplay, which satisfies a certain deeper need within the photographer, both emotionally and intellectually. Our own critical rationality may find this unquestionably self-evident through photographic images, which may be philosophical-psychological in their makeup. Consequently, the projection of this aspect of the image presents a reciprocal situation involving the observer with more than aesthetic questions. That is not to say that aesthetics are nullified by philosophical-psychological, sociocritical, or psychoanalytical aspects of the image, but that whatever aesthetics do exist are further enhanced by them. Indeed, they are often one and the same even though they may be understood as distinctly separate strata within the totality. The initial reading of a photograph generally, however, introduces these two aspects as one unit. Beyond this point, observer participation moves toward the need for ritual, and this we may recognize in ourselves through the photographer's way of thinking, feeling, acting, and will, which may itself become ritualistic.

But where does the photographer really stand as a human being and artist, in relation to questions of revelation of the self, of the language of photography to the public, and its connection with reality? And where do we stand as observers of his action and production? Is the photographer's autonomous action as a human, recording inner and outer realities, of personality, and of environment through the experience of light, more problematic than we think, or to be understood as one kind of human development within another person whom we recognize as an artist? However we attempt to answer these questions through our own identity and situations in life, it must be kept in mind that these and other complex issues concerning creativity are and will continue to be persistent and essentially unanswerable questions which are part of reality. Neither art, photography, the artist, nor the photographer can supply the definitive answers to and about reality, nor can they supply any amount of the definitive security we seek. Even though the enigma of reality cannot be fully or satisfactorily answered, art and photography can reveal and enlighten segments of reality which we do or do not understand, of every new and old human situation, the affairs of humanity, and of daily lives composed and routinely carried out within our fragile, changing environment. Human behavior and the environment are the realities we come closest to understanding in spite of our differences, and it is the medium of light, photography, which has become in our time one of the very best creative tools in achieving a better understanding of these realities. Photography as art, indeed all art, is circumscribed by these realities; they are reciprocal, and form the first and innermost ring of our being. Existentialist philosophies and political adventurism (witnessed in art) are viewed as attempts to reach another level of understanding, leading to the optimal goal, the ultimate understanding of reality. As powerful and persuasive as they are, these attempts always fall just short of their goal.

Like all other creative and scientific endeavors, photography shares a role in this quest for reality, and reflects the continued struggle of human existence. The human experience of life generates an unrepeatable, individual comprehension of reality, as distinct and individual as works of art are from one another, while still forming part of the transient, regenerating whole of life. The truth of reality we wish to understand comes from and through living the many-faceted, multicolored, magnificent gift of life.

4 THE VISUAL ELEMENTS: Tone, Shadows and Cast Shadows, Shape

Light creates tonality, and tonality assists in building such formal visual elements as volume, plane relationships, texture, space, shadows, and cast shadows. But tone can also be the generator of mood and the support for individual statement. During the Italian Renaissance, the term "chiaroscuro" (light-dark) was born, and chiaroscuro became an established method in formal studio procedure to create those variations of light such as highlight, reflected light, shadow, cast shadow, and the core of the shadow (a darker area within the shadow). (In art criticism, the word chiaroscuro is sometimes mistakenly used to mean "tone" when in reality referring to the qualities of light in painting and drawing.) When gradations of light are rendered in paint or charcoal, it is possible to give a sense of volume to objects and give the illusion of space, atmospheric effects and, in general, an illusion of the third dimension on a two-dimensional plane. When considering chiaroscuro, the "value scale" must be mentioned. The value scale traditionally accepted by artists starts with white and runs about seven graduated greys to a black. Once artists understood the principle of chiaroscuro and the arbitrary value scale, they could manipulate the value scale and the light procedure any way they wanted to suppress or accentuate extraneous details, expand or reduce volume, and create the illusion of deep or shallow space. Dramatic lighting effects could be established, aerial perspective executed in a variety of ways, and new and expressive methods made possible for painting and drawing.

Tone

For photography, the term "value" is replaced by "tone," or more often, "zone." The zone scale, like the value scale, is a simple series of tones arranged from white to black, covering about eight greys. The photographer who understood the zone scale and the zone system, as created by Ansel Adams, could—like the painter or draughtsman—manipulate the zone scale at will to create images high in contrast; low-key, high-key, or middle-key. High-key images are composed of zones from the light end of the scale and low-key images from the dark end. Manipulation or modification of tones may be accomplished by exposure adjustments, through control exercised during the processing of film, and through printing techniques as well as changes in grades of paper.

Under normal lighting conditions, nearly all subject matter will contain many gradations of tone between black and white that extend beyond the zone scale. The range of tones depends upon lighting conditions and the properties of the materials, such as color, density, transparency, texture, and the ability to reflect. One of the most valuable tonal functions is to convey a sense of volume and form. A wide range of tones that gently moves from one zone to another can be most effective in creating a sense of volume and in establishing the illusion of the third dimension. When lighting conditions are hard and come from a single direction, exposures averaged from the lightest and darkest areas will produce a wider range of tones without losing details and definition. Low-key tones can produce images which evoke a sense of the mysterious, the forbidding, the unknown. High-key images, on the other hand, tend to give a sense of space, softness, and delicacy.

In Western culture, we tend to associate black with death, mourning, evil, sadness, and mystery, and white with happiness, innocence, hope, and good; such associations are reinforced by our own art forms and become clichés. Some of the most inventive and paradoxical images have been those that have violated the stereotypical tone relationships used in support of the accepted conventions.

January 1, 1972, Martinique by André Kertész (Figure 4-1) appears at first glance to be composed of three or four tones but, with time, one discovers that the image is a collection of many greys, black, and white. The composition, based on a picture-plane division of thirds, also functions as a method that divides the major tones into three distinct areas. The compositional-tonal division lends strength to the simple geometry and, combined with the depth of field, brings the image close to the picture plane. Light passing through the large pane of glass on the left is softly diffused by texture, so that the contour of the figure leaning on the railing on the other side of the glass becomes diffused rather than sharp-edged. The tone, which is constant within the shape of the shadow figure, slowly begins to dissolve along the contours into tones of a higher key until they merge with the overall tone of the glass. Through light and tonal diffusion, the shadow-figure becomes something of a mystery, its gender unclear, and its soft form associated with the grey-toned clouds drifting above the horizon line between sea and sky. The dark tone of the sea with its sharp-edged horizon line comprises one-third of the image, while the waves produce an overall texture resembling the textured glass. Superimposed on the dark tone of the sea is a railing of geometric shapes

Figure 4-1   ANDRÉ KERTÉSZ, *January 1, 1972, Martinique* (© André Kertész)

and gradated tones topped by a thin strip of white. The white edge of the railing leads to a contrasting dark tone of the thin edge of the glass, which becomes another division in the composition. The sky comprises nearly all of the high tones within the rectangular shape it occupies and enhances the other tones within rectangular shapes. Light diffused by glass, partly absorbed by wood, reflected by water, and scattered by clouds forms a range of tones in which an introspective, dreamlike mood prevails throughout the photograph. Kertész makes subtle use of tones within the highly structured composition to produce a sense of timelessness through anonymity. The figure could be anyone, the body of water could be any body of water, and the place could be any place. But there is an interesting twist to this image: It fluctuates between a believable third dimension and two-dimensionality. On the left, the tones are diffused and unmodeled, thus producing a flat plane ending with a thin, sharp, dark line. On the right, the sky, clouds, sea, handrail, and tones combine to model and give the illusion of space. It is the paradox of the two aspects side by side that breaks with conventional seaside photographs. Kertész's photographs are consistent in presenting the unexpected visually and in content. He is a master of his medium, ingenious in his perceptions and unsurpassed in his stylistic methodology, and his creations have withstood passing judgments of men and time. In many respects, *January 1, 1972, Martinique* is the summation of Kertész the photographer and, in all respects, one of the finest examples of tonality put to maximum formal and expressive use.

Shadows and Cast Shadows

Shadows and cast shadows, like any of the other visual elements building an image, are best understood by taking the time to observe them, especially through a variety of changing artificial and natural lighting conditions. They, like photography, cannot exist without light. It is the quality and the angle of light that will determine some of the fundamental characteristics of shadows and cast shadows. Penumbra, luminosity, transparency, density, elongation, and contraction are characteristics of cast shadows that depend on light and surrounding reflecting surfaces. Cast shadows may create mood, be an important consideration in composition, give a greater sense of volume, build space, and heighten the illusion of space through perspective. Shadows and cast shadows can be a vital part of the photographic image and can turn the ordinary situation into a dramatic or extraordinary one.

Imogen Cunningham's environmental portrait, *John Winkler, Etcher,* 1958 (Figure 4-2), shows what could have been a rather dull asymmetrical composition

Figure 4-2   IMOGEN CUNNINGHAM, *John Winkler, Etcher* 1958 (Imogen Cunningham Trust, Berkeley, California, and International Museum of Photography at George Eastman House, Rochester, New York)

transformed into an asymmetrical composition with visual excitement, radiance, and grandeur. By the use of a single cast shadow from an oculus window, this portrait takes on an air of an event, an event of historical interest for all of us. Certain areas of this photograph are so filled with light that sections of the columns and hanging curtain have lost most of their detail. Cunningham has used the cast shadow to compensate for the absence of detail. The cast shadow creates a certain pattern and yields form and definition where they are lacking. As the lines of the cast shadow move over the column's curving surface, they arch with changing degrees of tension to describe the smooth roundness of each column, as well as their slender elongation. While some definition appears in the curtain, large areas remain without definition, and here the cast shadow has been used to describe the soft, undulating folds and to give weight to the hanging curtain. The radiating lines of the cast shadow burst forth from the upper center of the composition, uniting all parts, while at the same time providing the image a secondary focal point, which accents the figure without competing for attention. The section of wall in which the oculus window is supported casts a shadow upon the lower half of the composition, giving further strength to the ground plane, and helps to bring our attention back to the figure, which is the real subject. He has been placed off-center, his head out of alignment with the central section of the cast shadow so as to maximize the cast shadow for special effect, and the juxtaposition of light and dark tones. Cunningham has put together an environmental portrait with the greatest finesse and ingenuity by the intelligent, sensitive use of a single photographic visual element, the cast shadow.

Through powerful artificial light in the studio, Charles Sheeler created a photograph that is in many respects very close to many of his paintings. It was through the sale of his photographs that Sheeler was able to continue to paint until the market made it profitable for him to spend most of his time painting and to leave photography as a pastime and form of note taking for his pictures. Sheeler took great pleasure in depicting clear, airless light, light that defined forms as sharp and clean-edged. In *Cactus and Photographer's Lamp,* 1931 (Figure 4-3), he demonstrates his preference for precision, clarity of form, and airless space. The cast shadows have been treated like positive shapes; each shadow is as carefully considered as each object. The placement and relationship of object to cast shadow are sure, absolute, and firmly fixed for what seems to be eternity. While some of the cast shadows have been allowed a space to exist between them and the object casting the shadow, others are connected with the objects which cast them. The artificial light has been so arranged as not overly to elongate the cast shadows, but to repeat closely the shape of the shadow's source. Several changes in the plane relationships of the wall have been used to emphasize the geometric shape and to create a new shape from the original object's shadow.

Through the arrangement of objects, light, and cast shadows, Sheeler has created a composition of the utmost perfection, carefully balanced, interlocking, and permanent. Each cast shadow, object, and placement has been so carefully considered and is so correct that one has the sensation of an unreal world, where nothing could be changed or moved a fraction of an inch without upsetting the entire balance and harmony. Here is a world of constructivism, precision, and coolness that radiates total control over each fragment of the photograph. Shapes repeat shapes playing off one another, shadows move from sharp to softly

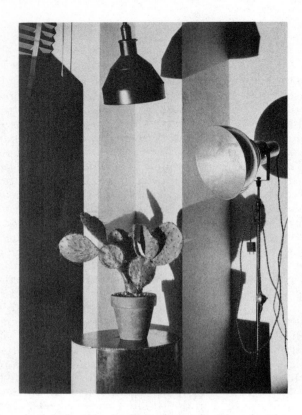

Figure 4-3 CHARLES SHEELER, *Cactus and Photographer's Lamp* 1931 (By permission of the William H. Lane Foundation. Collection, The Museum of Modern Art, New York. Gift of Samuel Kootz)

modeled, cast shadows from dense to luminous, and forms are spaced predictably. Yet, it is this strange, relentless regimentation that appeals to the eye and releases a mood of well-being through order and rightness. The feeling of permanence generated through the elements that Sheeler was so fond of is, in the final analysis, the magnet which draws so many to this type of photography and art form. It offers a world of security and protection, where nothing is left to chance and nothing may be misinterpreted. Visual and intellectual challenges are at a minimum; things are what they are. But, for an artist like Sheeler, such problems are not really important, since a personality of great strength runs through both aspects of his artistic activity with equal force and conviction.

In *Self Portrait with Rock* (Figure 4-4) by Judy Dater, a low, natural, raking light produces shadows and elongated cast shadows, giving the image the sensation of total horizontality. This surreal image depends almost entirely upon the cast shadows to create a richly patterned field of alternating dark and light shapes upon which the sensuous nude figure rests in the center of the composition. Directly in front of the figure is a rock, slightly larger than the others and broken in half. The fractured rock appears to emphasize the fleshiness of the figure, at the same time strangely reducing the female form to the appearance of another rock in the open field, but one that has been polished smooth by the elements of wind and rain. The light producing the magical cast shadows also creates deep shadows on each rock so that they stand out in sharp contrast to the flat field appearing to be alive, moving across the barren landscape like small creatures from another planet. Each cast shadow functions as a shape forming a pattern within the totality of the image, its penumbras clear so that textures may be read

Figure 4-4 JUDY DATER, *Self Portrait with Rock* (Courtesy of the photographer)

with ease. The changing dark shapes of the shadows' form, movement, and pattern show the photographer's complete understanding of the whole phenomenon of light and shade. What appears to be a simple, easy composition is in fact a stunning example of the photographer's sensitivity to light, transforming an ordinary landscape into a symphony of varied shadows, a memorable photograph, which lingers in the mind's eye long after direct visual contact has ended.

Dater's brilliant, imaginative, original study demonstrates that often one visual element can be the framework for an idea, mood, or style. *Self Portrait with Rock* is like all of Judy Dater's work, highly integrated and fusing the visual elements, the basic idea, and personality of the artist into an image of an unforgettable photograph.

Graceful, winglike cast shadows are cleverly used in Michael Northrup's *Blue Butterflies on Brett* (Figure 4-5) as a contrast to the masculine torso, adding a touch of wit to the image. The high contrast of the tone relationships and the diagonal placement of the shadows on the torso give a sense of movement and an air of summer sunlight while emphasizing the full volume of the male figure's rib cage. By photographing the torso at eye level with a wide-angle lens and a blue flash, its shape and form-projections take on a certain monumentality. Rather than relying upon the natural phenomenon of cast shadows to object surface, Northrup creates his own by placing a pair of hands in front of the light source (the sun) and the figure. The hands are spread flat, fingers extended, thumbs touching, in order to give the illusion of a fluttering butterfly hovering above the figure, ready to descend lightly on the back of the unsuspecting

Figure 4-5   MICHAEL NORTHRUP, *Blue Butterflies on Brett* 1981 (Courtesy of the photographer)

individual. Within the shell of the rowboat a pair of oars cast their shadows downward, projected as a curving line which emphasizes the shape of the boat and functions as a compositional method to hold the observer's vision at mid-point in the image. The illusion of space is increased by the single curved line of cast shadow; without it the spatial relationships tend to condense, resulting in a rather flat effect. Overall, they confer upon the image a mood, a season, temperature, and whimsical elusive sexuality. What might have been just another ordinary photograph of a male torso has been transformed into a strongly individual, personal, and highly imaginative image by the unusual application of cast shadows.

Shape

Shape in image-building is often considered a fundamental visual element, since it is shape that one reads first. Identifying an individual or object from a distance prevents the reading of such specifics as facial features or any other surface characteristics; it is the shape or contour that is used in identification. Shape is essentially a two-dimensional element, but with light, tones are created, shape turns into form, and form indicates volume, which, in turn, gives the illusion of the third dimension. However, light can also give the illusion of destroying form by creating black shadows, merging many shapes into one, and eliminating graduated tonal relationships, texture and detail, so that nothing but flat black-and-white shapes remain.

To lend strength and interest to a shape, it can be placed against simple, contrasting backgrounds, or the basic means of repetition and variation can be used. If a shape is silhouetted against a contrasting background, volume is eliminated and shape is emphasized. Manipulation of shape can be achieved through mirror images and the distortion of forms by reflection in uneven surfaces. Distortion, mirrors, and uneven window glass are two methods commonly used to create new and unusual forms and shapes. Shape can be the subject and can also be used to bring attention to the subject.

Mirror images formed by still water can often be employed to give the illusion of doubled shape, building new outlines and presenting a variety of spatial relationships. Edward Weston's *Iceberg Lake*, 1937 (Figure 4-6) depicts the mirror image of a slope partly covered with snow and ice, with a variety of shapes formed

Figure 4-6   EDWARD WESTON, *Iceberg Lake* 1937 (Collection of The Art Institute of Chicago. © 1981, Center for Creative Photography, University of Arizona. Used by permission.)

by the land mass revealed through snowless areas. The reflection in the still water gives the illusion of a vertical plane in the background, while doubling the number of free-form shapes. Ice floes of irregular contour float on the motionless water and echo the dark shapes from the background mirrored in the water. The water functions as a flat plane, extending toward and beyond the picture plane like a sheet of reflecting glass. The dark and reflected shapes are intersected by white, floating shapes, creating a gentle cross-movement within the frozen stillness, at once beautiful and remote. It is a majestic, tranquil environment in which shape and form coexist in air that is crystalline pure. Sharp, ragged, disintegrating, and soft edges add visual interest to open, partly open, or closed shapes as they float and reflect. As they contrast to the smoothness of the water and flowing striations in the snow and ice-covered slope, they reemphasize themselves as the essential visual element. *Iceberg Lake* offers many visual investigations and delights through shape arrangements, composition, and variety within the unity of the single-shape element. It is an outstanding photograph, almost phenomenological in its singularity of approach. Yet it remains fresh and new each time it is reexamined.

Two Callas, 1929 (Figure 4-7) by Imogen Cunningham depicts two calla lilies that are gently modeled by light and assume volume as their paper-thin walls, forming a spiral, end in a single lozenge shape projecting from the center of the flower. Lighted from above, the leaves form curved shapes, echoing the sensual curving forms of the lilies as they touch and overlap. Their whiteness is accentuated by the uncluttered dark background, and their shapes are clearly and easily read as they project from the rich, deep black background. Cunningham chose shapes that are the same, but with subtle, graceful differences. One is open, the other slightly closed, with curving shapes linking one with the other and contours that shift directions as they course through space. One is

Figure 4-7   IMOGEN CUNNINGHAM, *Two Callas* 1929 (Imogen Cunningham Trust, Berkeley, California, and International Museum of Photography at George Eastman House, Rochester, New York)

larger than the other, and one has a more tightly curved spiral than the other. The S-shaped leaves in the background also differ in their curvature, one with greater tension, the other with less. Like the flower and its simple but elegant shape, Cunningham composed the leaves with simplicity and elegance so as to bring out their essential characteristics of transient, delicate, sensual beauty. Turning the photograph upside down, one finds that the repetition of shape and interlocking rhythms through form becomes more quickly apparent. Because of the reflected light within the lily on the left, a quality of fleshiness begins to appear that is absent from the other lily because of the brighter light and smoother surfaces. The shapes a photographer selects can often speak of his aesthetic, be an extension of his personality, and tell more about him than a direct verbal statement. The qualities of shape found in Cunningham's *Two Callas* may also be found in many of her other photographs.

The flat, silhouetted shape of a piano is used in juxtaposition with the volumetric shape of the great composer in Arnold Newman's photograph, *Igor Stravinsky* (Figure 4-8). The background is also quite flat, high-key, and divided into two rectangular shapes. Newman's photograph is inventive and amusing. A repetition of shape is created by a number of means. Stravinsky sits in a triangular pose, a second triangle is formed by the negative space seen through the piano lid and the lid support, and still another may be discovered where the lid, support, and the two background rectangles meet—three triangles of different proportions, all linked to one another. The lid of the piano becomes a huge musical note floating in front of the rectangles. Newman has used geometric

Figure 4-8 ARNOLD NEWMAN, *Igor Stravinsky* 1946 (© Arnold Newman)

shapes in a simple arrangement referring to the geometry of music and, in particular, the music of Stravinsky. Stravinsky's suit lacks definition and becomes a silhouette referring to the piano. It is as if Stravinsky were growing from the piano, or were actually part of it, in spite of being dwarfed by it. The image is sharp-edged, clear, contemporary; remove the head and hand of the figure and the photograph could easily be a hard-edged color-field painting from the 1970s. Newman's portraits of well-known personalities in art, politics, or the social life always say something about the sitter through shape, light, and composition, and in a very distinct style that is Newman's and Newman's alone. His mastery over camera, medium, and technique and his ability to know and understand his subject are seen and felt in each portrait. But it is his natural understanding of the visual elements used to signify the sitter's occupation or personality that places him in the forefront of photographic portraiture. Bold and strong in style, showing a preference for geometric shapes, Arnold Newman's photographs stand as complete documents to the man and photographer.

When a photographer uses shadows and cast shadows as Northrup does in his *Untitled,* 1980 (Figure 4-9), they may be considered as major and positive forces in the composition. These dark shapes function as powerful elements in the image, building tension between one another, reaffirming the ground plane, framing the image, and building spatial relationships. The sculpture, located in the center of the composition, would have appeared isolated if it had not just

Figure 4-9   MICHAEL NORTHRUP, *Untitled* 1980 (sculpture) (Courtesy of the photographer)

slightly overlapped the cast shadow behind it; it is through this method of overlap that the tension between the foreground and background builds. Northrup's photograph, conceived as an abstraction through the stimuli of the geometry of the architecture, sculpture, light and shade, is particularly and resolutely authoritative as an abstraction. It is as though the photographer presents a new understanding of light and shade for the observer through his methodology. The self-realization and humanization, which are clearly set within the limits and conditions predetermined by the physicality of the environment, are to a large extent, if not completely, conveyed to the observer through the image with direct honesty and openness. Without abandoning his quest for perfection with the visual elements of photography, the photographer has empirically shown that his freedom of expression does not override the standards or responsibilities of the craftsman-photographer.

The specific solutions that the photographer has worked out for himself in this modern image can serve as an acclimatization for those who have difficulty with abstractions, for here the immutable essence of the mind, spirit, and personality is melded to perfection and expressed through the photographic image.

Tone, shadows, cast shadows, and shape are all interrelated; all depend on light and all derive from the photographer's perception, comprehension, and experience with them, indeed, must do so if he is to bring into being photographs significant to him. Each one of the visual elements can be content, content can be shape, and shape can be content. Tone can become style, shadows and cast shadows shape and style, and style can be statement. Whether used as metaphors or simply as what they are, it is the photographer's understanding, manipulation, and execution of the visual elements as they compose part or all of the image that establish the external-internal viewpoint and stand as an article of faith in himself.

5 THE VISUAL ELEMENTS:
Line, Texture, Scale

Line

Since prehistoric times, when people drew animals on the walls of their caves and incised line into soft clay to represent bison, line has been the common, prevalent method of communication, through writing, drawing, and painting. In general, it has been the method through which ideas are transmitted to paper and passed to another individual. Museums, galleries, libraries, industry, art schools, colleges, and universities are storehouses of an endless array of types of line used for an infinity of purposes. But these manmade lines spring from perceptions of line observed in the environment and are refined to serve the artist, draughtsman, designer, teacher, and others. The use and refinement of line to form ideas and images requires primarily the observation of line, from childlike scribbles to the most complicated and sophisticated, but also line as it is found in the environment. The traditional definition of line is a dot moving across the surface of a support, but that definition cannot be functional when looking for line in the environment, because it simply does not exist. Our perception of line in the environment is determined by light, form, and shape. The contour of objects is read as line. Shape overlapping shape is read as line. Negative and positive shapes and spaces are perceived as line. Silhouetted forms that are narrow, thin, and elongated are read as line. Cast shadows elongated, jet streams, tree branches, a plowed field, the steel frame of a building seen against the sky; all can be perceived as line. We may find lines of an endless variety within the environment, each one possessing a different characteristic that may be used to reflect a mood or statement, express an idea, or project a personality.

Any line can suggest direction, begin a rhythmic influence, create pattern and texture, give a sense of movement and energy, give a sense of depth, volume, and weight, divide a picture plane into simple or complex compositions, and emphasize vertical or horizontal orientation to a support. Its limitations are only as great as those of the person making the line. Furthermore, line can have varying widths, tones, textures, and lengths; but, when a line begins to move in another direction, curved or angular, to change its width and tone, and its edges from rough to smooth, its descriptive and expressive power is increased considerably. With sensitivity and command over line, one can suggest, describe, evoke, and imply internal-external experiences as well as observations, concepts, and precepts.

Such classifications of line as broken, flowing, expanding, contrasting, clustered, modeled, encompassing, calligraphic, mechanical, and weighted are somewhat arbitrary and may be used to facilitate the investigations and explorations of other linear possibilities as well as personal linear invention. Line is not only descriptive, but expressive; the qualities of line that distinguish individual drawings, paintings, photographs, prints, letters, and diagrams betray attitudes and temperaments and can be modes of self-discovery reflecting the creator. Self-discovery on the conscious or subconscious, nonverbal level is important for the individual, for the artist, and for the photographer when finding methods and ways of working that are complete, satisfying, exhilarating, and personal.

Not only is line present in the shape and form of objects, but several objects may be positioned together so that they build new lines through interrelationships. Shifting the viewpoint can break and join line and alter direction, and vertical-horizontal line can be changed to diagonal by simple rotation of the camera. Once sensitivity to line is achieved, the creation of line through camera angle and position expands line vocabulary.

A broken or discontinuous line appears to be more spatially suggestive than an unvarying line. When used horizontally and vertically, parallel to the picture plane, the resultant space will appear to be shallow. However, when lines penetrate the picture plane diagonally, an effect of deep space is achieved. Many overlapping lines will give the illusion of greater volume than a single line. And when lines are grouped in a single direction so closely as to create a tone, the space will appear flatter than when the lines are not uniformly grouped. Lines repeated to form a pattern or texture will also flatten space. Analyzing line and its characteristics in subject matter, isolating it from the other visual elements, and making it the subject brings greater control over line, while furthering personal, ontological approaches to image making. For many photographers, visual ontologies can, and often do, have validity independent of verbal philosophizing. Such photographers as Diane Arbus, Harry Callahan, and André Kertész have attained a certain status as ontologists free of, and superior to, academic philosophers.

Harry Callahan's *Grasses in Snow,* Detroit, 1943 (Figure 5-1) allows one to read lines created by a high-contrast image as calligraphic. The weeds are seen as lines forming an abstract image of pattern and movement while establishing shapes marked off by lines that bend and curve back upon themselves as partial and complete enclosures. The weeds have lost their form-identification through loss of light by a calculated exposure, so that they have become silhouetted black lines dancing over a completely white surface. There is a kind of eternal validity established as the lines form two-dimensional structures and interpenetrate. As weeds, the image has an element of time and change that can scarcely be eliminated from the expression of the photograph, indeed, should not be if we are to gain a sense of truth from it, or if truth is to be served. Essential to the image is Callahan's sensitivity to line, observed in weeds projecting from snow. Seen and photographed simply as weeds, the image would have taken on an entirely different aspect, but as black lines which we know to be weeds, it can fluctuate between truth and myth. The calligraphic lines which change widths and tones, break, curve, bend, loop, and flow are visually exciting and are made possible by these changing qualities. *Grasses in Snow* has strong overtones of Oriental painting and calligraphy, yet is essentially Western, typically American in its energy, its boldness, its expressionistic approach. Callahan has created many images in which line is the dominant element: images of plant life, the human form, architecture, telephone wires seen overhead, sunlight on water, camera move-

Figure 5-1 HARRY CALLAHAN, *Grasses in Snow,* Detroit 1943 (Courtesy of Light Gallery, New York)

ment over a light source, painted lines on the road, trolley-car rails, a telephone pole; the observant eyes of Callahan seek and find line as the subject or as the one essential element among others in creating images that are distinctly Callahan's. He seems to know that the significance of line, any line, will arise from the way it can awaken echoes in the observer's mind of experiences connected with similar directions, at once actual and photographed, and that that meaningful connection can arise from the quality of line alone, whether it move downward, leftward, rightward, rise smoothly, or curl up within the image. Each of his photographs demonstrates a clear understanding of this principle; perhaps this is one reason why his work is popular with photographers and the general public alike.

Grain Elevator and Lightning Flash, Lamesa, Texas, 1977 (Figure 5-2), by Frank Gohlke, fully depicts the open vistas and long distances of the Texas

Figure 5-2   FRANK GOHLKE, *Grain Elevator and Lightning Flash, Lamesa, Texas* 1977
(Courtesy of Light Gallery, New York)

landscape in a rainstorm. Part of the illusion of great distance is achieved by his intelligent use of line. The telephone poles and lines read as black lines against the darkening sky that appear to recede and converge at a vanishing point off-center of the horizon line. A wet road surface, partly shiny and matte, breaks into linear pattern as it also moves into the deep space ending at the imaginary vanishing point. Thin lines dividing the grain elevator into seven parts add a needed horizontal element, while reinforcing the roundness of the elevator forms. A walkway atop the elevator adds a stronger horizontal line, preventing the eye from simply moving through the image directly to the vanishing point. The irregular line of the lightning flash offsets the straight geometric arrangements of line, while functioning as a counterbalance to the forceful forms of the grain elevator.

While the line element here is not as forceful as it was in the Callahan photograph, where it was the subject, it is nonetheless important as a unifying element. Space, form, and picture-plane division are established by line simply, grandly, and directly. The overall linear geometric quality of the image is subdued by the lighting conditions and reflections, but it is the two together that give this image its presence, sense of place, and condition. Gohlke uses mechanical line, indicative of the other mechanical objects, with great success. But even with the most static intent, there is a kinetic pattern of lines composed through opposing directions. Understanding their place in the whole context of the photograph depends upon the reading of the kinetic pattern they generate. The enclosures they form, as in the telephone lines, and the vertical-horizontal constructions near the cottages on the right reinforce direction and pattern effectively. At the same time, they echo other shapes found throughout the composition. These negative space enclosures formed by line are visual variations upon other positive shapes also defined by line, such as the grain elevator and the road. It is the parallel line enclosures, both positive and negative, that hold the image together visually and give relief from its straight-line aspect. The line of the road sets up a diagonal major axis, while the shorter lines of the grain elevator and the cross-bars on the telephone poles function as a minor horizontal linear axis. The distant telephone wires positioned between the grain elevator and the water tower also assist in establishing a minor horizontal axis. The leading lines of the road's edge and telephone wires lend a feeling of rightness to the various positions assumed by these elements and act as the major division line in the composition. Slight changes in line quality, such as width, tone, and lengths, keep the mechanical line from becoming lifeless and dull. Qualitatively and quantitatively, Gohlke has used line in his composition perfectly in keeping with subject matter and mood, all projecting his obvious pleasure in going out into the world and enjoying its visual delights. This photograph clearly shows a desire on his part to share those pleasures with us. What more need be said about an invitation to enjoy the breath of fresh air brought by a rainstorm and feel the grandness of open space?

Flowing, softly textured lines are combined into one liquid line in Margaret Bourke-White's photograph *Protective Pattern*, Walsh, Colorado, 1954 (Figure 5-3), photographed from a high vantage point. As two tractors plow the field, a linear, repeated pattern is created by dark and light furrows. Collectively, the lines form a single dark, sinuous shape against a light-toned field; together they

Figure 5-3 MARGARET BOURKE-WHITE,
Protective Pattern 1954 (Life
Magazine © 1954 Time Inc.)

function as negative-positive reversals. The image has the ascetic presence of a Japanese gravel garden in which the raked lines in the gravel encourage meditation. The soft curves resemble water, also associated with gravel gardens, yet what could be more typical of the American West than the endless wheatfields? Rather than appearing as a series of lines that move off into the distance, the space appears to tilt upwards, negating perspective. If the lines had continued to move up and out through the top of the image, deep space would have been achieved, but since they move through a quick curve to the right, the shape does not recede into space.

Bourke-White has suspended in time the landscape undergoing forced change, abstract in concept, representational in imagery. Line, the single visual element of first consideration, has been effectively used to generate shape, tone, texture, and mood, as well as composition. Scale is accomplished by attending to the tractors; they are the key to representation as well. The immensity of the distances cannot be understood until they are realized; cover them up with the fingers and the field could be a small section of fabric or the striations in a soft substance on a table top. The regularly repeated lines are relieved by the curves they form; brought together under the imaginative eyes of the photographer, they become magical. Simplicity, boldness, and irregularity are key factors in the success of Bourke-White's image. But more than these, it is alertness to the presence of line in the landscape that the photographer exhibits. Her sensitivity and careful observation have brought forth from an ordinary, common scene an image that is personal and universal. Margaret Bourke-White proves in this image that a striking subject is not necessary to a successful photograph; the most unspectacular scene can become the opposite when one looks and sees.

Texture

Textures can often evoke associations of past experience, and the reflection of past experience through the photographic image can make a considerable contribution to artistic formulations and structure. And, just like the other visual elements in photography or any other art form, it is not enough simply to stimulate the traces of past experience; it must be consciously combined in the image if it is to succeed in making a significant contribution or enhancement to the observer's personal interaction with the image as well as his personal life. Texture is generally understood as the surface of any object infused with a sensory, sometimes even emotional, quality that is conceived through sight and touch. Color is often considered in the same light, although associated less with touch than with sight. Smooth surfaces are often considered cool, remote, or cold; rough surfaces as warmer, more inviting to the touch. A great deal of mixed, broken texture can give the feeling of confusion and be disconcerting. Just as color may advance and recede through color temperature, texture may also advance and recede. Through scale, variations, density, and breadth, texture will advance, whereas a less defined, more open texture will recede. The surface characteristics of a subject can be related by texture, to give a greater degree of realism, to be used by itself as the subject. Photographed close up or from a distance, the quality of lighting is crucial in revealing the textural aspects of the subject. Harsh and angled sunlight emphasizes the strong textures of wood, fur, and so on, while soft, diffused light in shade and reflected light can bring out the textural qualities of the subject without creating dark shadows lacking texture. A rich tonal range of texture can be further developed through printing and exposure, but mechanical procedure is secondary to the primary consideration of seeing and fusing texture with the other visual elements through the perceptual process.

While some objects, such as wood, glass, hair, and so on, have their own intrinsic textural qualities, texture may also be created by other visual elements. Line of various qualities in repetition, patterns repeated, shadows, cast shadows, and shapes can all form textures under certain conditions of juxtaposition and light. Texture functions in different ways in different styles, and photographic styles, like any other style in art, depend on the manner in which the visual elements such as texture are perceived and acted upon in creating images and individual statements. Like musical sonorities, textures may also take on refinements expressive of each photographer's idea, so what matters finally is not that textures, or any of the other visual elements, exist, but what it is that the photographer does with them artistically and creatively.

The physical presence of an object may be stated through its textural qualities, and its textural qualities may also define it as a particular, identifiable object. Without sight, we can describe the texture of objects by touch, but with sight, we can recall the experience of touch and its particular associations without touching anything. The photographic image makes this possible, even if the object of association no longer exists.

The actual texture of a photograph is more often than not subdued, compared to painting and sculpture. Paintings may have a heavy build-up of pigment creating a tactile surface, and sculpture may often have rough or smooth surfaces inviting touch. The very materials themselves suggest texture, while photographic paper does not, especially when under glass. Such surface textures as matte, smooth, and stippled are actual features of surface texture in photographic paper, certainly less exciting than carved wood or scumbled paint. But recently, photographers have been creating their own textures by means of collage, assemblage, and drawing and painting on photographs. The approaches to texture can dominate a work and provide its reason for being, at least on the conscious level. But this sort of manipulation of the photograph is not yet common, so that the graphic arts, in general, have less effect than painting or sculpture through actual texture. Texture is a strong element: consider the difference between an exhibition of paintings with impasto surfaces, and an exhibition of unmanipulated black-and-white photographs. The exhibition of paintings appears to enter the space of the room, while the photographs appear recessive, subdued. One reason for our reaction to the paintings is that their surface textures reflect light at different angles into the room, causing a visual excitement, and their physical presence is tactile. These aspects, which heighten the visual experience in painting and sculpture, are lacking in the photograph. But the subtle, actual textures of the unmanipulated photograph can be as satisfying visually and intellectually if one proceeds without comparison to other art forms and accepts it for what it is.

Simulated texture is the imitation of real texture, to give the appearance of the actual thing, such as in trompe l'oeil painting. Not only does the trompe l'oeil painting imitate texture, but it gives the illusion of the third dimension as well. The Cubist paintings of Braque and Picasso also imitated real textures, but these were free from three-dimensional illusionistic concerns. Simulated texture for additional visual effect has been used by photographers along with collage and assemblage efforts—but so has invented texture, which does not imitate existing textures. Nonrepresentational texture of lines, dots, patterns of various sorts, and textures that symbolize actual textures have been added to the photographic image through paint, ink, crayon, and other drawing and painting materials. The photographer Lucas Samaras makes free and uninhibited use of textures, through a number of techniques that opened the door to new, exciting ways of expression through photography; other photographers were soon to follow his example. His combinations of invented, simulated, and actual textures create arbitrary space and unusual visual effects but, more important, helped to change the traditionally conservative attitude that the sanctity of photography cannot be violated either by physical addition or subtraction.

If texture can bring out the character of an object and emphasize its physical existence by association, so can it speak of the individual who created the image. *Church Door,* Hornitos, California, 1940 (Figure 5-4), by Edward Weston depicts a number of textures—wood, metal, and glazed ceramic—but is dominated by the texture of weathered, heavily painted wood. A strong diagonal light from above brings out the texture in high relief over the clapboard wall and door. Luminous shadows and cast shadows are transparent enough to allow one to read texture through them, and the high-key tone is punctuated by sharp, black cracks and joints in the wood. The doorknob, latch, and lock-hinge, all with different surfaces, playing a minor voice in a quartet of textures, allow the wood

Figure 5-4   EDWARD WESTON, *Church Door* 1940 (© 1981, Arizona Board of Regents, Center for Creative Photography, University of Arizona. Used by permission.)

to sing out its tactile qualities. The texture of the wood moves in vertical and horizontal directions, keeping it from becoming a monotone. Stronger, denser wood texture reads as a softer grey tone against the smoother, less textured surfaces which read as a higher tone, their surfaces reflecting more light. There is a mellowness, warmth, and nostalgia about the image that speaks of a rural America. It evokes a part of America that is fading before technological advancements.

Nail heads and holes offer brief visual stopping points within the irregular pattern of the wood texture and act as counterpoints to the flat and highly grained planks. Texture revealed by light establishes and identifies the material which, in turn, forms the object we know to be a weathered building. The slipperiness of the metal objects suggests warmth and comfort to the touch. The overall uniting texture of the wood with its heavy coats of paint offers no focal point; it is the black doorknob that the eye goes back to once visual investigation through texture is complete. Even though attention returns to the small, black focal point, it is the texture of the wood from which one draws deep satisfaction. In avoiding photographing his subject with total frontality, Weston accentuated the cast shadows and textures and prevented it from becoming a flat design by allowing a slight space to exist in the foreground. We feel this space by the angle of the building to the camera lens. Furthermore, the angle allows one to read textures as they move over plane relationships, thus reinforcing volume. All the visual elements have been carefully observed and composed, but especially texture, the fundamental aesthetic strength of this image.

Scale

Scale in the photographic image is rarely, if ever, discussed, yet its importance is undeniably clear when examining photographic styles and content. Through camera angle, scale may be changed: what is small can be made to appear colossal, and what is colossal, small. The change of scale may shift focal point, emphasize or deemphasize subject matter, and bring attention to content. Through manipulation of the negative, double exposure, and collage, ordinary objects may be taken out of context and placed in juxtaposition to one another through change of scale, quite often with surprising and unusual results. By changing the scale of one object in relation to another one, it is possible to bring new meaning to the objects, or at least allow one to interpret them in another way. Taking the objects out of their accepted, recognized context, in addition to changing the scale, brings greater expression. A master of this technique is the painter René Magritte, whose witty and thought-provoking paintings serve as a model for other artists who pursue this avenue of expression.

Photographing from below, underneath the leaves of low-growing plants in Ireland in 1972, Emmet Gowin has changed the scale of the plants, of the plants to the woods, and even our perception of the plants. *Ireland*, 1972 (Figure 5-5), succeeds in making us feel as though we are under the shady protection of a

Figure 5-5　EMMET GOWIN, *Ireland* 1972 (Courtesy of the photographer)

Figure 5-6   JERRY UELSMANN, *Untitled* 1968 (Courtesy of the photographer)

huge plant, looking up from the ground to the leaf, where light is diffused as it passes through its semitransparent covering, suspended by radiating veins and supported by a long, graceful, prickly stem. This simple, frail plant has become an unusually stout tree. It is another way of looking at the environment and our relationship to it. The change of scale is intensified by the circular format.

Normally seen from above, this sort of plant life is inconsequential, a green carpet for us to walk on, but turned around as Gowin has done, it provokes thoughts and questions about the interrelationship of humans and the natural phenomena of landscape. It is impossible to be indifferent to the image and the photographer's sensitivity to terrain. His investigation of scale and detail suggests deep feelings about his subject, manifested through careful craftsmanship and understanding of scale. By the change of scale, we have been placed in a position to examine carefully the complexities of design, precisely depicted for us, in the plant life. The image is more than a document of plant life, it is a poetical method of awakening our consciousness to the immediate world away from the imagined, to the astounding radiance of what it is. In this context, Gowin tells what there is to tell of what he perceives and what he believes.

Jerry Uelsmann uses the darkroom as a laboratory where postvisualization works to bring together fragments of images forming extensions of the subconscious reaching beyond logic and ordinary reason. His selections and combinations of seemingly opposed images, out of context with one another and often joltingly out of scale with one another, become fluid dream-pictures from a private world of his subconscious. But dreams and the subconscious are formed by the consciousness of reality. Uelsmann's *Untitled*, 1968 (Figure 5-6), depicts a pair of female hands rising up from the earth with fragments of soil still clinging to the folded, interlocking hands. Their scale dwarfs the landscape as they fill the black sky with their mass. Superimposed in front of the hands is an undefinable object that has certain organic references by its consistency and surface texture. It is as though the huge hands are regenerating life in the landscape by depositing the seedlike shape, one finger pressing down on the top of the oval shape, its smooth skin softly glowing, into the earth. The foreground is a negative, the middle and background positives; combining them has added a surreal touch in keeping with the scale juxtapositions. This creation, influenced partly by the myth that nature is female, partly by the physical reality of the landscape, and partly by fantasy, generates its own reality, one that cannot be found in our physical world.

Uelsmann stands alone among photographers in his personal inventive approach and style with image making. Each of his photographs belies the statement that progress in art has come to a standstill because all barriers to creativity have been removed. It is the rare individual who can claim that all personal barriers have been eliminated. The ultimate barrier is the artist himself, as he constantly overcomes the seemingly endless interior barriers to self-discovery. Through this process, photography, indeed all art, continues to evolve.

Extreme camera angle, manipulation of negatives, and double exposure are not necessary to give scale to individual objects or to the photograph. A simple shift or tilt of the camera can change standard scale into monumentality for the photograph without departing from representation into surrealism or abstraction. The scale of objects carefully studied as they relate to one another can also give the photograph a feeling of rightness and harmony without any special effects or camera shift. Scale, like any of the other visual elements, is simply a basic tool that may be used in the process of image making; it is not a question of why or how it is used, but the way it is used consciously in the creative process.

6 THE VISUAL ELEMENTS: Perspective, Space, Composition

Perspective

Over the centuries, a variety of systems of perspective have existed, each effective within a specific culture. In ancient Egypt, horizontal bands divided the picture plane into separate segments representing progression into space, the lower band reading as the frontal plane, the highest the most distant. In the Far East, isometric perspective was employed (a system often used by architects today), in which parallel lines do not converge on a vanishing point, requiring that objects diminish in apparent size as they recede into space. And in the Italian Renaissance, linear perspective, a formal, traditional system, was devised to project the forms and space of the physical world on a two-dimensional plane. The fundamentals of this system appear simple but are in fact complex and difficult, and detailed explanation is beyond the scope of this book. The basic principle is that parallel lines will converge to a vanishing point established on the picture plane. This effect may be observed by looking along the lines of telephone poles, railroad tracks, or any regularly spaced objects following a straight or curved line. The vanishing point is placed on a line called the horizon line, at the actual eye height of the viewer in relation to the scene depicted. Through this method, the foreshortening of objects is made possible. This theory rests on two premises: the eye of the observer is in a fixed position, and the surface of the support constitutes the plane of vision. The plane of vision might be compared to a pane of glass in a window, and the principle may be demonstrated by placing a section of tracing paper on the glass and tracing all that one sees. In the broadest sense, for photography, perspective simply means a point of view, referring to lines and surfaces on the flat film plane of the camera. But further, it also is the effect of size relationships and camera angle related to the viewer's interpretation of the image. This is one method by which the illusion of space is achieved in the photograph.

Related to linear perspective is atmospheric perspective, most probably discovered by the Flemish painters of the early fifteenth century, but fully realized by Piero della Francesca and Leonardo da Vinci in their landscape backgrounds. In Oriental painting, the effect has been used most effectively and with great sophistication. It is achieved by a succession of tones moving to a higher key as they represent distance, blurring both tonal and formal definition. The farther away objects are from the eye, the fewer tonal contrasts are used to indicate them, while the closer objects have greater contrast of tones. Atmospheric or aerial perspective is actually a function of chiaroscuro, as it was developed at the same time and by the same artists. This system of representing atmospheric space was devised by artists who lived in climates whose moisture-laden atmosphere produced such blurring effects. It is interesting to note that art produced by artists in dry climates, such as India and Egypt, usually lacks aerial perspective.

Using one-point perspective as the format in his photograph, *Queens, New York,* 1974 (Figure 6-1), David Plowden says a great deal about American life in the twentieth century. All the ground-plane lines of the road, curb, painted guide lines, sidewalk, and grassy areas between sidewalk and road converge upon a vanishing point situated on the horizon line just off-center to the right. The other upright structures, the row of houses, the lampposts, and automobiles follow in order as all their horizontal parallel lines converge on the same single vanishing point. All forms diminish proportionally according to the laws of linear perspective as they recede into the distance, and it would not be difficult to believe that they continued to infinity. It is all so perfect, so ordered that it becomes quite unreal, but this effect serves Plowden's purpose very well indeed. The commonplace has assumed a certain character through its banality. Regimentation is expressed by means of the architectural sameness, the monotonous landscaping, and the dreary planning of roadways. Undecided character, plastic, and polyester dominate the architectural style, reinforced by the mathematical lineup of houses. The uniformity and artificial organization imposed on the landscape have a crushing effect on the spirit of those who have to survive in such an environment. Plowden has picked up on this theme in his photograph and expressed it clearly, honestly, and without sentiment. Throughout his architectural studies, he demonstrates a complete grasp of the science of perspective and puts it to effective use formally, but more important than formality is his method of using it to serve his purpose of investigation into the new and old American commonplace structures. Photographing from high, low, and eye-level vantage points for the best point of view so that he may avoid perspective distortions, Plowden translates the fifteenth-century, Western invention of per-

Figure 6-1   DAVID PLOWDEN, *Queens, New York* 1974 (Copyright © David Plowden 1974)

spective into twentieth-century terms through the camera. He has accomplished this so well, so un-self-consciously, that the images have a surprising natural grace and purity, recalling some of the finest perspective drawings from the Italian Renaissance. Even the most unattractive structures that modern technology has imposed upon the landscape gain an element of visual interest through Plowden's method and his unrelenting pursuit of his subject. Aside from aesthetics, what these architectural studies through perspective have contributed, in the light of the developing history of photography, is to point out to us that we have become oblivious to banal structures. Living with them and in them, we no longer see them. They are not the architectural wonders we prefer to point to as examples of our society but, in fact, they are the typical examples. Plowden shows these common structures, which share our lives on a daily basis, as having the same ordinary frailties as the people who inhabit them. Unpretentious, idiosyncratic, more than symbolic, they are contemporary America. If you want to see America, Plowden says, look at these structures you no longer see, and if you want to see yourself, look to them. These structures, signs, and symbols are extensions of the spirit of the people who created them and live with them, and if we reexamine them, perhaps we may perceive them in a new and more tolerant light. As a photographer with a social statement, Plowden has succeeded with brilliance in his study of the commonplace structure in America.

The problem of perspective is approached by Michael Northrup in a very personal and amusing way. In his photograph *Gert,* 1980 (Figure 6-2), the vanishing point is located behind the large looming figure of Gert centrally located in the foreground. All perspective lines meeting at a single vanishing point in the distance appear to be radiating from the figure, thus identifying it with the vanishing point. At the midpoint of the composition a radio tower projects just above Gert's head as though she were a radio-controlled robot. To emphasize this joke the photographer does not allow the observer to see Gert's face, which is obscured by her hair like a space helmet. The wide-angle lens adds to the spatial relationships, already stated with a certain force by the radiating railroad tracks, railroad cars, and architecture. The perspective is easy to read, freed of visual entanglements or mere marginal visual clues.

Gert is a demythologizing of space, eliminating all references to "hi-tech" in which the photographer rationally paraphrases the surrounding environment into a witty narration, poking fun at the high priests of UFO and space technology. Northrup's view of reality is distinctive. It is at the base level that the distinctions between photographers are most clearly seen: in their personal in-

Figure 6-2   MICHAEL NORTHRUP, *Gert* 1980 (Courtesy of the photographer)

terpretations of the reality of life with its many conflicts, ideologies, and utopian dreams.

A night photograph of the Brooklyn Bridge by Andreas Feininger (Figure 6-3) brings together all the aesthetics of the bridge and the majesty of its architecture seen through aerial perspective. Silhouetted against the glittering lights of the cityscape, shrouded in fog and river mists, the bridge is sharply contoured and dark-toned in the foreground. As its span reaches across the river, the tone changes to a lighter key, and the forms become more indistinct until they merge with the cityscape. The lights on the bridge and in the cityscape also change their tones from high to low as they are softly diffused by the mists and recede into the background. Rays of artificial light scattered by the fog and mist are reflected in the river, which is modulated in tone from high to low following the laws of natural phenomena observed in aerial perspective. Conscious of the blurring and dissolving of shape and structure in this view of Manhattan, Feininger's background as an architect in all probability played a part in his decision to photograph these architectural forms under these particular conditions. But more than the architecture, it is the quality of light observed during the night hours that is the aesthetic element of interest in *Brooklyn Bridge*, 1948. Feininger's use of the long lens flattens space and objects, but emphasizes qualities of light, so that architectural elements appear as condensed, layered. His preference for the telephoto lens does eliminate extraneous detail, but it has also assisted in establishing a photographic style indicative of Feininger's work. His choice of spectacular views, from cemeteries to congested traffic on Fifth Avenue, clearly

Figure 6-3 ANDREAS FEININGER, *Brooklyn Bridge* 1948 (Life Magazine © Time Inc.)

demonstrates the changing qualities of light as a medium through which other concerns are made evident. *Brooklyn Bridge* is sweeping in its scope, grand, majestic, and still romantic, but its romanticism is achieved through careful consideration of the qualities of aerial perspective, point of view, and, most of all, by the photographer's attitude toward his subject matter.

Space

When discussing art, the word we hear most often is sure to be "space." Just what this word means in that context, or out of it, is difficult to say. Space is not an object we can grasp; we think it is limitless, and we know it to exist only by and through objects and their relationships to one another. Our response to actual space is formed through our own experience of the objective world. Objects functioning as signals in collaboration with individual educated responses give us some vague idea of what space is. And, while our ideas of space have changed considerably during this century, largely by the exploration of outer space through scientific methods, we still find it difficult to comprehend such space without reference to the bodies found within it. And "pure space" (whatever that may be) is only a noun, not a mystical concept, nor a visible or invisible reality. However, what the current explorations and discoveries in outer space have done is to replace our self-centered attitude to the world with a realization of our insignificance. These changes and discoveries have affected the work of artists, as is especially evident in their struggles to depict or give the illusion of space.

Because space is an essential ingredient in art and architecture, it is important to try to understand traditional and contemporary methods used by artists in establishing this illusion in their work. In architecture, structure builds space, or encloses a certain amount of it, divided into compartments called rooms which protect us from the elements. These enclosures may give the illusion of greater or lesser amounts of space depending on the methods employed in the design. And just as in the other arts, these methods will vary from culture to culture, depending on climatic and social conditions, as well as cultural traditions.

In sculpture, we must move around, through, or over the work to see it and to experience the sculptor's concept of space. In painting and the graphic arts, space derives from an illusion on a two-dimensional surface. No space actually exists, nor do most of the other visual elements in painting and graphic arts, only an illusion or a reference. Pictorial space may be illusionistically three-dimensional, ambiguous, or flat, depending on how the artist employs the visual elements and his individual perception of what space is all about. Pictorial depth can be achieved by the visual elements, cofunctioning or singly. Spatial relationships are essential in traditional art in building the illusion of space, that is the illusion of depth, volume—the third dimension. In some contemporary abstract images, where the picture plane is denied, the spatial relationship between the visual elements is of little value.

Working on the two-dimensional plane, a single dot or short line will evoke the sense of space by the surrounding areas of blankness. But if another dot is placed near it, or another short line crosses over the existing one, another sort of space is indicated—primitive, but effective. Overlapping, the most common method used by artists to suggest space, may be found in both traditional and contemporary art. It is our reading of overlapping bodies in relation to the blank areas of the support that suggests space to us, negative space where nothing exists in the void. Because we know that objects appear to get smaller as they move into the distance, the size of any body will indicate distance, or the space between us and it. Placement on the support further assists in giving the illusion of distance and space. If placed at the lower section of the support, the body will seem closer, and the more it moves back, that is, higher up on the support, the more the distance appears to increase. Other methods of defining space are projecting a flat shape into an illusion of volume by linear perspective, employment of chiaroscuro, and shapes by association. For example, we know that the amount of space between a model's arm and torso as they overlap is small, but the overlapping of buildings may be accepted as a large space, and still greater between mountain ranges.

Two generally accepted categories of space are space as limit, and space as environment, terms invented by the French art historian Henri Focillon. The first contains within its own boundaries all the space it creates, and everything outside that space is of negative value. The other creates forms which move freely in undefined environment without specified limits and can extend into actual space. In Western art, we find Focillon's *espace milieu* clearly established in traditional and contemporary art, while Eastern art exemplifies *l'espace limite*. But all representations of space relate to one thing: our perception of depth and distance as related to the ground plane indoors or outdoors, and extending to the horizon line. Consciously and subconsciously we continually measure distance by it, calculate size, and "feel" or experience space. In traditional art, the presence, or implied presence, of the ground plane is essential in presenting the illusion of space, whether deep or shallow. With the changing movements in art, the ground plane as a measure of space and distance assumes different forms, such as in Baroque art where clouds become the reference point for space and distance. And in the still life paintings of the Impressionist period, the table top is the reference point. In contemporary abstract art, the ground plane shifts its position to the vertical and new, ambiguous spatial relationships are formed.

The term "personal space" is often heard. For many, the definition would be difficult to articulate, yet we know when our personal space is violated by another. How would one represent that space? Each one of us experiences space differently; there can be no one definition of it any more than there can be a single representation of it that everyone would agree upon. Examining works of art from a variety of cultures and from different time periods, there would be, in all probability, certain overlapping of concepts, methods, use of media, rhythmic sequence, and approach in visually representing space. However, no matter what culture or time period an image comes from, the represented objects inevitably act as spatial references, whether they are as evasive as a cloud or fog, or as solid as rock outcroppings.

Approaching the question of space in a more limited and restricted way related to our immediate environment, it seems that geographic locations and the changes wrought in the environment by imposing cultural values upon the natural world through city planning, industry, architecture, and landscaping are the elements which build the space we perceive, and that our perception of space is always in flux, due to social, economic, and political change. These changes cannot be sidestepped by the artist since they are the forces which shape the space he experiences and, in one way or another, represents in his work. It has been scientifically proven that character and amount of space allowed an individual affects his social interaction as well as his character traits. In observing the way that space is represented in works of art, it can be said with certainty that the way space is represented, not the objects, is indicative of content, mood, statement, state of mind, or temperament.

The great frescoed ceilings of the Baroque period were not intended just to give a greater sense of space to the interior of a church, since most of these architectural wonders already enclosed great spaces. These paintings, often depicting the open heavens with clouds, architectural elements, angels, saints, and light were new, romanticized versions of church dogma, floating in heavenly space. This depiction of space was part of a stylistic movement, but what was the origin of the style? A change in attitude toward dogma by the church. These new representations of space were intended to draw the observer into the experience painted, and were sometimes brought forward by the addition of stucco figures to enhance the sensation of the activity actually extending down into the space the observer occupied. Every visual spatial device known to the artist was used to draw the observer into a state of union, through his vision, with the intensity of the action. The space of earlier frescoes depicting church dogma was quite different in concept. In many paintings, the actual architecture of the church was extended into the paintings by means of painted illusion, but the space was closed. The observer was not invited to participate in the depiction of the scene; he was to remain an observer, looking at the events from a distance. There were clearly two separate spaces: the observer's, and the space he looked into, intended by artist and patron. But even in the Baroque frescoes that depict limitless space, reference had to be made to relationships between objects in order to achieve such an illusion.

Van Gogh never depicted space in which nothing was at rest or anchored to the ground plane, and never a vacuum in which things merely existed (Figure 6-4). Space became as one with the other objects, fused with them, solid, measurable, inseparable. Light and light-auras never reveal form and shape to create distance and space, rather they negate space. In Van Gogh's paintings, space does not fragment into smaller spaces, or shapes into smaller shapes, or color into smaller fragments of unrelated color. His conception of space is thought of as an entity, a whole that unites all parts, although nothing in his work is conceived of in parts. There is an underlying wholeness that one senses immediately and completely, in which parts have knowledge of other parts, constituting an indivisible whole. For Van Gogh, the world, the universe, and his relation to it are a complete unity undivided by space and time. Such modes of thought and work eliminate any chaotic and meaningless conflict in his representations of physical reality, freeing his vision from antagonisms and cross-purposes that collide, limiting vision and energies. A person makes an idea or a principle visible and gives it form and shape that others can share. Van Gogh makes his ideas and feelings visible in his depiction of space, which embodies his religious

Figure 6-4 VINCENT VAN
GOGH, *The Starry Night* 1889
(Kunsthalle, Bremen)

background and training. His spiritual longings expressed through his conception and depiction of space are not to be confused with his personality disorders, also manifest in this work through color and shape. The whole person of the painter is in evidence through his work, so that it is possible for these aspects of his personality to exist side by side in a single work.

An artist makes himself heard not just by what it is he depicts, but how he depicts it; we can misinterpret his voice by directing our attention toward objects rather than to their interpretation. For much of Van Gogh's work, it is the uniting of elements within a personally conceived space that is his voice. For him, and for most artists, the creative act is a temporary refuge that later becomes a permanent imprint of the artist's personal perceptions and conceptions, a concrete symbol of the individual. It is this symbol that may summon from us, the observers, a kinship with the artist's perceptions and experiences. But unless we approach these symbols as individual interpretations of outer reality based on inner realities, they have no authority, no voice, they are mute.

Grant Mudford's *Los Angeles,* 1978 (Figure 6-5) depicts urban development in which space is compressed, then released, specific to a single location, culture, and time. The space is formed by contemporary structures, partly or entirely within the image. From the foreground to the middle ground a series of structures looking like prophecies of the space age shape and compress space within the geometrical configurations they form. In the foreground, a vertical, perforated structure functions as a screen, which begins the enclosed space but allows us to see into it and beyond and, in the middle ground, another vertical structure defines where the space ends. We are led into this first layer of compressed space by a handrail to the left of center. The handrail functions as a straight line

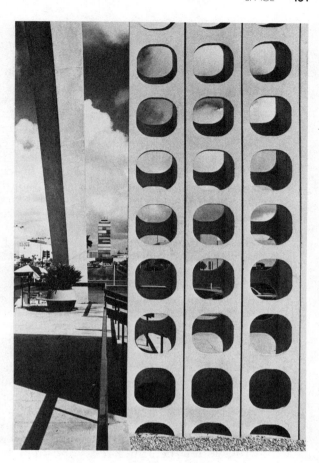

Figure 6-5   GRANT MUDFORD, *Los Angeles* 1978 (© Grant Mudford. Courtesy of Light Gallery, New York)

leading the eye through this space and into another space which is open. The line of the handrail joins visually with the road in the open space and forms a single major axis through the composition. In the open space, the perspective lines of the road and buildings lead to an unseen vanishing point situated at the base of the vertical structure in the distance.

It is at the skyscraper where the terrestial demarcations for space end and infinite space begins. Natural and artificial forms diminish in size as they recede into the distance. Textural aspects of plant life, concrete, and pebbles are clearly defined in the foreground, but diminish in definition, and tonal shifts from black to white in the foreground slowly change into lighter tones as they too recede with little diminution of clarity due to aerial perspective. Overlapping forms heighten the feeling for space, while the cast shadows in the foreground restate the ground plane as the measure for distance and general orientation, assist the major lead line of the handrail by restating it, and encourage the eye to follow all the visual elements as they lead into the open space ending at the skyscraper. Light, which enters from the upper right side of the composition, is brilliant, reflective, and crystalline, enhances the space, and adds further visual excitement.

This space, largely shaped by architectural elements, is punctuated by the organic forms of trees, offsetting their geometrical nature. Variety within the whole is felt by the irregular compartmentalization shaped by the organic forms. Mudford's knowledge and use of the visual elements has created a sense of space familiar to most urban dwellers. But his depiction of this space is personal, made so by defining different kinds of space existing within the totality of a single enclosure. His observations, calculations, and judgments all add up to a specific and highly individual interpretation of space but, to us, it looks right, knowable, experienced, and true; if this is so, then there can be no doubt that as an artist, he has reached us; we have heard his voice.

Like Van Gogh, whose longings were made evident through his depictions of space, the compassionate, humanistic aspect of Mudford's personality has made itself felt through his perceptions of space. We can best interpret his space by observing his efforts to change the existing unfamiliar chaotic space into an ordered synthesis where one may find grandeur in place of confusion. Playing compressions against opening space within the total space, Mudford's interpretation has allowed the scale and drama of the modern contemporary structures to form brilliant displays of pattern, linear relationships, light, shade and cast shadow to dazzle the eye. The artist's reshaping of space according to his will has served his needs, and ultimately it is the artist's method of constructing space that we recognize and empathize with, not the photograph as a document of a place or situation. The space depicted is an ideal environment, where order rules, where everything is in logical arrangement, in which humans may exist and move freely through uncluttered areas. The sequence of concepts intuitively grasped and intellectually arranged within the deliberately controlled space indicates an artist whose perceptions and experience are synthesized in an image that serves as a bridge between the observed and observer. Space is the crucible for the artist's ideas and thoughts, which are freighted with previous associations beyond the specific elements seen in the photograph.

Throughout the history of art, the artist's concept of space has been the one constant thread inextricably woven into the fabric of image making. He may eliminate other visual elements such as texture, volume, line, and shape, but he has maintained a tenacious hold on representing and using space. Whether space is a drawn, painted, or sculptured illusion, or a physical reality used outside and around the work, it remains a fundamental concern in which visions of an open or closed universe, non-Euclidean geometry plausible beyond the third spatial dimension, or human spatial experience are made manifest. The boundless advances artists make in their work often go unnoticed by the spectator and obscure his understanding of the artist's creative progress. The eventual complexities that such works of art contain are at times greater than the individual who created them. The perception and conception of space are phenomena which fit together in a homogeneous manner through the visual world and through our imagination, which is a constant condition of being human.

Composition

Perceiving and understanding the visual elements individually and collectively is essential in forming compositions. From this base of understanding, through continual unbroken development, one may approach a beginning to the achievement of significant works of art, including photographs. Each artist demonstrates through his work a sense of form, differentiated by his ability in organizing the various components. The organization of the components into a comprehensive order is designated as composition. It is through this structure that we may perceive the artist's intelligence, but also a deeper, more significant aspect: his meaning. This meaning may be directly observable through representation of pattern or form, or may be implied, unspecific, an intellectual connection. The photographer as well as the painter must isolate his subject from the stream of physical reality or thought. In a sense, to extract the subject from the general mix so that it may stand within the matrix of the compositional form is a kind of purification.

But that is not to say that the matrix is reducible to diagrams or procedures. The composition may serve as the matrix which reflects isolated experiences or existence, observable in a single image or related multiple images. The image is composed of an interaction or cofunction of thought and vision, united by composition. It is here in composition where perception and conception meet and enlighten one another, united into one and the same experience. For the observer, all these aspects are revealed through the photograph as a single experience—as the expression of the photographer.

The process of composing, on the conscious or subconscious level, continues for many artists even outside the hours of active production. It is a mental, visual, perceptual procedure that functions without the objects and tools needed for creativity. No other element of artistic production seems to exert such force, for it is composition that is the container of ideas, germinating themes that become structures allowing each artist to speak in his own individual way. Each composition is not only the sum of its parts—content, movement, all the academic and nonacademic aspects of creativity—it is, in a way, the artist's language. At times, content and composition are independent of one another, and at other times, they can merge, transforming the production into a powerful statement and image. The basic creative activity we call composition, then, could be said to be an orchestration of the visual elements that make up a work of art. Whether it is called design, placement, arrangement, layout, or choreography, composition for all artists is a major consideration.

Obviously, there are no rules to follow in composition or, for that matter, in the use of any of the other visual elements. When ironclad rules are set up, enforced, and followed to the letter, they lead to a blind alley of imitation and repetitiveness. There is no secret formula or procedure that would lead one to successful image making. However, during the Italian Renaissance, a number of compositional approaches were established and have been in continuous use by artists since. These approaches may serve as guide posts or starting points, but are best left behind once understood, or once their format has been used in creating other inventive compositions. And while it is true that the photographer's language is visual, we must not overlook the fact that other forms of communication have been incorporated into the visual image that may further our understanding and appreciation. It is a mistake to believe that only through a visual approach may one find pleasure. Treatment of the subject does have something to do with the value of the photograph as art and expression. Otherwise, art has been reduced to mere decoration, the frame rather than the photograph, the mat instead of the drawing. To understand and increase the appreciation of any individual photograph, much can be said, for often individual works are pivotal in an artist's departure from a movement, or instrumental in a change of style, or revelatory of the makeup of the individual personality. Furthermore, all the principles of an art movement may not often be found within individual works, even though the artist is part of a given movement. Composing is one way to bring expression and meaning into visual existence, and we may understand wholly or in part just what the artist means by giving consideration to his composition.

It would be a mistake to speak of composition without considering past compositional methods, since some of these methods are the basis for expressive compositions current today. And while it is true that a great deal of composition is approached intuitively, much of it is carefully considered on the conscious level, taking into account such problems as placement of forms, movement, scale, proportions, spatial relationships, and division of the visual field. Photographers who employ the tripod use it for other reasons in addition to stabilization of the camera. With the tripod, careful adjustments of distance from subject, angle, and organization of the visual elements within the visual field are methods used to form intentional compositions.

The choice of compositional format is highly personal. If one were to trace the compositional development of a single artist, a source, or sources, would emerge for his preferred compositions. Composition often is as much a statement about the artist's personality as is the content, and quite often, one may find that composition is independent of content, presenting its own meaning. Through a variety of compositional techniques, the photographer can, and often does, manipulate the observer in a number of ways, emotionally and physically. The observer's responses are brought about by placement of form, perspective, divisions of the visual field, and careful use of the other elements within the composition. Throughout history, artists have constructed a wide variety of compositional methods through which they may be understood. Those methods continue to be used and expanded upon. This process goes on with each new generation of artists as they search out new and experimental ways in which to make their voices heard, their ideas and perceptions made visible. Each composition is more than the sum of its parts—all the academic and nonacademic aspects of creativity—it is the artist presenting himself to us.

From the past, a small group of compositional formulae are mentioned as reference: The Golden Section, dynamic, radial, symmetrical, assymmetrical, and geometrical. The Golden Section is a canon for ideal compositional proportion, or more precisely, the perfect and ideal mathematical proportion. This idea seems to have begun in ancient Mesopotamia; from there, it moved to Egypt,

Greece, and Italy. It was during the Italian Renaissance that many canons were developed and the concept of mathematical proportion reached its zenith. In 1479, Fra Luca Pacioli wrote *De Divina Proportione,* in which he stated that the whole is to the largest part as the largest part is to the smallest (I : X = X : I−X). Dynamic composition is based on a force which produces motion throughout the composition. Radial composition is movement and form relationships radiating from a central point in the composition. Symmetrical composition is relationships of form and movement equally mirrored, vertically or horizontally. Asymmetrical composition is an unequal balancing of movement and form, vertically or horizontally. Geometric composition is form and movement contained in or related to geometric shapes as the underlying structure of the composition. Some of the more recent compositional approaches are negative and positive reversals, reversible image, field or overall reading, grid systems, and figure-field.

Negative-positive reversals or reversible image compositions are based on the optical illusion of black and white (or color) grounds or shapes interchanging their spatial relationships. In field compositions shapes are distributed evenly throughout the picture plane so that the image appears to continue beyond the edges of the picture plane. Grid compositions are based on the division of the picture plane into equal or unequal parts, and are often defined by a linear construction of vertical or horizontal lines. The linear construction may be curvilinear as well. Figure-field composition comprises a shape resting on a field devoid of other shapes.

Birthday Party, 1979, by Larry Fink (Figure 6-6), uses a dynamic composition to assist the photographer with his interest in depicting social functions. The gestures and postures of the figures show us their social interactions at a birthday party. The camera is tilted so as to accentuate the feeling of overall movement, but especially to activate movement in the architectural elements of the screen door and wall. As the woman moves through the doorway and under an extended arm, carrying a birthday cake topped with the number eight, a countermovement forward is established without separating from other movements. Each figure is animated; arms, hands, heads, facial expressions, all combine into one sensation of movement, reflecting the source motivating the action, the birthday party. Fink depicts human movement and sets it in an overall movement by means of camera angle, but he has revealed to us the real world in which we may recognize ourselves as well as the photographer through movement in social interaction. By dynamic compositional methods he says we are one, that everything is in continual motion, transient, constant, and unified, and that human social interaction, fundamental to all people, is expressed through movement. Each figure's posture represents a different aspect of movement, the woman's movement is slow, tense, and balanced as she concentrates on the cake.

To the right, another figure we do not see, except for an arm, is in graceful movement, the arm extended, the hand reaching over and holding the door open with several fingers. A young boy holds up his hand with five fingers extended, seemingly in contrast to the number eight on the cake, demonstrates swift angular movement, and in the foreground other types of movement are expressed by body angle. Each movement, expressing an inward mental state, is different from the others yet part of the whole, caught by Fink's rapid observa-

Figure 6-6   LARRY FINK, *Birthday Party* 1979 (© Larry Fink. Courtesy of Light Gallery, New York)

tions of the situation on film. This composition meshes with the photographer's intention, interests, and perceptions. Unity of idea, situation, movement, and the visual elements are strongly and firmly conveyed through Fink's photograph by his selective vision.

While this photograph depicts a certain social class at a particular function, one does not feel that it is an impediment to the recognition of deeper human responses experienced by everyone. It is a purposive and selective image allowing cognition, an instrument from which our responses spring. All of its features are indispensable to the whole if it is to fulfill the artist's intent, and our responsiveness is made possible by intent manifested through the visual elements, especially the artist's use of the dynamic composition.

Compositions based on geometric shapes as an underlying structure, or objects used to form geometric shapes, is a compositional method employed in paintings and drawings of the Italian Renaissance, and has been in use ever since. Today, photographers use this geometrical structure in their work, greatly simplifying it or giving it greater complexity. Arnold Newman's photograph, *I. M. Pei,* 1967 (Figure 6-7), is one of his superb environmental portraits, demonstrating an updated, sophisticated, bold use of this format. His composition is severe and yet fully effective for his intention. A rich black field is used to float a triangle, square, ellipses, and rectangles. These geometric shapes fully express the basic and common denominator of his subject, who is posed in the long horizontal rectangle. The rectangle is divided into fourths by the figure and a

Figure 6-7 ARNOLD NEWMAN, *I. M. Pei* 1967 (© Arnold Newman)

door. Each division is proportionally different from the others, adding visual variety to the rectangle. The door forms a square, the door knob assembly a vertical rectangle, placed in harmonious juxtaposition to the rectangle which contains them. A soft modulation of tones within the rectangle turns it into a shallow negative space, alternating with the positive shapes. In the top third of the composition, three ellipses of various proportions form an isosceles triangle with its point shifted to the left edge of the photograph, while the horizontal rectangle is placed at the right edge. The opposing positions of the two geometric shapes generate a lateral thrust and movement while further dividing the field. These geometric shapes are architectural elements, a window and overhead lights, transformed by Newman's metering of the lights so that a high-contrast image resulted.

The isolation and transformation of these elements is part of his method in building an extraordinary photograph, reflecting a kind of social algebra in reference to the personality and occupation of his subject. The visual grasping of these shapes leads to the comprehension of the reason why Newman imposed them upon structural features of the stimulus material, the architecture and figure. Thus, our perception of these geometric shapes operates at a cognitive level of idea information arrived at through cultural and social background, learning, and biological maturation. The intense intellectuality of this image limits its accessibility. These limitations do, however, suggest, if not prove, Newman's use of a geometric type of composition through his intellectual powers, a new direction in portrait photography that he has consistently pursued for nearly two decades. The result has been a highly personal style few have dared to imitate. His photographs, geometrically based, stand unique and firm against the changing tides of fashion and trends in the art world.

The grid system as composition is a recent development used by painters, photographers, and printmakers, and taken by itself, offers a statement about contemporary society as dehumanizing, technological, and regimented—permitting understanding and contact through limited ritualized channels.

Ray Metzker's *Nude* 1966 (Figure 6-8) is one example of the various grid systems he uses to establish his compositional format, and produces through his unusual technical means. The multiple permutations of the figure are the result of the photographer's method of making exposures. First the entire roll of film was exposed, then rewound, then exposed once again. Later the film was cut into seven segments to form a single image which has the effect of seeing an entire roll of film or individual frames at once in a single image. The result of this grid system is a series of small compositions within a larger one.

Within each frame a segment of the figure is seen in high contrast, which at once unites the individual frames through identity of zone or tone into a single unified image, and is a forceful denial of the picture plane's limits. There is no focal point in the image, and the shapes, both black and white, appear to continue beyond the limits of the photograph.

Nude is without a center of interest, no frame has priority over any other in any way, and its high-contrast technique of sharp black and white shapes turns them into negative–positive reversals and neutralizes the space. Each segment of the grid may be read as a separate experience, and seen together, all add up to a total, as if each frame were a snapshot of a different figure, but placed side by

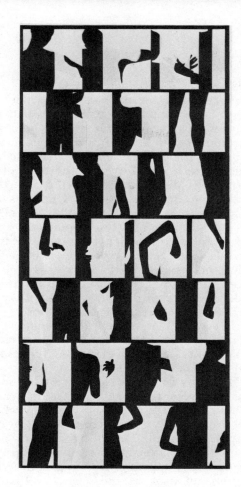

Figure 6-8 RAY METZKER,
Nude 1966
(Courtesy of the photographer)

side all fuse to become the same figure seen in graceful motion. It is this am-
bivalence that reveals Metzker's message and places him in a vulnerable position.
However, this very vulnerability becomes a strength which we ultimately admire
and respect. While each part of the grid imposes a formal rigidity upon the
images, the compartmentalization works as a faceting, allowing one part to move
into the next, a dissolving effect that gives great animation and movement to the
total image. Metzker weaves a realistic image, in spite of the flatness and graphic
designlike quality, both sensual and human, over the grid composition that is
mesmerizingly realistic, establishing a viable bridge between observer and observed. Each compartment of the grid allows vision to act as an invisible finger
with which we may move through the spaces and touch surfaces, trace contours
and borders. The multiple images, each in its own compartment, form a spontaneous experience by the eye, extending to an active psychological process of
vision. Through the grid system, our vision imposes a conceptual order on the
information it receives from each part. For each individual the conceptual order
will be different according to the individual readings of the material presented.

However, as in all visual scanning or screening, each viewer will expedite
the processing of the images from each segment of the grid into a totality
dependent upon cognition of the message conveyed by the photographer. With-

in this visual processing, visual selectivity will function, restricting choice of segments to form the whole. This selectivity is merely an extension of personal background which makes the reaction faster and surer. But that is not to say that the process of perceiving this image is accomplished suddenly; the fact that the grid system is over, around, and on the image partly prevents it. The observer starts from somewhere, and in the case of vertical–horizontal orientation formed by the grid, the Western tradition of reading encourages one to start at the upper left and move across to the right, dropping down to the next line and proceeding in the same manner. Once this overall reading through the grid is accomplished, random visual exploration takes over. The grid then becomes a method of offering a starting point to the observer as he orients himself to the skeleton of the work. After the framework is understood and read, it then may elicit visual–intellectual response within the totality of the work, illuminating or assisting the meaning of the work. Throughout the photograph a middle-grey tone or zone sets up a movement that offers a visual guide. After the movement is understood within the total context of the composition, the viewer begins to experiment with further visual explorations beyond the general framework of the grid system. The power of individual vision begins to organize the various elements discovered beyond the grid into personal rearrangements, so that while one system organizes and orientates, it does not prevent the dominance of individual orientation.

Metzker's work reaches us directly by supplying us with what we ask for, by saying that the more strongly we insist on reality the more we are immersed in it, and the more deeply we are affected by what we see and experience through reality pressing in on us. Perhaps the test for each of us is the manner in which we handle that reality, which impinges on us every day of our lives, with ourselves, and with others. If art and photography can offer us this challenge, as they continually appear to be doing—through photography in particular—then this combination of art and science will have served us as no other art form ever has.

The visual elements in themselves are simple and passive; but when activated by a creative mind and placed in the context of a particular medium of expression, they form a universal language. As we perceive the world in its context of change, by which it is modulated, the photographer may, if he chooses, show us that we are part of that context, modulators as well as modulated, in which we may recognize ourselves. More deeply and simply, we possess the unique quality of thinking and reasoning which sets us apart from every other form of life. One of our greatest rewards is thinking about what we see. This simple process has enriched our culture and enhanced our lives. Part of that enrichment and enhancement comes to us by and through the special language of photography.

7 PHOTOGRAPHY AND THE OTHER ARTS

Almost from birth the camera and the photograph have exerted an undeniable effect upon the other arts. At times this effect has been strongly evident, changing the visual appearance of other art forms, while at other times the effect has been less pronounced. As our society becomes more and more strongly influenced by technology, still and moving photographic images have become an integral part of our ever-advancing technological age. To many photographers, the exchange between photography and the other arts presents a threat to photography as a pure art form, yet it is this very interaction that prevents photography from ossifying. Some of the most original and visually exciting photographic images have been those in which this interaction is most keenly felt and made visually present. To date, no comprehensive study has been made of the relationship of photography to the other arts, although this is a fertile area that deserves attention.

In spite of this interaction, photography and the other arts have not been judged by equal standards until recent years, when it has become clear from the economic reality of photography and from the proliferation of photographic exhibitions that this discrimination has largely been eliminated. Whether this economic phase is transitory remains to be seen. In the process, however, photography has made enormous technical and aesthetic advances, offering both to the other arts, which have not always used them to their own best advantage.

The mechanical image is an enticement offering easy, quick solutions to some of the other arts, and yet from time to time sincere efforts have surfaced, clearly demonstrating originality through this incorporation of the photographic image. The traditional distinctions between the arts have largely disappeared as artists look freely to a constantly increasing variety of artistic disciplines for techniques and materials, which they use to form new and fresh images, objects, and environments.

The present period of photographic history has gone beyond Stieglitz's expectations, hopes, and wildest dreams. It must be remembered that the relationship between photography and the other arts does not always produce physical and tangible evidence but may result in intangible effects that contain the promise of a future art. Such intangibles as changing methods, concepts, ideas, and interpretations generated by the visible physical realities of the interrelationship of photography to the other arts are the energy source representing the continuation and regeneration of art. And outside this circle of artistic creative expression stand the observers, who are emotionally, intellectually, and psychologically affected for better or worse.

While certain aspects of the relationship between photography and the other arts may be easy enough to see, there are theoretical aspects that are less obvious and difficult if not impossible to demonstrate. All human actions are open to interpretation, as is all art. Of course there are exceptions in both cases, but art life is a continuous, gradual, rational and irrational attempt of humanity to attain a higher degree of development. The meshing of ideas, concepts, and art forms within any society is just one phase in this process of development and is a fundamental part of human existence.

The new breed of art, which is the consequence of the interaction between photography and the other arts, must be considered dispassionately and in the light of artistic evolution, just as we must do with any other aspect of human development. Even unsuccessful creative efforts must not be judged as setbacks, but as part of the entire, unconditioned natural process of development within the community of arts, and the community of humanity of which it is an integral part.

Some may view human enterprise as governed by sociopolitical systems alone, but it must also be seen in the entire context of historical, artistic, and scientific influences. To do otherwise is to be unreal, isolationist, and defeating. Likewise a concept of art controlled by systems established in the past does nothing to promote artistic development and may effectively block it. The recent cross between photography and other disciplines is not a matter of mere technical gymnastics, but has resulted in new perceptions, new self-motivations, and new self-actions postulating our new identity in the twentieth century.

Drawing and Painting

Drawing appears to be inextricably wedded to photography, more so than any of the other visual arts with the possible exception of painting. From the first camera obscura to the present camera, artists for slightly more than four hundred years have used the light image as an aid in efforts to reproduce with more accuracy the illusion of physical reality. However, some artists have used the photographic process to reach beyond the representation of physical reality and to depict an inner reality.

It was in the tenth century that the first camera obscura was invented by a famous Arab mathematician and scientist, Alhazen of Basra, and used by him to observe the eclipses of the sun. Alhazen's treatise and work was known in Europe during the thirteenth century, when the lens was invented. This was a period of great excitement. Artists were working for a more accurate means of representing their physical environment, and an intense investigation into the problem of optics was taking place. Scientists were looking toward the artists whose investigations and perceptions, methodically followed, were bringing science and art closer together. By the fifteenth century, linear perspective was brought forth as a science by Filippo Brunelleschi, and Leon Battista Alberti's treatise on painting had heightened the public's interest in the illusion of believable space and objects on a two-dimensional surface. It was Giovanni Battista della Porta, in his *Magiae Naturalis* of 1558, who first recommended to artists that they use the camera obscura in their work. At this time the camera obscura was fitted with a double convex lens; later della Porta suggested the use of a concave mirror so that a magnified image could be reflected back right-side-up onto a wall. By 1646 a small portable camera obscura was invented by Athanasius Kircher. This camera obscura allowed the artist to enter it through a trap door and trace the projected image on transparent paper that hung opposite one of the lenses (Figure 7-1). With time and further adjustments the camera obscura became smaller until it reached table-top proportions. Johann Zahn's reflex-box camera obscura (1685) was quite close to the easily portable camera obscura of the early nineteenth century. Arnold Guyot's table camera obscura (1770) had a lens and reflecting

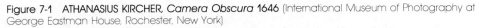

Figure 7-1 ATHANASIUS KIRCHER, *Camera Obscura* 1646 (International Museum of Photography at George Eastman House, Rochester, New York)

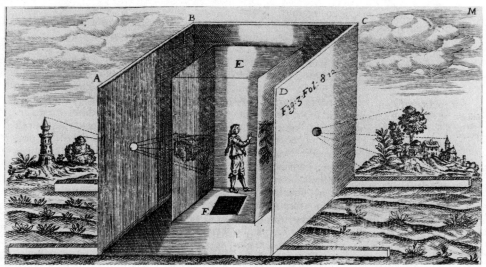

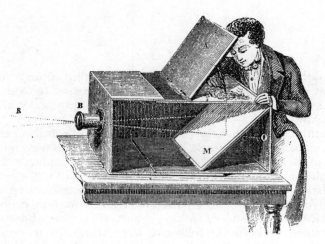

Figure 7-2 ARNOLD GUYOT, *Camera Obscura* (International Museum of Photography at George Eastman House, Rochester, New York)

CHAMBRE CLAIRE
selon Amici.
Perfectionnée par Vincent Chevalier.
Quai de l'Horloge 69, au Microscope Achromatique.

Figure 7-3 WILLIAM HYDE WOLLASTON, *Camera Lucida* 1806 (International Museum of Photography at George Eastman House, Rochester, New York)

mirror which allowed the image to be projected onto a piece of ground glass, where the image could then be traced (Figure 7-2). William Hyde Wollaston invented a device known as the camera lucida (1806), depicted in an engraving made four years later in London (Figure 7-3). This apparatus consisted of three telescoped tubes mounted on a table clamp, a 45° prism, and an adjustable sight with a spectacle lens for individual vision. These forerunners of the present-day camera aided the artists in their drawing pursuits and even allowed some amateurs to achieve drawings that had a certain credibility. An example of the kind of drawing that could be made with the aid of the camera lucida is Sir John Herschel's drawing of the Temple of Juno at Girgenti in Sicily (the modern

Agrigento), dated 1824 (Figure 7-4). Linear perspective, proportion, and chiaroscuro effects are recorded with accuracy, and yet the drawing has a certain flatness even though Herschel's touch is light and freely worked in the trees and foreground with some drawing conventions of his time.

Once the camera as we know it had been developed and the photographic image made somewhat more permanent, the controversy of photography as art began. Many statements were being made for and against photography as an art form, most notable among them those of John Ruskin, whose opinion shifted from one extreme to the other. In the end he did little to disguise his dislike for photography, even though he collected daguerreotypes and used them in his own landscape and architectural drawings. In *Elements of Drawing,* published in 1857, he suggests that artists use photographs taken of sculptures in French cathedrals so that they might draw the folds of drapery, and that photographs of landscapes would be of value when drawing and working out value changes, for here the delicacy could be clearly observed. For the most part, artists were no longer just tracing images or making precise copies of photographs but using them as sources for their work. Often segments of photographs were used and incorporated into larger compositions, and photographic studies of nudes were used as models for more complex drawings and paintings. Sketches made by Eugène Delacroix (Figure 7-5) from photographs by Eugène Durieu (Figure 7-6) give an example of one way that artists were using the photographic study. But the photograph was serving the artist in other ways than simply for accuracy in recording objects. Some of the qualities inherent in the camera itself, such as blur or in-and-out focus, attracted interest and appeared in the work of such artists as Corot, Courbet, Daubigny, Dutilleaux, Fantin-Latour, Ingres, Millet, Manet, Rousseau, and Eakins.

With the studies of locomotion by Muybridge and Marey, and Disderi's *cartes-de-visite* in production (1854–1866), photography and art interacted as never before. Degas's work appeared to have been affected most of all. His

Figure 7-4 SIR JOHN HERSCHEL,
Temple of Juno at Girgenti, Sicily
(Science Museum, London)

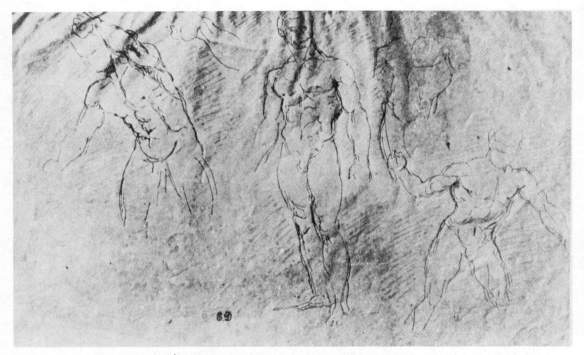

Figure 7-5   EUGÈNE DELACROIX, *Sketches, Nudes* c. 1854 (Musée Bonnat, Bayonne, France)

Figure 7-6   EUGÈNE DURIEU, *Nude, Male* (Bibliothèque Nationale, Paris)

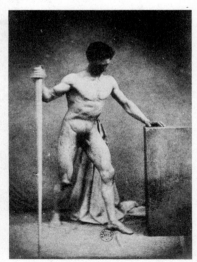

compositions have the same sort of cropped look to them as the instantaneous image. Cinematic progression appeared in his compositions, in which sequential poses of dancers were placed horizontally in his drawings and dancers were caught in graceful leaps into the air (Figure 7-7). The work of Muybridge and particularly the chronophotographs of Marey appear to support, and perhaps even inaugurated the Futurists' concept of simultaneity and interpenetration of forms. Balla's pencil-on-paper studies for the painting *Rhythm of the Violinist* (Figure 7-8) depict the movement of the fingers and hand as they create the illusion of blur, transparency, and the interpenetration of forms. Some of these characteristics may be observed in Marey's chronophotographs of men and women in motion, but in all probability relate more directly to Anton Giulio Bragaglia's work in photodynamics of c. 1911–12. Bragaglia's photograph *The Typist* (Figure 7-9), published in *Foto Dinamismo* in 1912, coincides with the beginnings of the Futurist movement and records many of the Futurists' concerns. Bragaglia, who was an important personality in the cultural and artistic circles of Rome during this period, directed and supported many of the Futurists' activities. His photography, however, had an important effect upon the painting and drawing of the movement. Balla, who studied the violin as a child, certainly would have known by experience the finger positions for the violin depicted in his study, and yet there is an interesting relationship between Balla's drawing

Figure 7-7   EDWARD DEGAS,
Le Pas Battu
(Buhrle Foundation, Zurich)

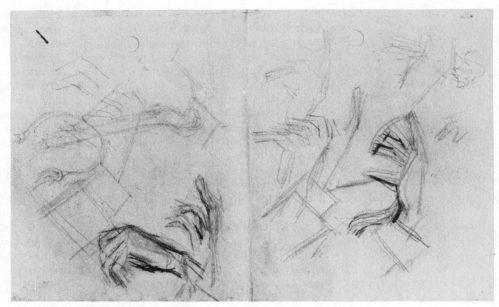

Figure 7-8   GIACOMO BALLA, *Two Studies for Rhythm of the Violinist* **1912** (Courtesy of Miss Elica Balla and Miss Luce Balla)

Figure 7-9   ANTON GIULIO BRAGAGLIA, *The Typist* (Courtesy of Antonella Vigliani Bragaglia)

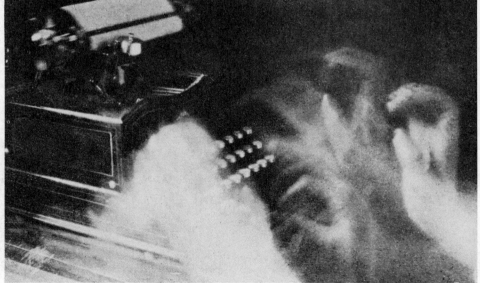

and Bragaglia's photograph, even though the study may have been made during a practice session on the violin.

Some of the distinct visual characteristics of Futurism, such as transparency, interpenetration of forms, and negative-positive shape relationships, were to appear later in Cubism. Photography reaches into Cubism indirectly through the Futurist movement.

The New Realists were never a movement, but sprang up independently of one another in different sections of the United States. Photography and the traditional arts of this time, about 1970, were bound to one another more strongly than in the case of the Futurists. But the two relationships are entirely different. The Futurists used the photograph as a source, and the New Realists placed themselves in a position of total reliance. Interestingly enough, since the mid-1970's photography has rapidly grown in public popularity throughout the world. Whether this new acceptance and chic has anything to do with photography's recent affiliation with drawing and painting remains to be answered.

One artist who made ample use of the photograph in his paintings and drawings during the period when the new realists were at the apex of popularity was Chuck Close. As a "portrait painter," and one has to use this term in the broadest sense when applying it to him, his work shares a common ground with that of Ingres. Both of these artists maintain a surface tension at once breathtaking and surreal. Although there is no factual information that Ingres did use photographs in his work, all visual evidence tends to point in that direction (perhaps the daguerreotypes). But unlike Close, Ingres used photographs as a source not only for accuracy in physical likeness and speed in working, but for drawing out those qualities that may be considered humanist. This is the major difference of intent between the two. Close maintains emotional distance, refraining from comment or interpretation of the person. His major concern is process rather than likeness, making use of the grid as the primary image-forming device in translating the photograph. The photographs he uses are generally of his friends, and the photographic genre tends to be either the snapshot or the identification format. The drawing *Robert* (Figure 7-10) is a restatement of monocular vision, which maintains all the distortions and in-out focus characteristics of close-up photography. The people portrayed are anonymous through the artist's emotional distance from his work, but one must remember that the photograph is the subject and not the individual depicted. Close's faithfulness to the photograph's inherent qualities is the startling aspect of his work, not to mention the scale. Often the work is more than five times life size, magnifying not only human proportions, but enlarging the generally accepted scale of a snapshot to the dimensions of a billboard. Suppression of surface texture, demonic attention to the finest detail in translation from photograph to painting back to photograph make this period of Close's work an unbelievable tour de force that leaves a lasting impression.

In some respects the artists of the New Realist group mimic the camera by their unblinking recording of photographs without comment or interpretation. For these artists the photograph is essential; without it, their work would not exist. Accurate rendering of form, light, color, and flattened space through the use of photographs speaks highly of a cold, steely skill. The important role that the photograph plays in their work may have been the result of a reaction to the

Figure 7-10 CHUCK CLOSE,
Robert/104,072 (Collection,
The Museum of Modern Art,
New York)

highly charged emotionalism of Abstract Expressionism and the intellectualism of Pop Art. But one must keep in mind the sort of photographs the new realists choose to work from. They tend to gravitate toward subject matter that would hardly stimulate the intellect or touch the emotions. Their selection of subject matter is not guided by any photographic ideology, individual, or group, but by their own emotional, psychological preferences. The photograph as photograph found acceptance by these artists because it appeared to dispense with the traditional concepts found in studio art, and therefore allowed them to disengage themselves from content as well as bypass the difficulties of reference to other works of art. One could lose oneself through process rather than invention and achieve anonymity. (Could this be interpreted as a statement of significance for our time?) The mechanical appearance of the photograph offered an undemanding subject to work from, something one could take from and not give to, no questions asked.

Yet for all the non-statements claimed by the artists who produced the New Realism, collectively the work seems to bespeak if not reflect an era of contemporary American society: the "me decade," in which noninvolvement and the breakdown of interpersonal relations inside and outside the family unit could easily have served as illustrations for New Realist paintings and drawings, with few exceptions.

Finally it seems that it is the triumph of the photograph over manual skill in New Realist painting and drawing that is in the last analysis the contribution that remains for us to contemplate.

As artists found that the camera obscura, the camera lucida, and the present camera could aid them in drawing, they also discovered that these mechanical instruments could assist them with painting. Some of the paintings produced during the period of the camera obscura and camera lucida differ greatly from the sort of painting produced today with the aid of the camera and photograph. Artists' intentions are different now, but the fascination with mechanically produced images continues.

Leonardo da Vinci, whose multitude of scientific investigations covered many disciplines, speaks of the camera obscura in his notebooks when discussing the problems of light and optics. In the section entitled *"Precepts of the Painter"* he refers to his projected book on painting in which he proposed to demonstrate how light transmits "the images of the bodies and colors of the things illuminated by the sun through a small round hole in a dark place on to a smooth surface which in itself is white. But everything will be upside down."[1] He says in the section on "Light and Shade":

> The boundaries of the images of any colour which penetrate through a narrow hole into a dark place will be always of a more powerful colour than its center. But if the surface of the said interposing object shall have within it some small hole that enters into a room dark not on account of its colour but through absence of light, you will see the rays entering through this small hole transmitting there, to the wall beyond, all the traits of their original both as to colour and form, except that everything will be inverted. The way in which the images of bodies intersect at the edges of the small holes by which they penetrate: What difference is there between the manner of penetration of the images which pass through narrow apertures and those which pass through wide ones or those which pass at the sides of shaded bodies.[2]

Leonardo knew that aperture adjustments would affect the projected image, producing a soft or sharp focus. Although there are no facts to support any claim that he used the camera obscura for his painting, it seems odd that an artist of such great intellect with a seemingly endless interest in science would not have done so. He consistently searched for new scientific information concerning pigments and vehicles and experimented with them ceaselessly. The logical step would have been for him to use the physics of the camera obscura. His paintings give no evidence of its employment, but it is possible to use the camera obscura and so adjust the painting as to conceal any traces.

Vermeer's *The Girl in the Red Hat,* c. 1660 (Figure 7-11) gives all the visual appearances of having been produced with the aid of a device like the camera lucida. Tiny points of light throughout the painting often gather into circles of confusion, especially on the girl's shoulder and on the lions' heads in the foreground. The scale of the painting, which is $9\frac{1}{16}'' \times 7\frac{1}{8}''$, seems to be correct for the sort of work that could be successfully accomplished with a device like the camera lucida. Furthermore, there is the question of the manner in which bright light diminishes details, as in this painting. Traditionally, painters tend to lighten the pattern or texture of any form suffused in light, while darkening the portions in shadow. This practice results in an interesting painting, but is not accu-

Figure 7-11 JAN VERMEER,
The Girl in the Red Hat c. 1660
(Andrew W. Mellon Collection,
National Gallery of Art,
Washington, D.C.)

rate in reality. Bright light striking a surface tends to obscure detail and disintegrate form. When the camera records this phenomenon, these brilliant areas are referred to as "hot spots." The clothing the girl wears in Vermeer's painting, especially on the sleeves, shows these "hot spots." Finally there is the in-and-out-of-focus aspect. The background area tends to be in focus; shapes, lines, and details are read with ease as they appear to be clearer than the forms in the middleground and foreground. In these areas forms are softened and slightly blurred. Even though one may clearly see the brushwork of the painter, the presence of a mechanical optical device is strongly felt in *The Girl in the Red Hat.*

The camera obscura and camera lucida were not mechanical devices on which painters depended during the early stage of photography, when an image could be permanently fixed; they were aids or sources that remained secondary to the act of drawing and painting. But it was in the 1840s and 1850s that photography had an immediate and what appears to be a lasting effect upon painting. Painters began the move toward photography and photographic reality with determination. There are many reasons for this move, but besides the obvious mechanical advantages there is a possible psychological reason. Could it be that photography as an emerging art form posed a threat to the established painters? Certainly portrait painters felt this more than the others. What better way to deal with a rival than to absorb the clear advantages he enjoys? Imitation

of photographic reality quickly spread and was accepted by the established sa-
lons of the day, while the photograph was excluded.

   The Pre-Raphaelites were a cohesive group of painters who were particularly affected by the photographic image. Their work translated photographic
reality into acceptable pictorial imagery. The physical world seen in detail
through the lens and recorded by means of brushes and pigment remains with
us often as an array of odd romantic impossibilities. John Everett Millais' composite *Ophelia*, 1851 (Figure 7-12) demonstrates the use of photographic reality;
a strange lack of idealization and generalization haunts the painting. The face of
Ophelia, as she floats in the stream on her back, appears to be the focal point,
which is an inherent quality of the camera. The composite painting of this period
imitated the composite photographs of the 1850s, when story illustration was
popular. Rejlander's composite photograph *Two Paths of Life* (Figure 7-13) is a
composite of thirty negatives. In both painting and photographs executed during this time there appears to be an unsettling stiffness of pose and exaggeration
of expression that verges on theatricality. Part of this peculiarity rests in the fact
that time exposures had to be made since the camera was not equipped for
speed. Those who had to pose for the camera, did in fact pose and wait. This
photographic disadvantage then became a mannerism of painting.

   It is well known that Gustave Courbet thoroughly embraced photography
in his painting. The tightly knit groups of figures that appear in his pictures,

Figure 7-12   JOHN EVERETT MILLAIS, *Ophelia* 1851 (Tate Gallery of Art, London)

Figure 7-13   REJLANDER, *Two Paths of Life* (International Museum of Photography at George Eastman House, Rochester, New York)

with no reasonable relationship to the space they inhabit, are the result of the inability of the camera lens at that time to effectively record a large area of space. Those who posed for the camera had to stand close to one another to accommodate the camera lens. The figures in his paintings look as if they are glued onto the canvas. This is particularly true of his early painting *The Stonebreakers,* 1849, and of the slightly later paintings *Village Maidens,* 1853, and *The Portrait of Max Buchon,* 1858, in which Courbet makes no attempt to deal with a believable space for the figure. The ground plane, middleground, and background fuse into one undefined space resembling some of the recent techniques of fashion photography in which a seamless backdrop of a single color is used. Some of these photographic effects may be observed in Manet's paintings as well.

By the late 1850s photographers were working with new approaches to composition and space, freely placing figures and objects within the frame. Fenton and Nadar worked with these ideas, moving toward compositions that gave the impression of moving out beyond the confines of the edges of the photograph. But it was Julia Margaret Cameron who established this compositional approach with the blur. It was about ten years later that these ideas appeared in the compositions of the Impressionist painters. Photographic advances were being made quickly; efforts toward stop-action, color, and stereoscopic photography were underway. Color experiments using large colored crystals on plates gave the impression of a rainbow of dots. It is quite possible that some of the Pointillists may have seen these efforts and that they played a role in the early stages of the Pointillist style of painting. The mid-1870s brought stereoscopic photography, which soon became a very popular entertainment; every family parlor had to have one. Seeing from two different points of view gave the sensation of the third dimension, and of being able to see around objects to other objects. Since the camera lens at this time was unable to correct perspective distortion, straight lines appeared as they naturally appear—curved. Surely the painter Cézanne must have seen the wonder of stereoscopic photography, and it is likely that what he saw affected his own work. His own drawing does not adhere to the principles of perspective, with straight lines converging upon a vanishing point, not because he had no awareness of them or could not execute them. His early work gives evidence that he understood these conventions. The thin washes of pigment he used partly to achieve space and form could be directly linked with the transparency of the glass slides and the illusion of the third dimension.

Stop-action in Marey's and Muybridge's studies of locomotion is one photographic device, among others, that appears in the work of the Futurists. The work of these two men provided the Futurists with visual facts concerning movement, which then became their hallmark. Blurring, overlap, transparency, and negative-positive shape relationships revealed in the photographs of Marey and Muybridge soon appeared in the Futurists' paintings. Some of the concerns of Futurist painting, such as transparency and negative-positive shapes, had also appeared in the work of the Cubists.

Photographing the unseen became an endless source for painters to draw on. Duchamp's *Nude Descending a Staircase* may be directly related to the locomotion studies of Marey and Muybridge, and with the invention of micro- and astrophotography the Dadaists and Surrealists were finding the forms and colors revealed to them an exciting stimulus for their own work. When Abstract Expressionism appeared in America it seemed that painters had finally moved away from the photograph, and that the subconscious had replaced that source. It was one of the most exhilarating and inventive periods of American art and has left a lasting impression on artists and public alike. But the apparent break with the photograph was only a surface illusion. Many of the abstract painters used the close-up photograph, which exposed a hidden world of shapes and color for them. Close-up photography of their own work inspired newer, daring compositions and space-form relationships that had gone unnoticed before.

The photograph reappeared in true form with the development of Pop Art. Many artists of this period used the photograph directly or indirectly in their paintings. Andy Warhol's acid paintings and silkscreen prints of personalities from the entertainment world were basically projected photographs, slightly manipulated with the addition of discordant color. Free interpretations of the photograph appeared in the paintings of Larry Rivers, and Robert Rauschenberg's fragmented compositions used photographs of works of art from the past as well as newspaper photographs. Roy Lichtenstein imitated the photographic reproduction technique of comic strips and later drew from photographs of works of painting, sculpture, and architecture. Optical and color field painting also found the photograph useful. The photographs of Dennis Stock, Arthur Siegel, and Minor White among others may very well have been sources for painters of these two movements to draw from.

Until the New Realists of the late 1970s eased into the limelight, painters had been slowly moving closer and closer to photographic reality; but suddenly it was more than imitation. Not only did the photograph offer, as always, new forms, colors, shapes, and textures; it had ideas to use, ideas that need not be restated, reinterpreted, expanded, or even paraphrased through paint and composition. Arthur Siegel's photograph from the series "In Search of Myself," 1951 (Figure 7-14), is an example of the photographic image containing the sort of material the New Realists use—reflections, storefronts, glass, chrome, all sorts of objects from giant tomatoes to used cars, with the human form playing a minor role. Comparing Don Eddy's acrylic painting *New Shoes for H.* (Figure 7-15), painted in 1973, with Siegel's photograph, it is as though the time span between them did not exist.

If the painters of the New Realist group sense a need to break away from the established classical traditions of studio painting by direct use of the photograph, we must note that the photograph has accomplished this for them already. Furthermore, it cannot be said that these paintings represent a new way of seeing, for the photograph has accomplished this also. And the composite paintings, like the composite photographs from the 1850s, are adding nothing that has not already been stated by the photographs. If we are asked to believe that the painter is making no comment about the subject and is simply affirming its existence, has this too not been stated already by the photograph? Copying another artist's idea does not make it yours, no matter what pains went into reproducing it. Making a painting for the sake of making a painting (whatever that means) may be the one real and honest reason to accept these paintings as paintings without question.

Figure 7-14　ARTHUR SIEGEL, *In Search of Myself* 1951 (Courtesy of Edwynn Houk Gallery, Chicago)

Figure 7-15 DON EDDY, *New Shoes for H.* 1973 (The Cleveland Museum of Art, Cleveland, Ohio. Purchased with a grant from the National Endowment for the Arts and matched by gifts from Members of the Cleveland Society for Contemporary Art)

It appears that as long as photography continues to exert an influence as fine art, painters will feel an underlying sense of competition with photographs and will continue to use them. Doubts once raised as to the status of photography as an inferior art or the servant of painting should be put to rest. Photography is an art form independent of painting and the other arts. It has its own inherent creative problems. The central issue with photographs, as it is with paintings, seems to be whether an artist's intentions are clearly formulated and projected through a creation which springs from the spirit. If we are able to read his intention and meaning, it does not matter whether they come from the conscious or the subconscious. What does count is that the meaning reaches us, that we find in it those qualities recognized as part of the self for better or worse, and that we can feel ourselves a little richer for having done so.

Printmaking

Since the Armory Show of 1913, printmakers have tended to align themselves with painters in approaching their work, but until recently they have not been as concerned with the photograph in their production as painters have. About the time of the Pop Art movement, printmakers began to make extensive explorations into new materials and processes, including the photographic image. Many of the graphic images were startling and extreme departures from the more traditional methods of print production.

There have been painters and printmakers who employed photographs in their prints before it became fashionable to do so. The painter, printmaker, and filmmaker Sir Hubert Herkomer used the camera obscura in his paintings during the 1870s and 1880s with great enthusiasm, and later used the camera for his lithographs. The photographic reality in many of Herkomer's prints calls to mind such portraits by Eakins as *Mrs. William Shaw Ward*, 1884, and *Mrs. Samuel Murray*, 1897 (Figure 7-16), where the identical photographic reality is felt. Eakins was an enthusiast of photography and made free use of it in his painting as well. However it was William Henry Fox Talbot who patented his method for making a photographic etching on a steel plate (October 29, 1852), which began the ever-growing relationship between photography and printmaking. It is from

Figure 7-16   THOMAS EAKINS, *Portrait of Mrs. Samuel Murray* c. 1897 (University of Nebraska Art Galleries, Lincoln, J. M. Hall Collection)

Fox Talbot that such processes as photoetching, photosilkscreen, photolithography, and photogravure sprang, giving birth to all of the subclasses of photoprinting that are with us today. It was photography more than any other force that changed printmaking, commercial reproduction and art, and brought about, beginning with Talbot, a Renaissance in graphics that has been gaining in momentum for over a century.

Until recently the major effect that the photograph had upon the printmaker was that the photograph offered unusual angles and points of view that were later expressed in prints through composition. The works of George Bellows, Mabel Dwight, Howard Cook, Rockwell Kent, Charles Demuth, and Charles Sheeler all reflect the camera's influence in new ways in dealing with the picture plane and composition. During the 1950s and 1960s, printmakers began to move toward larger dimensions, replacing the more restrictive format that had been the hallmark of printmaking. A profuse use of the photograph began about this time also, further liberating the print from its previous conservative past. It also became three-dimensional, taking on sculptural appearances. But it was Andy Warhol who made use of the photograph as never before in silkscreen processes. His multiple and single portraits of such popular figures as Marilyn Monroe, Elizabeth Taylor, Jacqueline Kennedy, and others (Figure 7-17) were

Figure 7-17   ANDY WARHOL, *Marilyn Monroe* 1962 (Tate Gallery of Art, London)

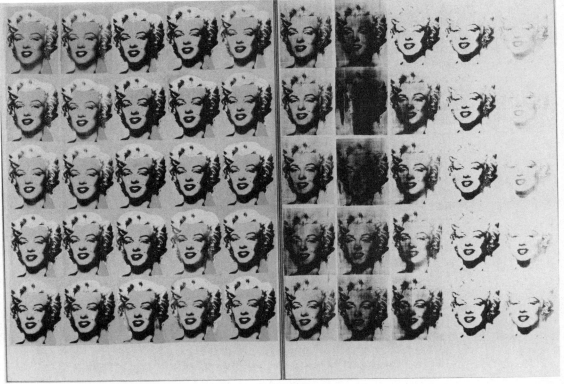

photographed and silkscreened into vertical-horizontal grids on canvas, paper, and other materials, monumentalized forever. At times Warhol made slight color and tonal changes within the grid pattern containing the photographed idols, but that did little to disguise his total surrender to the mechanical process. Personalities from the sports and political spheres also served as his subject matter, as well as ordinary objects like soup cans, soft drink bottles, and Brillo boxes. The repetition of triviality began to take on monumentality and soon it became compelling, demanding our attention. Warhol's process and method of production speak of his own attachment to the mechanical, reflecting a mechanical society immersed in materialism and shaped by the unrealistic world of entertainment through movies and television.

Political statements made by the Spanish Social Realist, Juan Genoves, through his prints made ample use of photographs depicting groups of people as though they were seen through a telescope. A circular format served as a support for what appears to be the confused, unorganized movement of masses of humanity caught in physical, emotional conflict. Social upheaval, political turmoil, physical violence, or impending disaster are themes which course through his prints and paintings.

It is in the prints of Robert Rauschenberg that the photographic image in printmaking takes on a nonmechanical look, in contrast to the work of Warhol. Rauschenberg often uses newspaper and magazine photographs as rubbed-off transfers to lend a more "handmade" look. At times the photograph may be washed over with a thin glaze of paint so that the image has coherence with the other freely painted areas. The fragmented surface made up of photographs, glazes of paint, dripping pigment, or pencil-charcoal smudgings gives a discordant, transitional image, filled nonetheless with painterly puns and personal comments. Although the parts of his image appear to be shifting and in constant movement, they effectively engage us as do other photographic images that fill our daily lives. The collagelike appearance of his prints is like the kaleidoscope of images that one might find in the subconscious if it were possible to make it visible.

Booster, a lithograph dated 1967 (Figure 7-18), is a 7' × 3' print made up of life-size, X-ray images of the artist combined with charts, photographic prints, and other images freely drawn with pencil, charcoal, and ink. The scale alone points to efforts printmakers are presently making to reach beyond conventional limitations. This print breaks with all traditional approaches to portraiture, beginning with the title, a double play on words and image. In this contemporary self-portrait, Rauschenberg reverses things for us; instead of an outward physical appearance that may speak of an inner world, he shows us the physical interior by X-ray. It is an inside-out portrait. The other photographic images, smudges, splatters, and drips of drawing materials tell us about the inner life of the artist that would have been indicated by facial expression in traditional portraiture. Mechanical photographic images which surround us, he seems to say, may be fashioned into new images regardless of their originally intended use. The overwhelming mass of photographic realities that reach us each day is summed up in the microcosm of this single print, which so eloquently speaks of engulfment by our own technological creations.

Today more prints using the photographic process are being executed in

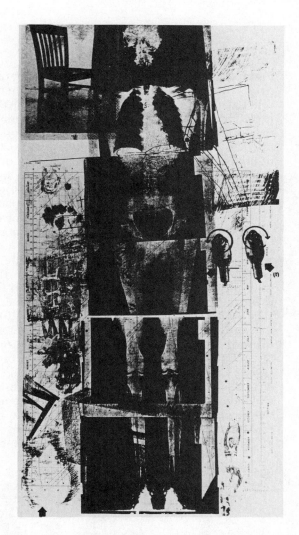

Figure 7-18 ROBERT
RAUSCHENBERG, *Booster* 1967
(© Gemini G.E.L., Los Angeles,
California, 1967)

more inventive ways by more artists than ever before. The photograph, once
held in suspicion by printmakers, has now been totally embraced and absorbed
into the printmaking process, not because it appears to be an easy road to image
making, but because the photograph offers an additional method to extend our
perceptions. It is not technical or mechanical processes that need concern us in
any art form, but the mainspring, which is personal perception. Printmakers
who have understood this axiom have demonstrably elevated the discipline
above the level of technical appreciation. Innovation, which may be considered
the father of originality, has craftsmanship as a companion, but let us not confuse the two. Innovation in aesthetics, perception, and expression cannot be
eliminated from any art form without reducing it to craft. The adoption of new
technical advances does not in itself guarantee success, but it does open the door
for those artists who have a strong belief in individual perception to stronger
realizations of their ideas.

Naomi Savage is just one artist among many who are working with photographic images in printmaking, and using other technical advances to produce prints of unusual character. Her photoetched plates are often mounted as bas-relief sculpture in which her depictions of the human form become idealized through the process from photograph to finished plate. The photographic portrait of *Philip Roth* becomes a near abstraction in her print (Figure 7-19). An out-of-focus print was reprinted and then photoetched, producing a sculptural plate of high relief as mysterious as a mask from an ancient Greek play. When printed as an intaglio or an embossment, the image becomes softened, almost dreamlike, with greater reference to the original photograph. The shadowed areas of the photograph have been dropped out in the plate; in the intaglio they become part of the negative space in which the head appears to emerge and yet is fixed. Like much Oriental art it is a beautiful understatement in which the observer's imagination fills in what is gently suggested.

As photochemical advances were made, such as the use of ferroprussiate, artists began to sensitize materials other than paper for printmaking, and soon photoetching on cloth, styrofoam, and plastics of various sorts allowed the print to become soft and three-dimensional. Catherine Jansen's *Soft Bathroom, with Satin Sink and Taffeta Toilet* (Figure 7-20), with photosensitized fabric sewn and stuffed in life-size proportions, becomes an amusing sculpture, photograph, drawing, and print held together in an environmental construction. Unlike Claes Oldenburg's mammoth soft sculpture of ordinary objects exhibited as single pieces, Larson's step into three-dimensional experimentation does not give us a larger scale work of art as a monument. Instead she keeps it all within human scale and the softness takes on a different meaning from that of Oldenburg's sculpture. The routine and symbols of the bath are scattered throughout the environmental piece. This common human activity is the subject of her work, and all the objects become as fluid as the subject.

Figure 7-19 NAOMI SAVAGE, *Philip Roth* (photoetching) (Courtesy of the artist)

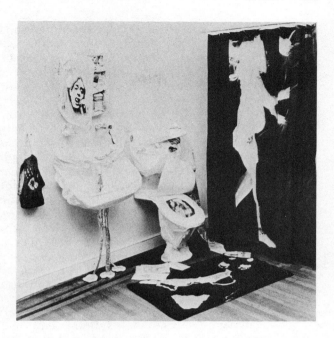

Figure 7-20   CATHERINE JANSEN,
*Soft Bathroom, with Satin Sink
and Taffeta Toilet* (Courtesy of
the artist)

As the traditional demarcations between art forms become less defined and the new materials flood into the artist's studio, the old classifications of art forms and media appear to have less and less importance to artist and collector alike. All the arts have begun this transformation, and the most exciting original works today are those that have accepted and utilized new materials and technical advances as well as assuming a nonconforming attitude toward traditional tools, materials, and equipment. As the new parameters are loosely defined by contemporary artists, nontraditional processes increasingly aid in greater self-expression by facilitating the production of new images. The print and the photograph have swiftly moved into the new dimensions with mutual benefit without keeping one foot in the past.

Cinema

Any attempt to trace the early history of the cinema to a single source is an impossible task. Just before the turn of the century, many photographic discoveries were made quickly and simultaneously, not only in America but in France, Germany, and England. The ideas, inventions, and technical problems often overlapped, sometimes resulting in claims and counterclaims as to who got there first. Some of these inventors had but one goal, the moving picture. Still photography was a new and astonishing form of image making during the 1850s and was the foundation for the moving picture. The cinema is a form of photography. Some of the primitive moving pictures were just that, still photographs set into motion to create the illusion of movement, such as the two-disc Phenakisto-scope constructed by the Belgian scientist J.A.F. Plateau (c. 1824) (Figure 7-21). Even though the cinema has become the most popular form of entertainment in the world today, the still photograph has not been eclipsed by the cinema as an art form if we do not measure one against the other in terms of economic success.

The studies of animal and human locomotion by Eadweard Muybridge and E. J. Marey around 1880 were not originally intended to be studies for moving pictures, but they do without question prefigure the cinema, especially the Zoo-praxiscope of Muybridge, and the Chronophotography of Marey. These studies and inventions stimulated the public's interest in movement during the period when the Industrial Revolution and the internal combustion engine changed ideas about movement. Until the appearance of the engine, movement and power were solely associated with the forces to be found in the environment. Now human beings had created their own sources of power and movement, much to the excitement of the world. These sources were instrumental in pro-moting the growth of the cinema within an extremely short period of time, less than a century. Photographers, scientists, and inventors such as Cook and Bon-nelli, Goodwin, Daguerre, Eastman, Edison, Jassen, the Lumière brothers, Niépce, Plateau and Talbot, to name but a few, made the conception of the cinema a reality that we now enjoy. Some of these men worked toward the goal of moving pictures, while others unknowingly contributed to it.

Cinema is an extension of still photography with many similarities, and yet with distinct differences. Two important aspects of their relationship have not changed from the beginning, and give no evidence of changing. They are

Figure 7-21 J. A. F. PLATEAU, *Two Disc Phenakistoscope* (International Museum of Photography at George Eastman House, Rochester, New York)

(1) that both tend to record the physical reality of existence (whether this trait is part of tradition or an inherent quality of the medium remains to be decided), and (2) that the recording of existence is perceived through the inescapable framing device of the camera. From time to time photographers and filmmakers have tried to avoid the physical and psychological presence of the frame by stylistic change, but for the most part these efforts have been unsuccessful. During the early periods of filmmaking, and in still photography as well, subject matter was approached as though it were on a stage, or as if one were looking through a window, which only emphasized the frame. Overall compositional readings were also attempted, but the frame remained as a sign that only bits and pieces of physical reality could be selected and presented through film. So in the final analysis it is the viewer who must fill in what has been presented only in part. If the viewer must supply what the photographer and the camera cannot completely, does the viewer have a greater sense of actuality if the image contains more, or less, of physical reality? Japanese filmmakers appear to have an instinctive way of approaching this question in their work through austerity in composition and editing. This tradition in current Japanese art stems in large part from their cultural history. Hiroshi Hamaya's *Children in Snow Country On Their Way to a January Festival* 1965 (Figure 7-22) exemplifies technical proficiency that has reached new heights, as well as delicate balance between precise content and visual clarity.

If we assume that the inherent quality of photography is accuracy of recording, specifically of physical reality, do we then judge the product by this

Figure 7-22   HIROSHI HAMAYA, *Children in the Snow Country On Their Way to a January Festival*
(Magnum Photos Inc.)

standard? While it is true that the camera will record what light allows it to without interpretation or comment (an individual photographed in eighteenth-century clothing is just that and nothing more), all we have is a record of the reality, not the reality itself. Bringing this resemblance to the viewer via film or paper only allows him to identify it through projected association or recall. Do we then judge the product by its resemblance to the "real" thing?

Other techniques of still photography found in the cinema are the close-up, double exposure, soft focus, two-dimensionality (except for certain three-dimensional effects), and film as a receptor for images. The instantaneous photograph and candid photographic approaches are in all probability the clearest evidence we have of the legacy from still to moving photography.

The two strong points which separate cinema from still photography are that (1) film can give the illusion of movement, while still photography may only depict movement in a fixed image; and (2) film can give the sensation of time-space adjustments within a given amount of actual viewing time, which has its own set limits of a beginning and end. Another advantage of cinema is the ability to record events in which motion and sound are intrinsic parts of the performance, such as dance, the opera, or stage plays. Although certain photographers have attempted to build a story or plot by the addition of script to their work, it does not achieve what film does with plot and story line. Film relies on artificial light for projection and other mechanical devices, and whatever the film has to offer an audience is dead until the moment of projection. The still photograph does not depend on any assistance in order to reach the viewer other than its own objectness. Content may be contained in a single frame, and digested as the viewer paces himself. Film content covers many frames and paces the viewer, and content most often cannot be grasped until a certain time period is covered.

Documentary photography implies that accurate recording of physical reality is inherent in the medium by the apparent lack of visualness and reliance upon message. Does this then make it the purest form of the medium by producing resemblances to the "real" thing, therefore bypassing aesthetics and photography as art?

Other forms of photography, when manipulated by adding paint to the photograph, double exposure, overexposure, underexposure, tinting, toning, and other technical special effects, are instantly associated with the other traditional arts such as painting and drawing. As soon as this identification is established, and especially when the image is nonrepresentational, judgment, evaluation, and aesthetic standards that are applied to the other arts are then applicable to the photograph. And what of the film or photograph that records physical reality and does not use any of the effects mentioned, and yet is judged a work of art? Are we to use a separate aesthetic for each, and term one non-art, the other art, and the last quasi-art? The photographer's intention is the first priority. Whatever the medium's inherent quality, in any of the visual arts, is not a prime consideration; to make it so reduces art to a common denominator of trivial dimensions.

A central psycho-physical correspondence between still and moving photography is that their images or story line may function as symbols for other intended meanings. Edward Weston's *Cloud, Mexico,* 1926 (Figure 7-23) may be said to be the equivalent of his *Nude,* 1925 (Figure 7-24), in that the sensual

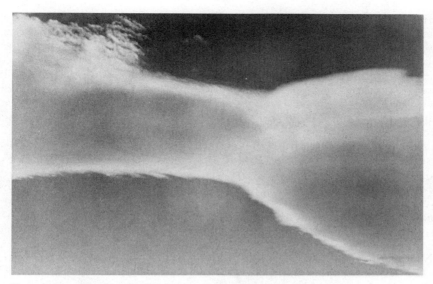

Figure 7-23   EDWARD WESTON, *Cloud, Mexico* 1926 (© 1981, Center for Creative Photography, University of Arizona. Used by permission.)

Figure 7-24   EDWARD WESTON, *Nude* 1925 (© 1981, Center for Creative Photography, University of Arizona. Used by permission.)

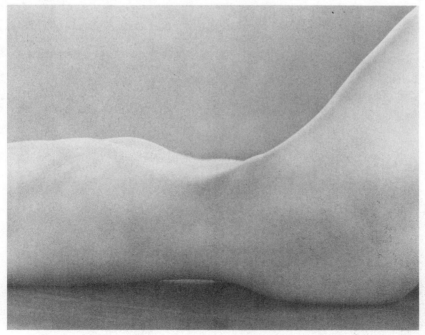

curves of the nude are found in the cloud. The softness of the cloud speaks of the softness of female skin and flesh. And a correlation between floating and sexuality may be drawn with little effort. Or, as we see in Akira Kurosawa's still from the film *Rashomon*, Machiko Kyo's face registers repulsion to the advances made by Toshiro Mifune (Figure 7-25), but the expression only masks her desire. Often these metaphors may be found in everyday human experience, such as the frightened person who laughs hysterically when faced with an unexpected situation of potential danger, and the person who weeps with joy rather than sadness. The switching of colors may also function in the same manner; black is customarily considered to represent evil, and white innocence, but these may also be turned around to touch off an endless variety of mood changes, emotions, and meanings.

The still photograph exerts its presence in film today in a number of ways. As promotion material for films and the advancement of film personalities it has been highly valuable, assisting in the financial success of films and in bringing obscure individuals into prominence. Photographing film personalities has been brought to the level of art by certain photographers, and today some of these photographs are shown in museums and galleries. They are highly prized, as collectors vie for them and their value increases. John Kobal's work has achieved a high aesthetic level in this sort of portraiture, and Richard Avedon's photographs, while not primarily concerned with the promotion of film personalities, have nonetheless extracted the greatest intensity from this kind of photography.

Special effects in film have relied on the still photograph for economic as well as aesthetic reasons, and as an archival source it has been of special use in

Figure 7-25   Still from *Rashomon*, Machiko Kyo and Toshiro Mifune (Courtesy of National Film Archive/Stills Library, London)

costume and set departments for period pieces. Such historic films as Victor Fleming's *Gone with the Wind,* John Ford's *The Grapes of Wrath,* and Ingmar Bergman's *Wild Strawberries* relied on the documentary, portrait, and landscape photograph in presenting degrees of authenticity to costumes, sets, and attitudes for their films.

Film has yet to achieve what still photography has, a universal that every individual can respond to. Edward Steichen's exhibition called "The Family of Man" evoked a worldwide response not because there was a special photographic quality about the exhibition, or because anyone could recognize his own likeness. Steichen achieved this unrivaled success by revealing the spirit of humankind that links us with one another. Steichen's work crossed all seemingly impossible barriers and found none when the spirit was reached. From among two million prints sent by photographers from every corner of the globe, his own understanding spirit and searching eye selected the prints which radiated the beauty he sought. For five years the exhibition toured the world as an affirmation of what is best in humanity.

Still photography bears a closer relationship to the other traditional arts such as painting or drawing than it does to film. Audiences who attend films generally expect to be entertained, to be caught up in a story that will transport them from their daily existence. Yet that same audience, if attending an exhibition of photographs, will not proceed with the same frame of mind. Perhaps the exhibition is a diversion, but essentially it is understood that in addition to looking, a certain amount of intellectual participation is required. For many this is not considered being entertained, and not a sure means of escape. However, both forms can extend vision disconnected from content. The physical circumstances for viewing each form are different and therefore help to build a psychological state of being before engaging with the images. In the darkened theater the film comes to life on the screen, and the individual can feel isolated from everyone else in the audience and from the outside world. This sort of psychological transport and engagement is impossible for the photographic exhibition where an awareness of the physical surroundings is constantly intruding on the observer. The photograph, like a painting, is an object that may be looked at, held in the hands, and admired for its physical characteristics, but the film has no physical identity for the observer. It cannot be hung on the wall to be admired for content or physical distinctions. The images are projected by light, are fleeting and transitory, and may be seen again only by attending another performance or by recall. For most moviegoers, image and content are experienced again by recall. These images cannot be collected and used as symbols or signs of one's being. Perhaps this is an advantage that film has over still photography. It effortlessly accomplishes what the artists of the conceptual movement attempted to do, elimination of the object in favor of the idea or concept. Films may be collected but not in the same sense that one collects paintings, drawings, or sculpture. With the uncollectability of films it seems that there is an advantage not extended beyond some of the early films. The early films of Lumiere, *Le Dejeuner du Chat* and *The Card Game,* demonstrated this advantage by little concern for the inherent qualities of the medium, and engagement of the audience with content. The freedom from commercialization during this period allowed for a freshness of expression that is rarely if ever experienced today.

Film has, however, continued to move toward the concept that was so dramatically expressed through the exhibition "The Family of Man." It has also begun to bring one of the strong points to the public with increasing awareness, the capacity to materialize that which may be imagined and the unseen.

The future of film, like that of still photography, rests with beginners, and with the future photographers who have the strength to resist the dogmatic approaches and suppression of ideas and experimentation, and to circumvent the self-appointed prophets of doom who, from time to time, build short-lived reputations on prophecies announcing the death of whatever discipline they choose to undermine. The overcommercialization of film not only weakens its artists, but in the long run destroys the medium. Film can continue to shape our consciousness and extend our vision by bringing forth issues of political, social, and aesthetic significance when unrestricted by established conventions, and is in direct communication with a public ready to receive the energy from this powerful medium.

Two films from the silent era which should be mentioned for their particular contributions to cinematic history, albeit for totally opposite reasons, are Carl Mayer's *The Cabinet of Doctor Caligari* (1920), and Carl Dreyer's *The Passion of Joan of Arc* (1928). Mayer's film, often considered an example of German Expressionism of the 1920s, is an art movie within the category of fantasy cinema. Siegfried Kracauer, the historian of German film, suggests in his book *Theory of Film* that the German films of this period, in particular *Caligari*, whether intentionally or not, encouraged the rise of Nazism, although this idea is open to debate among other cinema historians and critics. *Caligari* concerns an insane psychiatrist who exhibits one of his patients, an uncontrollable somnambulist, at a fair, and directs him to murder a number of people.

Many of the sets for this film were constructed and mechanized in an Expressionist style popular a few years before the film was produced; however, Expressionism was dying out by the time *Caligari* reached the general public in Germany and America. Intended for export, this movie was well received in America, but had little success in Germany. The sets were nonetheless quite effective for dramatic purposes, and have remained one of the strong visual points of the film. In a sense, the film could be considered something of a designer's movie, since several designers and painters were employed and the sets, without a doubt, leave a lasting impression on the spectator by their highly imaginative approach to fantasy. An outstanding aspect of the movie is that the audience is placed in the role of detective and remains at a loss to resolve anything from the great variety of confusing clues.

The open question about this movie, even today, is whether it is to be thought of as the hallucination in the mind of one of the characters, with the moving and shifting sets and camera work supporting this view, or whether any insane person has seen the world in the way in which it is depicted, as angular, shifting, and transparent.

Caligari is Mayer's attempt to produce an art film, to bring art to the general public, but is also more than this. Perhaps *Caligari* should be considered the counterpart of the wave of German neo-realist films of the 1970s and 1980s, which are expressions of underground German anti-Nazi movements before and during World War II. Two examples are Werner Fassbinder's early films, *Katzelmacher* and *Recruits in Engellstadt. Katzelmacher* (1969) is an intricate but deliberate Socialist attack on the German petty bourgeoisie. Actors playing various social types were placed in front of a stark white background, and emoted directly to the camera in a stylized manner. To a lesser degree *Recruits in Ingellstadt* (1971) is the continuation of this theme, but is not as stylized as *Katzelmacher*, nor is it as pointedly anti-Nazi. Mayer's movie may have been cited as degenerate art because of its criticism of the National Socialists rather than as the work of a degenerate artist.

Carl Dreyer's *The Passion of Joan of Arc* (1928) is a skillfully composed movie in which the semi-abstract compositions focus on a variety of faces intended to bring out human spirituality as well as the lack of it. Dreyer's compositions are almost entirely close-ups, and the first twenty-five minutes of the film show only faces, before any indication is given of the courtroom in which the action is taking place. This film represents Dreyer's belief that mankind can be best understood through the human face, and in *Joan* he plays the bewildered, tormented spirituality seen in the face of the actress against the rough features and probing eyes of the other actors, her accusers.

The camera work keeps up a narrative momentum throughout the film in such a way as constantly to shift and change the atmosphere that seems almost unforgiving, and this in turn affects the actors so that they reflect this attitude also. Dreyer's interest in faces as windows to human motivation and action is powerfully exemplified throughout the entire movie. He projects Joan as physically worn out, and even psychologically broken, by the long interrogation and torture, but in an ultimate sense triumphant in her peasant simplicity over her worldly and corrupt ecclesiastical judges. In many respects the more recent work of Richard Avedon parallels that of Dreyer's thoughts about the human face. Avedon's portraits free his subjects from extraneous distractions of the environment. Their faces are shown at a moment when those inner qualities that define the person are frozen forever in the blank white space determined by Avedon, and as he says, "Amen, that's how it is."

The Passion of Joan of Arc, which was directed in France, is considered by many historians and critics of film to be a masterpiece, and Dreyer's best work. For their time, and for the unusual techniques explored and established and used by other filmmakers since, both *Joan* and *Caligari* have made contributions to film and to art that are still being discovered. While both of these movies are masterpieces in their use of unusual techniques and processes, it is their expression of the human experience which stands out above all else. The main source of energy which emerges as the vital force is the depiction as well as the unseen consciousness of the human condition manifested in the spirit of the films, which characterizes all of us one way or another.

Within the category of narrative film two efforts stand out as turning points in the history of filmmaking: *Citizen Kane,* and the more loosely although not strictly narrative associated film *Un Chien Andalou.* Orson Welles' film *Citizen Kane* (1941) brought many new and valuable cinematic devices and atmospheres, which permitted greater freedom in the interpretation of images and no longer manipulated the spectator to a point of a single interpretation, as did most earlier narrative movies.

Such devices as multiple images (for selective image reading), deep-focus photography, and thought-narration (rather than strict dialogue), were among the many inventions which broke with cinematic conventions and put an end to one kind of filmmaking while beginning another and opened the doorway to the more personal, freely interpretative styles. While *Citizen Kane* is filled with an abundance of stylistic devices, some of which were to be used later by the neo-realists, it remains a landmark in stylistic development rather than just a film which did much to promote naturalism.

Un Chien Andalou (1929) by Luis Buñuel and Salvador Dali, a Surrealistic film, plays content off image and image off content as no movie had done before and concerns itself with impulses from the deeper layers of the psyche. The work was intended to shock the spectator but also to lead him into those deeper psychological aspects of the unconscious forgotten during day-to-day activities. Like many other Surrealistic films, this work is based on the concept that personal inner reality is far more important than the physical material world. For Dali and the other filmmakers of this genre, the materials of the physical world provided a passageway into the chambers of locked dreams, visions, reveries, and fantasies. These were the only things that mattered to them; physical reality was a series of signs and symbols which functioned as equivalents, transcending concepts of a one-dimensional man to the multidimensional man. It was at this level that the Surrealists thought that the convincing truth of inner realities of the psyche could be revealed through the living matter of the physical world.

The ideologies and technological advances the Surrealists had promoted through film helped in the evolution of the cinema, but *Un Chien Andalou* certainly established the medium as fine art, that is in the sense of painting and drawing. It also liberated film from the story or conventional narrative. But beyond this aspect it may be said that rather than alienating itself from nature, or "nature in the raw" as Siegfried Kracauer calls it in his *Theory of Film*, it actually draws us into it, if we consider humanity to be part of nature. Those aspects of the inner reality expressed in this and other Surrealistic films are deeply rooted in nature. It may be by choice that we depict the physical environment or hidden aspects of the psyche, but it is fact that they form a cohesive single unit. The human psyche and nature are interdependent, and join to form human character. The complexity and diversity of the human psyche was an aspect of the unseen part of humanity that had not yet been sufficiently explored through photography and surrealistic images. Dali's efforts in this largely unexplored area produced movies which not only proved that the cinema could be art, but that it could also bring to a wider audience some universal human questions. Ernst Bloch's main work *Das Prinzip Hoffnung* tries to answer such questions as Who are we? Where do we come from? Where are we going to? What are we expecting? What is awaiting us?

Beyond narrative cinema one may find a wealth of ideas and expressions through the visual explorations of film by the new wave of independent filmmakers and art films. Through the creative work of these people, the cinema may in fact be forming a new identity. Despite the difficulty in the availability of screening for their work, a new generation of moviemakers have continued on their own initiative to produce an astonishing number of works outside the narrow confines of commercial entertainment, and these works are reshaping the previously restricted concepts of cinema.

Cinema and live performance, film as image without references to time, space, inner or outer realities, and various animated images assisted by computer are just a few examples of the current creative activity which is pushing cinema beyond the common and commercial concepts of traditional and standardized avant-garde moviemaking. Conventional terms such as abstraction, narrative, surrealist, experimental, and documentary are not applicable to the new energies forging the shape of cinema for the future. The silent revolution taking place now with the intensive work of young filmmakers in universities and colleges as well as the independents, promises a decisively changed cinema.

For most spectators the cinema has always been aligned with the theater, or the novel brought to life by movement, but especially when sound and image were coordinated. These superficial associations may be simply dismissed when one considers basic cinema techniques such as "close-ups", "mid-long shots", "mid-close-ups", the manifold fragments of time and space variations, or the ability of film to change objects through changing proportions, juxtapositions, and dissolves. The transformation of the exterior physical world on the screen into signs and symbols (as in the study of semiotics) has always been an integral part of film. Semiotics, an inherent part of all art including the cinema, cannot be simply dismissed if we consider each work of art as an equivalent, sign, or symbol for something else.

On the other hand some believe that the cinema is merely a series of still photographs set into motion, and technically it is. Andy Warhol's two films *Sleep* and *Empire State Building* represent another important step in the history of cinema. The moving picture in this case becomes a still photograph. These two films do not treat movement; they are for the most part still images representing the movie as something other than entertainment. *Sleep* runs for eight hours and has no beginning, middle, or end, nor any of the generally accepted structures of traditional narrative cinema. These two productions do not align themselves with any other film, nor do they imitate any other art form. Furthermore, they are not attempts to record the physical exterior reality. They are essentially single images, open to free interpretation by the spectator, but they also take on other meanings entirely their own.

Virtue, real or imagined, arises from necessity, and the ability of Warhol to profit from the weaknesses of commercial cinema speaks emphatically of his unusual creative abilities and originality. His success as a filmmaker, in addition, points to the fact that cinema is not an autonomous art, and that the movies can, when intended to do so, transform any material, idea, wish, or fantasy.

These movies were made during the Viet Nam War, a troubling period in American history, which triggered some of the largest demonstrations the United States had ever experienced and saw the beginning of the disintegration of the American Dream and the growth of a drug culture in which more and more youth were "turning on and tuning out." The political and social crises were to have immediate and long-lasting repercussions in every direction. A mood of helplessness, disillusionment, anger, and pain touched the lives of many and changed them forever.

Sleep and *Empire State Building* powerfully project the artist's alienation, as witnessed by the intensity and strangeness of the films but also by their dehumanized lack of constructive dynamics. *Sleep* depicts a person involved in an essential activity, while *Empire State Building* presents a fixed gaze providing escape into blank nothingness. The artistic and personal alienation represented by these movies may be the outward sign of the breakdown in the creative psychology of the artist, a form of schizothymic estrangement (defined as temperamental introversion or, in creativity, a breaking up of artistic conventions, and the reformation resulting in an unusual style, image, or form). This is the opposite of schizothymic transcendence, in which the artist may achieve an extension of humanization in his work, as the late work of Rembrandt illustrates. Such work can become universal as well as deeply personal.

The intensity and strangeness of the Warhol productions, achieved through blandness and a noncommittal image, may be seen as representing the fragmentation of the creative process. These films may be appreciated for these particular aspects alone since they ultimately possess no hint of greatness, nor even very high quality. Although they were considered to be underground movies, many were drawn to them as spectators, feeling similar pressures to those the artist experienced, sharing with him the sense of dislocation and extreme uncertainty produced by the pressures of a time of great anguish and anxiety.

The emotional colorations of artistic and personal alienation in Warhol's work are not uncommon in art and may be observed in other periods of the history of art in which political or social tensions and crises exerted their forces upon the artist. Further, it is not that the films deal with the breakdown of the creative process or alienation that makes them noteworthy, but that the method, or the reformation of cinematic approaches was entirely new and has not been repeated since in exactly the same way. These are isolated works of art, removed from the mainstream of filmmaking and filmmakers. Their isolation is due in part to the fact that they deny one intrinsic characteristic of film, which is movement, and revert to still photography. And in other respects they are closer to drawing and painting. In the final analysis, these films are in certain ways parodies of older films, while at the same time asking to be accepted as radically new.

While it is true that Warhol's films never did really have an enormous effect upon the work of other filmmakers, they cannot be dismissed as oddities produced during a period when it was fashionable for many to protest in unusual ways, parodying more serious and sincere efforts. The contribution of these films to the history of filmmaking has not yet been fully realized. Their importance as mannerist works of art related to a period in our social history remains to be recognized and understood.

Many of the new filmmakers who face the pressures of the twentieth century, the ultimate of which is the threat of total extinction by nuclear warfare, are producing an astonishing number of radical and unusual works in cinema which are windows through which we may observe the same breakdown of the psychological and creative processes seen in other works in other times. The mirrors these artists hold up to their faces reflect their own psychological condition and also our own deep uncertainties. It does not matter what age works of art come from or whether they are characterized as golden, warlike, or regressive. Whatever they yield, be it hope, yearning, unfulfillment, or alienation, we the observers are the beneficiaries, perhaps recognizing our own dilemma crystallized in a visual form.

Within the same milieu, other artists are able to transcend creatively even the ultimate threats, tensions, and pressures, and transform taste and style while at the same time bringing about new human metaphors in which universality is expressed through works of great daring and conviction. Independent filmmaking and art films are breaking new ground continually through films that explore our physiological and psychological makeup but also attempt to explore realities beyond our apparent disposal. For many of these filmmakers physical reality is not the exclusive domain of film, and still photography is no longer the place where film takes over to accomplish what still photography cannot. These barriers and classifications do not exist in the newer realms of filmmaking. For many filmmakers the interconnectedness of still and moving photography is a reality through which their expressions are not merely ideologies trying to mask the physical realities of the exterior world in any way, but may be seen as more complex extensions of that reality superseding conventional concepts. The psychological and metaphysical points of view expressed in art film and independent films are in fact often redirecting our own thoughts and visions back to physical reality so that new perceptions of that reality become a process of rediscovery. This process of rediscovery may bring to light those aspects of reality either forgotten or not observed.

One of the more important points being made by this group of filmmakers is that film is an art form like any other in respect to the realities of the physical world and of the psyche, and can be dealt with in the same manner in spite of media differences. There is no ideology reserved for the cinematic medium that separates it from other arts such as painting, even though the creative materials for image making are different from one another.

Charles Dekeukeleire, critic and historian of the cinema, commented, "If the senses exert an influence on our spiritual life, the cinema becomes a powerful ferment of spirituality by augmenting the number and quality of our sense perceptions."[3] Seen in a broader perspective than mere relation to physical reality and the cinema, this analysis accurately supports cinematic efforts which do not strictly record physical reality, but activate the sense perceptions directly through means other than representation. Indeed, spiritual life is not based on material things of this physical world, but on qualities which may or may not be derived from or through material things. The flame of spirituality may be seen in people throughout the world by the camera's eye when directed by an individual who can show us that our similarities are far greater than our apparent differences. Our spirituality (whatever form it takes) is the single strongest aspect that unites as well as separates us, and may be depicted in endless ways through images, whether they be mechanical or not. If cinema, indeed if all art can serve humanity in this way, by boring holes through the physical realities of the exterior world to reveal those deeper aspects of ourselves, then what importance do individual ideologies of media really have?

It is impossible to discuss cinema without including the work of video artists, and video as a recent development in cinema as a form of expression.

This medium, which is rather new compared to still and moving photography, joins the family of software as a dynamic and highly versatile medium, which has not yet made full acquaintance with the general public.

The successful and innovative use of video in narrative film is exemplified in two rather recent films, *Lightning Over Water* (1979) by Nicholas Ray and Wim Wenders, and *One From the Heart* (1982) by Francis Ford Coppola. *Lightning Over Water* is an autobiographical film, which tells the story of an older director who is facing death and a younger director who comes to terms with mortality. Video is used within this film as part of the story line, in a documentary way, and is intelligently played off the film in a highly original style. Each is used in such a way as to bring out those qualities of the medium that are at once visually challenging, while at the same time demonstrating their differences and compatibility within an unusual work of art. The theme of *Lightning,* the search for identity, self-realization, and the human spirit's immortal quality, is beautifully followed through from beginning to end by the interplay of video and film.

Cuts from film to video stress the objective and the subjective tensions which underscore the film, and are vehicles for the shifting levels of reality. Throughout the film the juxtapositions of video and film images create unusual spatial relationships, but these are also quite clearly struggles to overcome the imposed rectangularity of the camera frame, which may be observed often in the work of still photographers. This film stands as a most powerful work exemplifying the transcendence of two artists, through their work, over the stress and uncertainties (death for Ray, and self-realization for Wenders) of life. *Lightning* is the visual, tangible evidence of the human spirit in art transcending those difficulties, bringing Ray's and Wender's work to the level of universality.

Coppola's use of video in connection with his film, *One From The Heart,* which is a musical staged against a background of Las Vegas reproduced in sound stages, was that of a painter using a sketchbook in jotting down ideas to be incorporated later in a major painting. Video utilized as a sketchbook proved for Coppola to be an economical method to previsualize scenes which were to be finalized later on film. Although video was used on two distinctly different levels by these directors, they nonetheless proved that video has a place in the narrative form of entertainment in cinema.

Video artists who are now beginning to emerge as a powerful new movement in art have demonstrated that the non-narrative video can be an interface between painting, sculpture, drawing, and still photography through performance and installation. Lynn Hershman and Darryl Sapien are just two examples of highly gifted video artists among the growing numbers of this new breed. These artists are unquestionably forging an art form which will change conventional ideas about cinema, cinema as art, and the other art forms as well.

One of Lynn Hershmann's installations in the windows of Bonwit Teller in New York City in the late 1970s made use of still photographs, manikins, and other objects, videotaped with participation by observers on the sidewalk outside the windows, and is described by her as "time sandwiches." This highly colorful installation, which combines other art forms with video, is strongly individualistic as video art and depicts time past and time present between the layers of two realities. The reality of the existence of the physical exterior of now and the reality of video film are the layers which she uses to enclose her subject. The installations are at times surrealistic and extremely bizarre in their juxtapositions of the staged and the natural flow of existence as they interact with one another. Whatever values and ideals are expressed by Hershmann in her video work, they must be recognized as fundamental innovations in art, affirming eternal recurrence. And she shows us that recurrence without subtraction, without exception, of life even in its strangest and most bizarre manifestations. It is this inexhaustibility of life which her video work reveals. It invites us to realize ourselves through her art, to become part of that which we are, to venture into the undiscovered part of ourselves. The Bonwit Teller project does not ask for any justifications of life; it presents life as ambiguous, mendacious, and terrible, just as Hershman experiences it through event and fantasy. In the final analysis, this work which, one would expect to be repulsive, is not. One is drawn into the images, slowly but surely, and they must be coped with just as one must cope with the everyday occurrences in life. Hershmann's free spirit wings through the video project, reveling in the joy of life.

Darryl Sapien's work tends to move toward performance; his recent video work depicting a version of ballet is clean, crisp, and pure. But the ballet Sapien depicts is not classical dance, nor is it what might be termed modern or contemporary. One example of his ballet, performed in San Francisco and videotaped, consisted of a group of men in white costumes resembling space uniforms, suspended from ropes, attached to the outside of a building high above the street, and was performed during the night hours. The result of Sapien's choreographed dance was elegant ballet performed by dancers who could not see one another, but were in communication with one another through a predetermined set of vocal signals. The purity and abstractness of Sapien's work stands out in sharp contrast to Hershmann's work, and yet like Hershmann's work, it demonstrates a vitality and originality missing from much of today's art.

Video, the newest and freshest expression in art today, is being produced by artists brought up in the medium, but by also artists trained in the traditional disciplines of painting, sculpture, and still photography, who have turned to video as a medium which offers greater speed and flexibility for their particular needs. It is clearly evident that the video artists are supplying what traditional narrative film has lost through commercialization and mechanical advancements—the artistry of artistic expression.

> It may seem surprising that mankind should produce in large number works based on a principle that represents such a radical artistic impoverishment if compared with the available purer forms. But is such a contradiction really surprising at a time at which in other respects, too, so many people live a life of unreality and fail to attain the true nature of man and its fitting manifestations? If the opposite happened in the movies, would not such a pleasant inconsistency be even more surprising?[4]

Architecture

Occasionally one may observe the direct effect of photography upon architecture, but for the most part the interaction has been minor. As a teaching aid, the photograph in the classroom has brought the entire world of architecture into the immediate experience of architecture students. It has with little doubt promoted what is generally recognized as the International Style and allowed students to draw upon the past for inspiration within their own work. As tools, the camera and the photograph have been invaluable in the production of site plans, architectural models, sights, elevations, texture studies, and the recording of outdoor natural phenomena for design and structure placement.

The New Bauhaus, 1937, later the American School of Design, established in Chicago in 1939, included still and moving photography as part of a constant reorganization of the architectural program. The photography workshop, along with others in the fine arts, formed part of the Bauhaus concept of the *Gesamtkunstwerk,* or the "total work of art." Many architects, but in particular Gropius and Le Corbusier, both associated with the Bauhaus, approach interior space in their work as the camera sees it. The sense of framing, a mechanical characteristic of the camera, and the flattened space of the photograph may be observed in the view of the vestibule and staircase in *Sommerfeld House, Berlin-Dahlem* (Figure 7-26). Sommerfeld House was a collaborative production between Gropius and Adolf Meyer with Carl Fieger, who made the drawing for the design under the direction of Gropius and Meyer (Figure 7-27). The interior is heavily textured, in particular the walls with a herringbone effect carried out in teak. Joost Schmidt carved the staircase decorations, which further add to the overall textural aspect. This was the kind of collaboration that was central to the Bauhaus policy that each individual share in the product by contributing his own particular talents. The transitions from flat drawings to the actual third dimension of the construction, then back to the flattened space of the photograph, no doubt did have an effect upon the way interior space was conceived. During the 1920s photography, Cubism, and architecture were interacting at a level that was never again achieved between the arts. Space and form were approached from nearly the same attitude.

Le Corbusier, who made and collected many photographs, was an astonishing photographer in his own right. His photographic compositions, whether achieved through the viewfinder or through cropping, have a strong sense of orientation, firm negative-positive relationships, and are thoroughly architectural in approach. His photographs of ships, automobiles, mechanical parts, airplanes, and carefully selected objects all have the sublime sense of proportion and placement that appears in his architecture. Even though some of the machines are clearly dated, a strong sense of timelessness persists in the photographs. *Air Express* (Figure 7-28) achieves a certain monumentality and grandeur through convincing camera angle and the picture plane divisions that one rarely finds even among the most accomplished photographers. Moreover, there are structural elements and form relationships in his architecture that may be traced directly to some of the subjects found in his photographs. This relationship appears to be more than mere accident.

The central entrance to the Palace of Assembly at Chandigarh (Figure 7-29), the new capital of the Punjab in India, repeats structural elements found in the airplane in *Air Express.* The double wing and double row of wing struts with eight in front and eight in back between the wings are reborn in the main entrance of the Palace of Assembly. Although the spacing of the verticals at the entrance is even compared to the struts on the airplane, the same sense of

Figure 7-26 *Sommerfeld House* Vestibule and staircase 1921. Gropius and Meyer (Bauhaus, Archives, Berlin)

Figure 7-27 Drawing for *Sommerfeld House* Vestibule and staircase (Bauhaus, Archives, Berlin)

Figure 7-28   LE CORBUSIER, *Air Express*

Figure 7-29   LE CORBUSIER, *Palace of Assembly, Chandigarh, India* (Artemis, Architectural Publishers, Zurich)

tension and support exists. At the entrance they become broad and flat, huge slabs of concrete with double openings that pierce their massiveness. The lower openings refer to the windows of the airplane, square-shaped with slightly rounded corners, and the upper openings are very close to the shapes of the wheel struts. The roof they support is the redesigned airplane wing, still suggesting lift and flight. And the odd jog in the wing tips reappears as the double base which appears to float upon the water of the reflecting pool rather than rising from it. Whether Le Corbusier actually used his photographs when working out the architectural designs cannot be said with any certainty, but it is clear that they were sources he drew upon consciously or unconsciously.

Close-up photography allowed artists to observe new forms and form relationships never before seen from which they could draw ideas for their own work. Such photographs as the one depicting a cross-section of a termite nest (Figure 7-30) bear a striking resemblance to Frederick Kiesler's *Endless House* (Figure 7-31). The interior connecting egg-shaped cell chambers of the African termite architecture create a space that is without wall, ceiling, or floor. This sort of flowing space, eliminating corners, moldings, and other angular architectural details, appears in the *Endless House,* where the unbroken surface is the major characteristic. Through photographs of animal and insect architecture and other organic structures and substructures, architects such as John Johansen, Paolo Soleri, Richard Hamilton, and Marvin Goody, to name just a few, appear to use natural design elements to enhance their own original designs, often appearing in Expressionist architecture.

Finally, the photograph has in all probability served architecture best of all in its role as an archival tool upon which restoration and reconstruction have depended. While paintings, drawings, and engravings have also served architecture in this capacity when photographs were unavailable, it is still the photograph that offers the most accurate record for the conservationist. Photographic accuracy was certainly instrumental in the reconstruction of historical sections of such cities as Warsaw, Vienna, Munich, and Pisa, and architectural monuments throughout Europe after the Second World War. Today we can enjoy the rebirth of the historical splendor of such places as Williamsburg, Mount Vernon, Old Deerfield, as well as a great number of other significant houses and cities whose restoration was made partly possible by photography. As we become increasingly conscious of our American architectual heritage and the importance of conservation, the photograph as a document in maintaining that heritage has become an invaluable source.

Lewis Mumford emphasizes photography's inherent ability to depict the "complicated, interrelated aspects of our modern environment." He goes on to say that "without any conscious notion of its destination, the motion picture presents us with a world of interpenetrating, counterinfluencing organisms: and it enables us to think about that world with a greater degree of concreteness."[5] Mumford's statements may be read not only as a testament to photography's quality to record physical reality as an abstraction, but its use as an aid to the architect to bring out those qualities of materials perhaps unnoticed. For the architect, the photograph provides an extremely important source of information, even stimulation, within the creative process of design considerations. Photographs by such artists as Aaron Siskind, Minor White, Edward Weston, or even Paul Caponigro could bring light to important visual design aspects such as

Figure 7-30 DR. KARL DAUMER, *Termite Nest* (Courtesy of the photographer)

Figure 7-31 FREDERICK KIESLER, *Endless House* (Courtesy of Mrs. Frederick Kiesler)

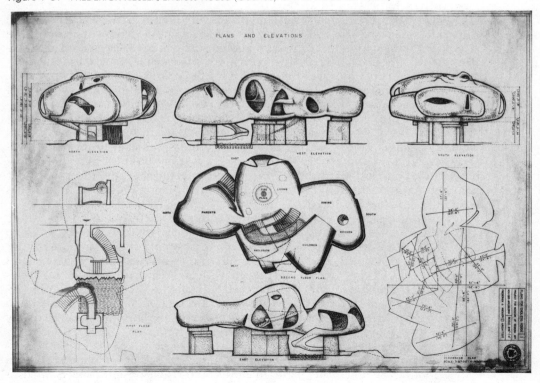

texture, material consistency, weight, and qualities of light reflectance or absorption in various materials to be used in a structure. It is often said that the most significant information and inspiration for any discipline come from outside it.

The proliferation of architectural photographs, some intended for use in the architectural profession and some not, has not only served the profession in a number of ways, but has also given rise to a growing number of exhibitions that have kept the general public in touch with the changing architectural styles and concepts throughout the world. For the architectural critic and historian these exhibitions have been a great aid as a convenient, quick, and easy way to practice architectural criticism without great expense of time and money. Throughout the history of art there have been those exhibitions which have been important, not only as examples of turning points for art, but also as landmarks of historical interest related to economic, political, or social issues. The Armory Show of 1913 in New York, The Cézanne Retrospective of 1936 at the Orangerie in Paris, The Surrealist Exhibition of 1935 and the Picasso Exhibition of 1981 at the Museum of Modern Art in New York are just a few examples of exhibitions which have in their way been highly influential.

There have been photographic exhibitions that have been instrumental in changing certain aspects of our social, political, economic, or aesthetic structures, often with results which had not been anticipated or expected. One such exhibition of architectural photographs was the 1932 exhibition titled "International Exhibition of Modern Architecture." This exhibition was sponsored by the Museum of Modern Art and organized by Philip Johnson. It consisted of a few photographs and models, accompanied by a book by Henry-Russell Hitchcock and Philip Johnson, entitled *The International Style.* During the time the exhibition remained at the museum in New York, 33,000 people saw it before it was sent on its way for a tour throughout the United States, where many more thousands of spectators evaluated the new architecture through photographs.

It was not until over forty years later that the results of this exhibition were to be known, or at least beginning to be understood. Without a doubt the exhibition has become an important element in the kaleidoscopic history of modern architecture. Some of the American architects represented in the exhibition were Russel G. and Walter M. Cory (the Starrett Lehigh Building in New York), Raymond Hood (the McGraw-Hill Building, New York), and Richard Neutra (Lovell House, Los Angeles). The Museum of Modern Art determined what the international style was according to an aesthetic established by the museum. Architectural photographs depicting structures that reflected the museum's definition of that aesthetic were part of the exhibition, and those that did not were excluded. The results of these decisions and the exhibition tour were not exactly what the museum had desired or imagined. However, the exhibition and accompanying book introduced the International Style to America.

> What this famous exhibition and the long-lived book that accompanied it did was to grant a certain legitimacy to a style that was coming, by virtue of forces far more powerful than those controlled by Mr. Hitchcock, Mr. Johnson or anyone else at the Museum of Modern Art, to play a larger role in shaping the cityscape. . . .

> Modernism continued to spread through this country for at least four decades after the exhibition, but not quite in the way the museum's proselytizers had hoped it would. Its acceptance was fueled less by esthetics than by the economics of the

postwar years, as glass curtain walls finally became cheaper than masonry, and as the decline in craftsmanship made it seem financially prudent to join the parade against ornament. By 1950 modern architecture had become the American corporate style, its clean, sparse lines ideally suited to the cool and anonymous world of American business in the postwar years . . . And as the style grew, however, it became harder and harder to tell what was the International Style and what wasn't . . . And thus there is, at this moment in architectural history, no clear sense of style at all . . . It is perhaps no accident that 50 years after the International Style's great exhibition the work of those architects with whom the International Style's practitioners felt in deepest competition, the eclectic architects of the 1920's, is riding a crest of popularity . . . The International Style was a kind of missionary architecture, and it is that, more than anything else, that sets it apart from the sensitivities of our age today.[6]

To say that any lessons had been learned from this exhibition or that it had set any sort of guidelines for future conduct would be shortsighted and nirvanic. These aspects of the art world have not changed and show few signs of doing so. The residue from this exhibition which persists as a reminder can be simply stated: the power of the photograph, without any human intervention, to plant an idea, to persuade, to change opinions and concepts often with unexpected results, has not changed from the early years of photographic history to the present. "The Family of Man" exhibition, also sponsored by the Museum of Modern Art, seen in the same light of power and communication, has remained in the memories of many who saw it or viewed it through reproductions as an example of the photographic exhibition in which some of the highest human ideals are demonstrated.

While the relationship of photography to architecture has not been of such strength that the effect is readily identifiable, it has in more subtle ways proved to be a continuing mutual relationship beneficial to the architectural profession, to critics, to historians, and to the public. If photography has assisted the architect in the rediscovery of Classical, Mannerist, Expressionist, or any other period of architecture, and aided in the reevaluation of current aesthetics, then it has served the architect very well indeed. And if the photography of architecture can reveal to the public the human spirit expressed through the art of architecture, then it will have assisted the observer's rediscovery of transcendence, or the redirecting of our perception of reality. The noble art of architecture is in many ways the reflection of the higher ideals in all of humanity expressed through the fundamental ordering of concepts, aesthetics, and materials, directed and asserted in the physical structure. The propensity for order in all of humanity is expressed through buildings, ranging from humble provincial structures to sleek skyscrapers. These expressions have been part of existence from prerecorded history to the present, and if photography can redirect our attention to this closely related materialistic diad in the twentieth century, we will have made an important step in a rediscovery of the self.

Basic human gestures expressed through tangible forms such as architecture are common to man and some animals, and when seen in the photograph serve as a reminder that the pressure of the age in which one lives, no matter how wretched, may be transcended through the recognized human instinctual gestures which unite us. The recognition of such gestures in images can be reconciliatory and comforting, and may even nullify the negative aspects of the period, even though the art may reflect and at times be said to contribute to them.

The great renewal of photography experienced in the late 1970s and early 1980s has brought in the wake of its astonishing success a heightened awareness of our values, priorities, and sensitivities to the other arts as well as a reassessment of the established aesthetics particular to each art. Furthermore, it has revealed that the interconnectedness of all forms of expression, especially art and, in this case, architecture, has a greater significance when seen in the light of human gesture and is a constitutive part of human consciousness.

The deep longing for renewal, regeneration, and new definitions, from the conscious and subconscious, is part of our makeup as humans. This longing is expressed in various forms in all cultures, but it is in art that it most often assumes intense, visible, tangible form, absorbed into culture as functional structures (architecture) or enhancements to life (photography) in which we may see ourselves reflected. The relationship of photography to architecture, no matter how strong or weak that tie may be, offers through the image questions and answers to some fundamental concepts of the totality of physical realities, but more important, it functions as a reminder of the human spirit and its relationship to physical reality, the creative process, and expression.

Sculpture

Although the effect of photography upon sculpture is less evident than its effect upon painting, nevertheless the power of the mechanical image is capable of reaching all the arts and leaving its mark. Sculpture more recently has moved toward the photograph with unusual results.

Auguste Rodin took a rather dim view of painters who used the photograph in their work, particularly in the problem of depicting motion. He was convinced that motion as depicted by painters was superior to photographs that stop time and show us motion as we do not see it. Photographic reality to him was not reality according to our vision. He strongly defended Géricault's painting of horses, for he believed his version gives us the reality we experience even if ultimately false.

Marey's and Muybridge's photographs of motion did, however, convince some sculptors that the photograph was a valuable source. Degas's own interest in photography gave rise to his use of the locomotion studies for his sculpture of horses and ballet dancers. Some of his horse sculptures have a direct pose relationship to some of the locomotion studies of horses by Muybridge.

Boccioni's sculpture of a walking man, entitled *Unique Forms of Continuity in Space,* 1913, was an attempt to bring together through sculpture the Futurist movement, and very closely resembles Marey's Chronophotograph of a figure during a "standing jump." But the sculpture's opacity prevents it from entirely solving the problems of transparency and interpenetration of planes. It was some twenty years later that Naum Gabo did solve them with his constructions of clear plastic. Simultaneity, interpenetration of planes, and transparency projected into the third dimension were the realization of the Futurists' concepts through Gabo's sculpture. *Linear Construction,* 1942–43 (Figure 7-32), by Gabo depicts the kind of line or overlap producing a sense of motion visible in Marey's photographic motion studies made during the 1890s. Some of these motion studies look like photographs of abstract sculpture made up of strands of thread suspended in space and supported by sheets of clear plexiglas.

The line drawings and paintings of Paul Klee, like the wire sculptures of Alexander Calder, specifically his witty linear sculpture *The Hostess,* 1928 (Figure 7-33), could very well be the result of having seen such photographs as Marey's stereoscopic trajectory of a slow walk, dated 1885. These photographs, with white lines twisting and curving, floating on rich black fields, were produced by a walking figure dressed in black with white lines painted on the clothing and photographed against a black background (Figure 7-34). In *The Hostess,* the same looping, curving line is used by Calder to create his walking figure, leaning slightly forward and holding a pair of glasses lightly between the fingers of one hand while the other hand is held out into space, limp at the wrist. This line drawing in space picks up Marey's methodical abstract study of motion and line, turning it into a mirthful animated caricature of looping, twisting lines of wire.

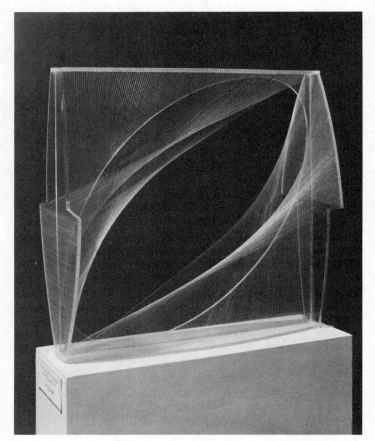

Figure 7-32   NAUM GABO, *Linear Construction, Variation* 1942–43. **Plastic sculpture** (The Phillips Collection, Washington, D.C.)

Figure 7-33   ALEXANDER CALDER,
The Hostess 1928 (Collection, The
Museum of Modern Art, New York.
Gift of Edward M. M. Warburg)

Figure 7-34   MAREY, *Stereoscopic Trajectory of a Slow Walk* 1885 (Musée Marey, Beaune, France)

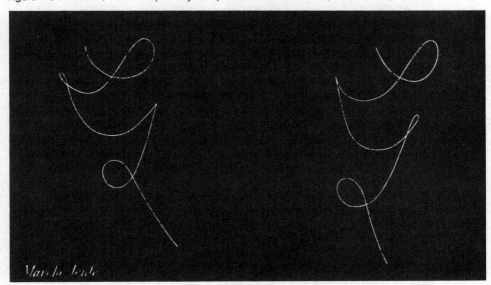

Microphotography, with its ability to record unseen forms and structures, had in all probability an effect on the work of Richard Lippold. His gold-filled wire sculpture, *Variation Within a Sphere, No. 10; The Sun,* 1953–56 (Figure 7-35), creating delicate symmetrical relationships from a central point into space, has a close resemblance to snow crystals in the microscopic world recorded by photography as early as 1910. Lippold states that "the fragile snowflake appears in more variations of form than any kind of permanent sculpture."[7] But the continual variation of the basic radiating structure of Lippold's sculpture just may be the equivalent of the fragile snowflake variations which he so admires.

Pop Art sculpture such as Marisol's painted wooden life-size sculpture uses the photograph in an unusual way. Her *Women and Dog,* 1964 (Figure 7-36), a five-piece sculpture, is a self-portrait in wood and paint, with a photographic portrait of the artist glued to the wooden head of one of the figures. Movement is indicated not only by the position of the legs but by the triple forms of the face on two of the figures, possibly observed in time-lapse photography depicting motion. This effect may be observed in the work of the Futurist painter Balla, whose painting *Dynamism of a Dog on a Leash,* 1911, shows the overlapping forms of the dog's legs and tail to give the impression of quick movement to the point of near coalescence. The face of the child on the right side of the composition appears to be drawn from a photograph covering the entire frontal portion of

Figure 7-35 RICHARD LIPPOLD, *Variation Within a Sphere, No. 10; The Sun.* Gold-filled wire. 1953–56 (The Metropolitan Museum of Art, Fletcher Fund, 1956)

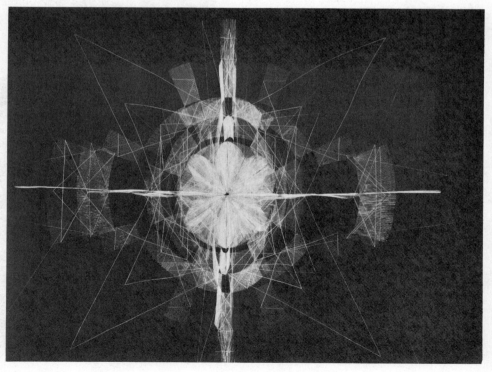

Figure 7-36   MARISOL, *Women and Dog* 1964 (Collection of the Whitney Museum of American Art, New York. Gift of the Friends of the Whitney Museum)

the wooden form, while the actual photograph occupies only the central section of the form on the other figure. The mélange of photograph, drawing from a photograph, painting, sculpture in wood, and the actual objects—handbag, ribbon, chain, and dog's head—creates a sculptural piece of surprising juxtapositions. Marisol brings all the elements together successfully while at the same time centering our attention on the reality that each represents for us as individuals and in art. It is a self-portrait that goes beyond physical resemblance, deriving at once from Cubist tradition and snapshot photography.

George Segal's sculpture combining plaster cast and found objects often fools the eye at first glance into believing it sees photographs. *Girl in Doorway,* 1965 (Figure 7-37), constructed from an actual doorway and a cast of a young woman, painted with aluminum paint so as to set her apart from the rest of the sculpture, emphasizes the human element and brings our visual attention to her by the use of the paint. Her head, slightly tilted with a rather wistful expression on her face as she leans against the doorjamb, is geared to bring us closer to the physical-psychological reality of the contemporary setting. The authenticity of the object, and the direct cast from a model, hardly altered by the sculptor, approximate photographic reality. Segal says that, "in freezing the gestures that are most telling is his biggest job."[8] This statement parallels what is often heard from portrait photographers. While *Girl in Doorway* could be any girl, it is also a specific girl, a portrait that successfully brings together the outward physical resemblances and inward emotional states not often found in sculpture.

Alfred Stieglitz's *Georgia Englehard,* 1921 (Figure 7-38) is a candid photograph that is in some ways close to Segal's sculpture. Both men are genre artists

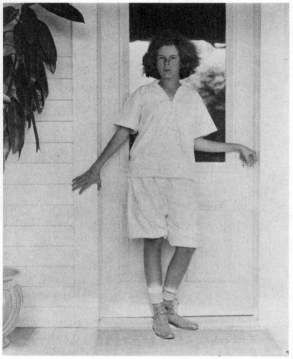

Figure 7-37 GEORGE SEGAL, *Girl in Doorway* 1965 (Collection of the Whitney Museum of American Art, New York)

Figure 7-38 ALFRED STIEGLITZ, *Georgia Englehard* 1921 (Collection, The Museum of Modern Art, New York. Gift of Georgia O'Keeffe)

with interests that seemed to have been guided toward social commitment. In both works there is the same physical, psychological presence of the subject, but Stieglitz's work is coolly taut, self-contained within the warmth of a summer's day. His subject's pose, setting her off against the architecture, is stated with great eloquence, while the girl stands, revealing details from a time past. Segal's portrait figure appears to be relaxed even though she stands erect in her leaning position with the door open behind her. This composition suggests contemporary change, flexibility, and an inner world of dimness, absorbing light rather than reflecting it. Stieglitz's clean, crisp composition speaks of an external world of light and air. Both works offer unusual insights into the artist, and some of the resolutions they found that were central to the issues that occupied them.

Among the New Realist sculptors there are two that stand out by their total control over materials and uncanny representation of the human form in sculpture. Photographs of their work can easily lead one into believing that the photographs are of living beings. Duane Hanson and John de Andrea have taken photographic reality and projected it into three dimensions. Although both sculptors work with the same materials and processes, fiberglass casts painted with lifelike colors, real hair, clothing, glass eyes, and other elements to create a startling effect of reality, they are quite different from each other. Hanson's work springs from the photojournalistic and documentary tradition that spans photographic history from the shattering Civil War photographs of Mathew Brady, to the photographs of Jacob Riis and Lewis W. Hine depicting the cruelty of child labor, the tortured images of Buchenwald by Margaret Bourke-White, Eugene Smith's photographs of demoralized Welsh miners, ending with current television and newspaper photojournalism. Hanson's selection of his subject matter, like that of the photographers mentioned, is a statement in itself, unlike the realist painters who are concerned with process and nonstatements. The human condition from its most depressing aspects to the most ridiculous is his well-expressed subject. Tourists dressed in outlandish get-ups with cameras slung over both shoulders, standing museum guards at rest, businessmen with particles of the day's lunch still adhering to their shirts and ties, overweight shoppers with plastic curlers in their hair—nothing escapes his searching eyes and probing mind. The accuracy of his perception to the smallest detail is often astonishing.

Bowery Derelicts, 1967 (Figure 7-39) is an example of Hanson's environmental sculpture that brings the physical-psychological reality of a given situation before the observer without sentimentality or overstatement. It has that ring of truth about it that one feels when viewing the nightly news or seeing a photograph on the front page of the newspaper. The same sensation of an unblinking, recording camera lens free of interpretation is present in *Bowery Derelicts.* So exacting is it that one finds it difficult to believe that it is not a photograph of three pathetic derelicts amid the trash, filth, and decay common to our everyday urban experience. Yet that ring of truth is softened when we learn that the photograph is of sculpture rather than the real thing. We tend to believe in the mechanical intervention of the camera and the photograph rather than an artist's careful reassembling of the same scene, no matter how painstaking and accurate he may be in reconstructing it. Once the viewer realizes this is a sculpture, it is difficult for him to accept it as truth. What accounts for the barrier? Is it a mistrust of the artist's ability to record, reconstruct, and paint without the intervention of his own personality? There is more to any image than mere physical truth; intellectual and emotional truth may carry a finality that supersedes the physical. Hanson brings his sculpture as close to physical reality as any sculptor ever has, a physical truth that is difficult if not impossible to deny. But the real genius of his sculpture rests not with his method and process in creating the physical reality which no doubt is truth, but in his extraordinary insight into humanity, without moral judgment. The sculpture is his insight brought into the third dimension, a mirror which he holds up for us to gaze into and see ourselves and those around us as they are perceived in the mind's eye. This mirror, like the camera lens, neither interprets nor lies.

Figure 7-39 DUANE HANSON, *Bowery Derelicts* 1967 (Courtesy of O. K. Harris Works of Art, New York)

Unlike Hanson, John de Andrea does not use environmental settings to complete his figurative sculptures; they are freely placed in existing spaces complementing the surrounding environment. Nevertheless they evoke the same jolting sensation of coming face to face with another live being. This sculptor is concerned with the positive side of physical existence, not social issues. The joy of physicality is conveyed through his subjects, who are mostly young and unclothed. Like the photographs of Lucien Clergue, depicting the female nude triumphant in her physicality, de Andrea's sculpture brings the same sense of pleasure through his male and female figures.

Déjeuner sur l'herbe (Figure 7-40) is de Andrea's take-off on Edouard Manet's well-known painting of the same title. Even though de Andrea has isolated the reclining figures from Manet's forest setting, and sets the three figures adrift in an interior environment, he has nonetheless accomplished what Manet himself intended, a modernization of a composition from a sixteenth-century design by Raphael. Further, Manet was striving for flatness in his painting and brought this about in part by illuminating the figures from the direction of the observer, thus eliminating mass. His attempt to shock his audience through depicting a nude woman with clothed men was in effect a way to say that it is not what is represented that is important, but the way in which it is painted. De Andrea parodies this statement by painting his sculpture various tones of dark and light grey, thus flattening the masses and aligning the work with the flatness of photographs as well as the zones in black and white photography.

The enigma of the pose in both the Manet and the de Andrea has in effect reduced the figures to inanimate objects, but especially in de Andrea's sculpture

Figure 7-40   JOHN DE ANDREA, *Déjeuner sur l'herbe* (Courtesy of O.K. Harris Works of Art, New York)

Figure 7-41   ÉDOUARD MANET,
Luncheon on the Grass
(*Déjeuner sur l'herbe*)
(Musée d'Orsay, Galerie du Jeu
de Paume, Paris)

since it is painted an anonymous grey. Although this monochrome is a departure for de Andrea, whose work is usually painted in lifelike color, it is in keeping with what he has to say about Manet's intentions for *Déjeuner sur l'herbe* (1863) (Figure 7-41), as well as his way of updating Manet's modernization of a Renaissance composition. The link between de Andrea's *Déjeuner sur l'herbe* and black and white photography is an example of the interconnectedness of all the arts today, deftly put and with a touch of wit.

Unlike many of the New Realist painters, de Andrea does not remove what could be considered distracting blemishes. No attempt is made to eliminate discolorations from the skin, moles, pimples, scars, or unwanted hair; all is left in place to enhance the lifelike quality he strives for.

Neither Hanson nor de Andrea uses the photograph directly in his work; it is the photographic image which leaves an impression later carried to the sculpture. These photographic impressions may be "picked up" from any visual source using photographs and transmitted to the subconscious.

The New Realist sculpture, in particular that of Hanson and de Andrea, attempts to reach beyond the photograph into a reality of its own, never satisfied with the merely decorative or academic, but establishing a new sculptural form that moves closer to all of us with information about ourselves that supersedes all other periods in the history of sculpture. Like the "Family of Man" exhibition, which carried a central theme recognized and embraced by people from nations all over the globe, New Realist sculpture may also succeed in reaching all levels of humanity with untempered, direct truths about ourselves. When faced directly, these truths may help shape our society and our future. If the work of these two sculptors succeeds in acting as the catalyst for this purpose, then they have succeeded in their sculptural intentions.

The Stage

What appears to be the most lasting technical effect of photography upon the stage is artificial lighting from the photographic studios. Cross-, down-, back-, and catch-lighting techniques transformed the flattened forms and performers through footlights into convincing projections of form. Slide projections of interiors and exteriors slowly replaced painted sets in many performances, adding to more believable environments on the stage. Special effects such as clouds, water, fire, and other neutral environmental effects appeared as the real thing through slide projections, and effectively cut the economics of set production.

In addition to being an archival source for set and costume design, the still photograph has more recently become the set. In the first production of *Boys in the Band* in New York, blowups of black-and-white photographs depicting the interior of an apartment were used. The apartment depicted in this play was furnished with contemporary furniture largely constructed of chrome, glass, and leather, and effectively worked as a visual psychological backdrop for the dialogue. A clean, crisp sharpness to the dialogue appeared to be echoed in the photographic set. For the musical *Annie,* the stage was transformed into a New York City street of the 1920s by blowups of photographs depicting buildings. Rather than use time-consuming and expensive makeup for the actor who plays the title role, in the play *The Elephant Man,* slides of the real-life Elephant Man were projected onto a screen on stage while the audience transferred the grotesque deformities of the deformed man to the actor. Such procedures are clearly economical in time and expense, but more important, they are far more effective in generating a sense of reality in the imaginations of the audience.

More recently, the Joffrey Ballet has filmed some of its productions outdoors. When projected during the stage performance the effect was an astonishing indoor-outdoor ballet of great visual excitement, of two separate realities held together by the dance.

The promotion of entertainment personalities and production is so much a part of still photography and the world of advertising that one tends to forget that the photographers are often artists in their own right. This kind of photographic advertising goes back to nineteenth-century American theater. In the 1870s, three photographers of unusual insight, Napoleon Sarony, William Kurtz, and José Maria Mora, who left a considerable photographic legacy to the theater and to the history of photography, had elegant, fashionable, and profitable galleries in New York, legendary in their own time. They specialized in photographic portraits of theater personalities which, in turn, attracted to their studios first-nighters and the beautiful and glamorous members of the social set. Portraits of entertainment idols and photographic *cartes-de-visite* established them as artists in their own right as well as making them wealthy along the way. It was Napoleon Sarony, however, whose famous studio was filled to bursting with an unbelievable collection of props he used to construct sets tailored to the characteristics of his list of star clients during portrait sessions, who remains as a unique photographer and personality. While he never did achieve the artistic success that he longed for during his lifetime, he did unknowingly form a complete visual document of American theater during the period of its early development. As a chronicler of late nineteenth-century stage in America and a portrait photographer of the great theatrical performers of his time, Sarony left behind an invaluable source for today's theater.

His photograph of *Sarah Bernhardt,* 1880 (Figure 7-42), shown in costume for her part in the play *Frou-Frou,* demonstrates his ability to bring out the personality of his subject and the part she projects in the play, supported by his props within a set. With the endless variety of props from his studio, he stages the photograph, filling it with textures, patterns, and light, without obscuring the profile of the actress. His subject is carefully placed so that her profile is centered in the upper quarter of the composition before an area free of competing material, so that above all the finely chiseled features of the actress leave an unforgettable impression. It is a subtle relationship of figure to environment that appears easy, but it took a photographer like Sarony who understood the individual personalities of show people and had the creative genius with light and props to bring it all together in a memorable portrait. For all its obvious staginess, there is a certain air of quiet that brings to mind the paintings of Vermeer, and like those paintings, the photograph has withstood time nobly.

On a theoretical level it is quite possible that dance was influenced by photography during the first three decades of the twentieth century when both photography and dance had similar concerns of light, space, movement, and rhythm. Alvin Langdon Coburn's photograph *Vortograph Number 1* 1917 (see Chapter Three, Figure 3-14) is an example of the sort of change that photography and dance were undergoing. A clear break with the past was being made, and the era of modernism was being ushered in. Coburn's photograph is an example of the work that was being produced by a group of artists known as the Vorticists. Such concerns as light and spatial organization were shared by the

Figure 7-42 NAPOLEON SARONY, *Sarah Bernhardt* 1880 (Reproduced from the collections of the Library of Congress)

other arts of this period, but on a new and experimental level. Loie Fuller was the American modern dance pioneer who created new dances with veils of fabric and light, possibly inspired by the work of the Vorticists. Isadora Duncan also experimented with new abstract dances, but the link with photography is in concept rather than an attempt to recreate the images and illusions of photography and painting.

Although Barbara Morgan has not shown any clear evidence of being interested in photographing personalities from the dance in America, her photographs of this segment of the entertainment world may just be accomplishing what Sarony's did from a historical standpoint. Without a doubt her interpretations of the dance have in one way or another aided dancers and choreographers alike, as well as being fine works of art. Although there are many photographers who are working in this vein, it is Barbara Morgan who seems to have the special ability to interpret and bring together personality and dance. She has maintained a strong individuality within self-defined artistic parameters, and yet has established a visual statement about the contemporary stage to be enjoyed by us as well as generations to come.

For thirty years Carl Van Vechten, the amateur photographer and dance critic for the New York Times and the first to review dance in America, produced and amassed thousands upon thousands of photographs of theatrical personalities which now serve as a near-complete document of the American theater from the early 1930s to 1962. His work is housed in the Dance Collection of the New York Public Library, The Performing Arts Research Center at Lincoln Center, and the Aldo R. Cupo and Karen Marinuzzi Library at Yale University, but it is the Philadelphia Museum of Art which has the largest collection. It was in the 1930s that Van Vechten's interest turned to photography and away from dance criticism. He photographed both the leading and the unknown dancers, writers, artists, and singers of his time. But it was the dance most of all which became his passion, both classical and contemporary. Although he often documented a complete dance performance, it is his portraits for which he is best known, and which reveal his interest in theatrical personalities.

Merce Cunningham, the dancer and choreographer who founded his own company in 1953, has been until recently outside the mainstream of classical and modern dance because of his unconventional ideas about art. His association and collaboration with artists from other disciplines, such as Robert Rauschenberg, Jasper Johns, Mark Lancaster, John Cage, Morris Graves, and Mark Tobey have kept him in touch with the avant garde in other fields and has in all probability influenced his work in dance.

His recent exploration into video and film as part of dance or, as he calls them, "events" has prompted him to reject video and film as a mere medium of transmission alone, but accept them as art forms for the dance.[9] In one of his planned events he would dance and carry a video camera, and as he danced this action would be recorded by other cameras and projected on two large screens. In this arrangement the spectators would see live video, prerecorded video, the live dancers, and the camerapeople. Consequently the spectators experience the mixing of opposing styles and movements and the mixing of two different realities, actual and recorded. This planned collage of movement and images is but one example of many which typify the interaction between the arts today.

The relationship of photograph to the stage has many aspects—set and costume design, archival and promotional value—and has in its way helped to shape the abundance of innovations on the stage today. If we look at this connection in a broader sense than that of a mutually beneficial interaction isolated from the mainstream of life, it is possible to see that the capacity for human development through the creative process is consistently manifesting itself not only in art, but in life as well.

The link between theater and photography represents the possibilities for these two art forms to explore our consciousness of intellectual, psychological, and technological realities. The commercialism evident in the theater, which cannot be used to measure in any respect the value or priorities of theatrical creativity, allows the relationship between theater and photography to exist and enables all of us to experience the often intensive and direct influence of new combinations such as these upon our society, our culture and ourselves. This exchange exists as a ground-plane support for human action and interaction and pointedly suggests a union of human action and reality in contemporary society.

8 PHOTOGRAPHY: PAST, PRESENT, FUTURE

Through our achievements we give affirmation to our existence and identify and justify ourselves. Each photograph is a confirmation of the photographer, from which he derives a certain satisfaction as an artist and human being. The moment he trips the shutter, the photographer brings an infinity of personal, technical, cultural, and social aspects to bear upon his medium. This extraordinary process, functioning on both conscious and subconscious levels, sets it apart from such disciplines as painting and drawing. It is specific to the photographic medium. Each photograph gives evidence of this process. The photograph is a realization of the self and of the environment. Striving for self-realization, each photographer concerns himself with reaching a goal of individual identification through style intended to set him apart from other photographers.

This is not an unusual task, but has become more difficult in our modern society, where a network of expectations, regulations, economics, controls, and demands have exerted greater pressure on the individual than ever before. While striving for higher personal ideals, the photographer is also part of the mania for achievement on which our society thrives. Personal achievement is a form of self-discovery that can offer great artistic and aesthetic rewards and progress, but to become part of the "achievement game" can lead to a multitude of frustrations, loss of individual artistic freedom, even loss of identity. Self-alienation through imitation is one of the byproducts of the high-energy game of achievement for achievement's sake. The dangers are obvious in this tremendous pressure competition, and one can only admire those photographers who have managed to maintain their individuality within the system that beckons in other directions. Those photographers who have asserted themselves, relying on their own resources—human beings aware of themselves—have achieved worthy contributions to the whole of society.

Achievements in themselves are nothing; they simply reflect the growing dehumanization of contemporary society. What does matter in achievement, however, is that the effort to achieve be more than a final self-centered goal of self-realization, and that it be something which offers another person the possibility of discovering something of himself—a link to others and to the environment. Photography, a principal vehicle of concepts, thought, observations, as a contemporary tool and visual language for artists, makes achievements possible quickly. The speed of the medium and the quick achievements within the grasp of every photographer can prevent one from utilizing this powerful tool in a manner that distinguishes it as a new art form capable of reaching everyone.

Photography's brief history shows us that some of the difficulties the medium has today have been with it from the beginning. Once the essential technical evolutionary process had nearly ended, the growing pains began, and that was a considerable identity crisis. However, as in so many of the new art forms, this crisis was not unusual, in fact, it was rather to be expected. The potential for an accurate form of documentation was acknowledged early in the 1840s; in fact, this aspect raised great hopes in industry, especially in the publishing business. Many photographers of the period were eager to capitalize on the predictions of photographic documentation's bringing the far corners of the world into the living room. They made haste, and an avalanche of photographs documenting Europe, America, and Africa streamed into the publishing houses and newspapers to be reproduced at first in the form of woodcuts or steel engravings. And while the process continued, the art and science communities were also recognizing the potential of photography as a form of recording that could be exploited.

But photography remained in a state of identity crisis, imitating the art of painting; even those photographs intended as documents were using compositions, lighting, and subject matter directly associated with painting. Adolph Braun's *Still Life with Deer and Wild Fowl*, c. 1865 (Figure 8-1), a tour de force of photographic technique, speaks generally of an attitude carried by many photographers in their work. Imbued with many of the attributes of still-life painting seen a hundred years earlier in French art and in Dutch painting of the seventeenth century, Braun's work remains faithful to those painting concepts. But there is a strange, unsettling quality about the photograph. The still-life paintings of the eighteenth century Dutch school were intended to remind the observer that life was transitory, just as the pleasure he received from eating and drinking was transitory. These paintings were often hung in dining rooms as a reminder of this fact. Braun's photograph excludes this central issue in the paintings and takes on an air of brutality.

Until the invention of photography, the only means of presenting optical sensations on a two-dimensional surface were painting and drawing. One must keep in mind that many of the very early photographers were painters them-

Figure 8-1   ADOLPH BRAUN, *Still Life with Deer and Wild Fowl* (The Metropolitan Museum of Art, New York, David H. McAlpin Fund, 1947)

selves, so that, without being overly accusatory about the identity crisis in photography, it was the painters who felt threatened by photography. The menace of photography became a reality when public taste moved toward photographic portraits instead of painted ones, since in the mid–nineteenth century detailed realism was in demand. Illustrators and other graphic artists also felt the results of the photographic threat as photography took over in the publishing business. For two generations before the perfection of photoengraving, many illustrators were reduced to the role of copyists, making woodcuts or steel engravings after photographs for newspapers and magazines, before disappearing altogether. At about the turn of the century, however, the best of them were resurrected when it became possible to reproduce their fashionable watercolors or drawings by photographic means.

For some painters, such as Ingres, the photograph came as a great aid, although many of them never did admit to using photographs in their work. For photography, a turning point came with the Impressionist movement in France. The French scientist Chevreul had discovered the method in which the eyes see patches of color, which was in theory the basis for Impressionist painting, although the Impressionists were not yet aware of his work. These research findings by Chevreul, carefully studied by the Neo-Impressionist Seurat, in essence gave the painter a new way of seeing and working, ending the obsessive rendering of endless detail, and the overshadowing of painting by photography ended for the time being. The identity crisis for photography had also come to an end. Nonetheless, some of the photographic effects, such as blurring and compositional methods, were used by a number of the Impressionists. By the end of the century, organized movements such as the Photo Club de Paris, and later the Photo-Secession of New York, headed by Alfred Stieglitz, forged ahead, establishing photography as an independent art form in its own right. Stieglitz's photograph, *The Steerage,* his own favorite, stands as a symbol amid the many different types of photographs made by members of the movement as being responsible for changing the public's original concept of photography as essentially a technological tool intended for documentation.

From this rich and fertile ground, abstract photography grew in abundance in the work of such photographers as Alvin Coburn, Christian Schad, Man Ray, and Laszlo Moholy-Nagy. Both Man Ray and Moholy-Nagy were painters, whose ideas as painters are often felt and seen in their photographs. It is almost as if one nourished the other, an unusual circumstance in the history of photography. From the early first steps taken by the infant photography, there appeared to be a certain innocence and straightforwardness about it that had a great deal of appeal. That innocence has now unfortunately faded, although without losing its central character of being human. One way or another, human expression makes itself felt through this medium of image making, which is what Stieglitz was saying when he insisted that photography was as much an art as was painting. Human expression is the foundation for art: not the kind of expression, but the expression itself. It is on this fundamental premise that we evaluate, judge, accept, or reject all forms of art, not by the technical means of forging that expression or the proficiency demonstrated through the tool chosen. Human will and expression, imposed on the medium, are as they are and as they should be in any form of image making. Just as language can describe the unseen, photography can reveal the unnoticed and unseen and supply that which cannot be described by words, spoken or written. Photography's past has made this possible, as does its present.

Since the early efforts by Nicéphore Niépce to fix an image permanently, photography has become, through rapid technological advances, an art form of enormous range and dizzying power, armed with an ever-advancing sophistication. It has recently been accepted enthusiastically as an art form with universal appeal. Photography as art enjoys an accessibility never quite achieved by the other more traditional arts, and its ubiquity through the multitude of publications, museums, galleries, and shops has enhanced that accessibility. It has become economically possible for nearly anyone to own an original. Yet in spite of the recent swift rise of photography and the secure position that it has achieved, it has not lost its sense of direction, its quality, or its standing as the art of new and of the future. Photography, which combines science and art, offers possibilities of limitless creative endeavor that are now being realized.

Today, there is a new spirit evidenced in photography in which every restrictive concept has been eliminated, giving way to total creative freedom. Yesterday's photographic visual and technical "mistakes" are being explored and put to evocative use in the stream of expressive consciousness. There have been those exceptional, temporary setbacks, however, when photography once again imitated the other arts such as painting and drawing (which had been imitating photography). But, for the most part, those who practice photography have fully realized its distinct and individual character and pushed it beyond what had often been considered clear-cut limitations. What characterizes so much of today's photography is the extensive range of expressive technical approaches and a determined resistance to categorical movements. Even within such specialized areas as photojournalism, documentation, advertising, portraiture, fashion, and industrial and scientific photography, there has been the equivalent realization. The relationship between art photography and the other specialized areas has been reciprocal, each benefiting from the other. The fine art photographers have drawn upon technology from the other areas, often turning it into poetical images and statements, while technological photography has used fine art photography with great success by turning straightforward images into visually appealing and instructive creations.

Our history of making visual images has been infinitely rich and varied from cave paintings to the present, a heritage in which each effort has assisted and brought into being the next. Each state and period has grown from its predecessor, through evolution or through revolution, and this interdependence springs from the indefatigable expressive variety of the human spirit. Photography is the present and quite possibly the future form which functions as visual evidence that the irrepressible human spirit can disregard natural environmental conditions and social repressions. Photography is now the vehicle for the expressive spirit residing in each of us.

Those photographers who continue pictorial photography as established by Stieglitz, who use the camera's technical means to interpret (a concept dedicated to the lens and exalting photography for photography's sake), seem to be at the opposite pole from those who work with photography as an ideal synthesis. And, while the straight photograph based in the experiential Gestalt, that is the sensory and extrasensory mental processes combined, perceives the totality of an experience rather than any isolated part, the most varied approaches are held together by a distinct existential discourse. Henri Cartier-Bresson's term "the decisive moment" best exemplifies the experiential Gestalt in photography by photographic images produced or taken at the decisive moment in which organized wholes are perceived, in spite of gaps, and experienced. The purist aesthetic formulated before the 1950s remains a part of the current general photographic milieu, although the practitioners of this style appear to be rather rare. Photomanipulation, radically different from photographic synthesis, is in all probability the most common approach today. Those photographers who have incorporated other art forms into the photograph, such as sculpture, painting, and technical-industrial techniques, have broken entirely with traditional photographic conventions. In their works, the photograph is a point of departure. Photomanipulation is indeed a combination of photography and other arts, yet it constitutes a step forward for photography.

Essentially, this sort of photography has stepped out of the darkroom into a current set in motion in the 1950s and 1960s, in particular by Robert Rauschenberg, who incorporated actual objects into his paintings. At that time, sculpture began to exhibit painterly qualities, so that the demarcations between the various art forms began to blur. This was a crucial turning point for art, and for our concepts about it. However, although this point in the history of art marked a clear and radical change that generated new production methods and ideas, this does not mean that the photographic synthesis is a repeat of that period in any way. The very use of the technical means currently available, such as the Graphic Sciences Teleprinter, Thermo-Fax, 3M VQC, Xerox, 3M Color-in-Color Systems, Thermal Transfer, Thermal-Forming Plastics, Emulsion-Printing Processes, and the SX-70 Polaroid Alterations, along with a host of other highly sophisticated technical equipment and processes, tells us that the idea generated in the 1950s was simply a point of departure for photography. Whether this current form of photography is art is beside the point; whether it is even photography is sometimes debated. The present period of photographic history indicates that there are no rules, and those who attempt to make them are held in the past by their own artificial bonds. Flourishing in their newly achieved freedom, photography, painting, sculpture, drawing, and printmaking, need no longer be qualified as such, but simply as art which concerns itself with the critical issues of our time.

The recent work of Siegfried Halus is a continuation of the experiential Gestalt within a framework of the narrative freely composed by his models. His highly introspective work balances the conscious and subconscious in such a manner as to suggest humanity's existence, primordial to present, within a single frame (Figure 8-2). Fundamental human characteristics indicated by movement are the continuum which transcends all time-space barriers; they are the central theme that Halus raises to an existential state, allowing observer participation in his images. He allows his nude models, photographed at night with a flashlight, to move freely in outdoor settings, each assuming basic postures and actions. He intermittently directs the flashlight beam to illuminate the stationary figures and makes a continuous exposure, sometimes up to six minutes or more. His background as a sculptor with particular interests in the human form is clearly carried over into his current work. Light, a major consideration in his sculpture, is now a fundamental concern in his photographs, moving beyond the illumination of formal relationships in the human figure. But it is a light that pierces darkness, the darkness of time both past and present, a generative force delivering the environment occupied by human forms. Halus's images, both opaque and transparent, become symbols of human activity held in a moment of time and perpetuated in the photographic image. Here we see human activities defined by movement and posture, carved by light from a darkness in which they had previously awaited hidden and undifferentiated, now becoming part of our very own being.

Halus's work with nude models seems particularly poignant at this time, in a complex contemporary social structure where the individual is obscured by layers of self-defenses which further remove him from social interaction. These images strip away all false structures, restoring the individual to the fundamental self. They reveal a desire reluctantly, if ever, expressed, in a world where pressures force a division between the self and the environment. Particularly significant is the depiction of human interaction in darkness, in which that interaction is highlighted as most strongly felt and needed. As a contemporary statement about the need for comfort, assurance, and warmth from others in a society

Figure 8-2 SIEGFRIED HALUS,
Fragments from a Collectanea
(Courtesy of the photographer)

growing increasingly colder and more distant, Halus's work strikes at the very heart of this issue boldly, frankly, even poetically, and entirely without sentiment. While in the past art served as a method of embodying church doctrine, or as a comment on political issues, Halus's work is a grand monument to a universal human issue, impossible to forget or circumvent.

Photographs which synthesize with other art forms are appearing with greater regularity, for example Shelley Farkas's *Meatpiece,* 1975 (Figure 8-3). Sculpture, photography, and actual functional objects are combined into a grouping of related objects forming a personal statement related to the women's movement. Farkas's statement is simple, direct, amusingly constructed, and dead true. A comment heard by women all over the globe today is graphically presented: the female is a piece of meat. Resting on the meat cart are parts of the female anatomy wrapped in transparent wrappers so that the contents may be observed. Each part—an arm, a leg, a torso—is given a label which identifies the cost of the purchase. Each sculptural piece is a flat cut-out upon which is mounted a pho-

Figure 8-3 SHELLEY FARKAS,
Meatpiece 1975 (Courtesy of
the photographer)

tographic image of an anatomical part. The edges of the parts are white to
resemble the outer layer of fat, while the interiors are darker to resemble the
meat fiber. Resting upright against the cart is one large package containing an
entire female figure, with one arm raised, the fist clenched in a gesture of
defiance. A smaller label to the right of this package reads, "Double Your Money
Back Guarantee." The figure is placed between the labels of cost and guarantee,
reflecting the male chauvinist attitude toward sexuality and the unrealistic physical-psychological demands placed on the female. Of particular significance is
that the materials used for this piece—hard plastic, chrome, reflective and transparent papers of various sorts—are all suggestive of coolness, indifference, and
remoteness. The photographs used as part of the synthesis depict the female as
rather soft in spite of the defiant gesture. In juxtaposition to the other materials,
the photographs are highly effective as a back-up support to the obvious statement. Artists working in this vein today have been acutely conscious of the
materials used and the way in which they are used, so that content, image, and
materials are a careful fusion that not only evokes a visual response but a reaction from the other senses as well.

Farkas's *Meatpiece* exemplifies the photographic synthesis process with
great agility, directness, and originality, and without a loss of personal identification. If anything, it seems that the process has assisted with self-identification, as
well as being a vehicle for the feelings of other women with the same concerns.
Farkas has created a work that is not restricted to the select few, but that speaks
to men and women of all social and economic levels. The piece may provide just
the stimulus needed to reevaluate any negative positions toward the feminist
movement. Farkas's observations, perceptions, personal statement, and clear
concern with social and political issues have been synthesized skillfully and
thoughtfully in an extraordinarily telling work.

Before the Xerox company called itself Xerox, it was known as Haloid. The
early equipment accomplished what the present form of Xerox machine does,
but with slight differences. The early equipment consisted of the Haloid Model 4
Camera, Fuser, and Processor, each an independent and mobile piece of equipment. However, to obtain a copy of an original, the process required the camera:

for enlarging or reducing, plate charging, development of the plate image, and image transfer and fusing. Control of the image before the fusing process was possible by manipulating the xerographic developer powder; this is impossible with present Xerox machines. This process of copy work was clearly cumbersome for the average business office and almost immediately became obsolete, when replaced by the present process. Charles A. Arnold, Jr., who explored the early Haloid process at the Rochester Institute of Technology, discovered that real creative possibilities were available to him through manipulation of the developer powder. Contrast, density, tonality, detail, texture, and a host of other formal and visual elements could be achieved with the machine at great speed but, more important, each image could either be different from the others, or they could all be duplicated precisely in great numbers. His investigations and productions with the Haloid process soon became known, and the Haloid machine was added to the other techniques and processes as a twentieth-century creative tool, another step in uniting technology and art. Other photographers soon discovered the process, and xerography became another photographic process with growing popularity.

Ron Talbott, who has made exclusive use of the Haloid process over a number of years, has produced a great variety of images from silver prints, his own drawings, and other Xerographs, each displaying the immediacy of the medium and the spontaneous poetry of the artist. His Xerographic prints, *Self Portrait*, 1979 (Figure 8-4), and *Nancy*, 1979 (Figure 8-5), are derived from silver prints photographed with the Haloid camera. Toner for *Self Portrait* was transferred with a negative electrostatic charge, which reversed the shadows and highlights and produced a soft flow of grey tones which form the head. *Nancy* was photographed at a slow shutter speed, resulting in a blurred image, and a severely scratched Xerographic plate was intentionally used to enhance the sense of movement. Talbott's images depict human qualities perceived by experience, where individual characteristics are integrated and transformed into the intended image. In Talbott's work, academic formalities exist as a grid in which horizontal lines of perception and experience intersect vertical lines of idea and thought. Superimposed on this matrix is the centric symmetry of romantic thought and character, particularly in these images.

Jill Gussow's recent explorations with photoetching on brass plates has resulted in witty images of sensory experience. Each plate is richly textured through the process she has investigated with logical freedom. The plates have a sculptural look, revealing her training as a sculptor. Looking like ancient artifacts recently excavated, the plates are rich and warm in material that the artist has successfully fused with her subject matter. *Backs and Trunks*, 1979 (Figure 8-6) is a visual, verbal pun in which the artist's free thought associations and visual perceptions are given substance. A series of unmanipulated photographs depicting a male figure, nude to the waist, are arranged consecutively in a horizontal line beneath the manipulated larger image of trees. Underlying these images are the disembodied sexual forces relevant to the artist. These images are symbols, not to be taken at face value, representing individual ideas interacting with experience. Gussow has taken sensory appearances and infused them with her highly personal ideas and thoughts to produce an image dependent on contemporary means of expression. These technical means have greatly assisted the pictorial analogue,

Figure 8-4 RON TALBOTT,
Self Portrait 1979
(Courtesy of the photographer)

Figure 8-5 RON TALBOTT,
Nancy 1979
(Courtesy of the photographer)

where the dynamic, animated male figure is played off the erect, still trees above him. The trees become the negative form mirroring the positive male form—generic forms held together in a cognitive statement, each complementing the other. Essential to the artist's work is the conviction that her images imitate nothing, mimic nothing, that they are eloquent, relevant symbols of life both specific and general.

Figure 8-6   JILL GUSSOW,
Backs and Trunks 1979
(Courtesy of the photographer)

Two photographers whose work bears close resemblance in technical approach are in fact quite different in content. Paul Berger and William Larson have both produced photographs reminiscent of Cubist painting in which all facets of an object are revealed, but the similarities end there. Both are concerned with shapes that grow out of one another, overlapping images, movement, and horizontal compositions based on what may be called double exposures.

Larson's series *The Figure in Motion,* 1980 (Figure 8-7) is achieved with a specially modified camera devised by the artist. The figure is photographed in motion through time exposures that last from six to twelve minutes. Each distorted figure (the same model for each image) appears to grow out of the other as if joined by bone and flesh, and thus the figure forms a horizontal and continuous ribbon of movement throughout the filmstrip image. Often the interlocking shapes produce minicompositions within the totality without a loss of dynamic movement. Arms, legs, torsos, and heads join in a syncopated pulsation which may be read either from the right or left of the image, since no attempt has been made to end the composition at those points. At times the figures merge in such a way as to form abstract images, however when the figure's limbs or head are recognized, the abstract image becomes representational. Larson's images may be more closely associated with the Surrealist paintings of Salvador Dali than with Cubist paintings, since the same kind of figure and object distortion may be observed in Dali's paintings.

In the late 1920s, Dali produced what he termed "hand-colored photographs of the subconscious," and these paintings were based on what he called the "three cardinal images of life: blood, excrement, and putrefaction."[1] While these paintings are interesting and germinal to his later work, they cannot be

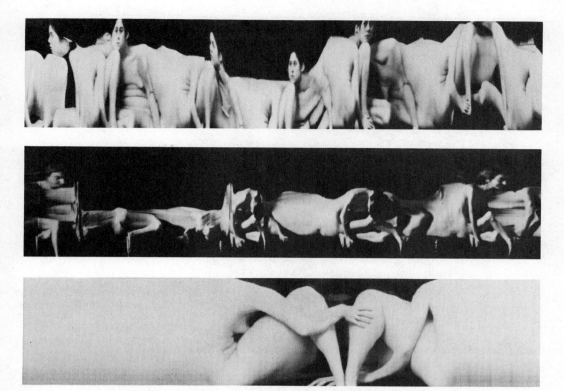

Figure 8-7   WILLIAM LARSON, *The Figure in Motion* 1980 (Courtesy of Light Gallery, New York)

said to have the historical and artistic importance of his work of the 1930s. While Larson's images from his series are sexual, they do not show the explicit sexuality rendered by Dali. Dali's *Soft Construction with Boiled Beans: Premonition of Civil War,* 1936 (Figure 8-8) depicts fragments of humans appearing to grow out of one another against a stormy sky filled with yellowish clouds. The image is at once frightening and sexual, as arms, legs, and hands interlock in combat and sexual pleasure. An old woman's head is thrust backward in pleasure or pain as a gnarled hand from below holds her breast in a tight clutch. Below, a small, fully clothed male figure gazes down at the ground as he stands partly hidden behind another hand.

Dali's desire to "materialize images of concrete irrationality with the utmost imperialist fury of precision" have resulted in paintings of extraordinary quality and originality of statement. This exactitude may be seen in Larson's images as well, but Dali's fury is replaced in Larson's work by the gentleness of female sexuality and physicality. However we observe the work of these two artists and whatever interpretations we may derive from them, both artists knew and understood the human form and character and imbued their work with the iridescent beauty of the human body and psyche.

The series *Camera Text or Picture* by Paul Berger (Figure 8-9) fuses texts, figures, landscape, and numbers by double exposure to unify these subjects into

Figure 8-8 SALVADOR DALI, *Soft Construction with Boiled Beans: Premonition of Civil War* 1936 (Philadelphia Museum of Art, The Louise and Walter Arensberg Collection)

Figure 8-9 PAUL BERGER, *Camera Text or Picture* (Courtesy of Light Gallery, New York)

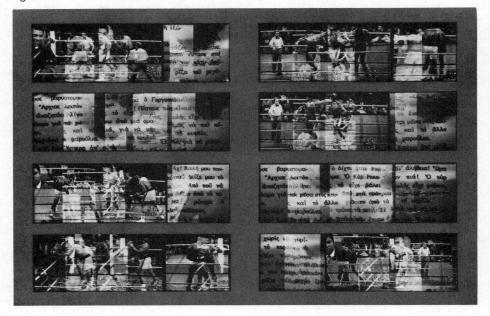

one shimmering and transparent image. The face of Muhammed Ali is superimposed over the figures in the boxing ring, with a different expression in each frame. At times Ali's expression reveals pleasure, at other times displeasure or puzzlement. He wears a suit and tie and is at once spectator and participating athlete. The reflections of trees in slightly rippled water may be seen in several images, while Greek writing is superimposed over these landscapes. Numbers indicating the round of the event have reached a high of 57 and are noted at the base of the images 21 times.

The Greek characters are printed and may be a fable or possibly a letter. Words and phrases repeated throughout the image are, "head" "pair," "caught," "outside over the trees," "he who is lost," "fleet-footed one," "the birds are eating," and "he who has arrived." We cannot know whether Berger intended these words and phrases to relate to the images or not, but they are easily associated with the landscape, the movement of the boxers, and Ali's well-known wit. The blending of the images, words, and numbers into a visual language is something of a game, mirroring the boxing event. Each filmstrip presents these individual aspects within a totality and at the same time sets them off against one another. The camera has recorded the physical movement of the fight, the Greek writing, and the landscape, and the photographer has superimposed them so that they become pictures of the photographer's thought processes.

While Larson's images are liquid flowing into one another, Berger's are fragmented and transparent, joining one another through a consistent style. Each photographer has used a slightly different technical and stylistic approach, but they reach a common ground when they reveal the extraordinary richness of human invention, while each one depicts a different aspect of human character.

Ray Metzker's *Fissured Foto,* 1978 (Figure 8-10) is one example from his series "Pictus Interruptus," which he carried out in Philadelphia and Greece. The series is consistent in idea and theme, which Metzker has gracefully followed through in each photograph, even though each is different from the other in composition, shapes, texture, and tones. The technique he uses to create his images is simple, original, and within the tradition of the "straight photograph," while at the same time extending that tradition. During the time the exposure is made, the photographer places a small object or objects—often a small piece of white paper—in front of the camera lens to interrupt the camera's monocular vision, taking care not to cover the entire lens but merely to block out parts of the subject being recorded. The objects held close to the lens are partly out of focus, while the remainder of the subject remains in complete depth of field, which emphasizes texture, light, form, and shape. This juxtaposition of objects in and out of focus poses an ambiguous and uneasy spatial relationship.

Cézanne's paintings do not entirely depart from physical reality but are interrupted by Cézanne's creation of shifting planes and carefully "adjusted" linear perspective, resulting in broken horizontal and vertical contours. Metzker's work follows this line of perception and creativity in a less formal manner. In many of Cézanne's paintings the picture plane has been denied through some of these techniques and inventions, and is a departure from the Renaissance assertion of the two-dimensional surface that functions as a frame through which a scene could be observed. In Metzker's photo the scene was constructed through traditional methods of linear and atmospheric perspective to give the illusion of depth and spatial relationships locked within the edges of

Figure 8-10   RAY METZKER, *Fissured Foto*
1978 (Courtesy of the photographer)

the paper or the canvas. But Metzker uses both the traditional formal assertion and the more contemporary denial of the photograph's surface.

The white paper held in front of the camera lens is not burned in later, but remains a "hot white," bleeding into the white borders of the print. The technique breaks through the picture plane and seems to continue beyond the confines of the horizontal and vertical edges of the two-dimensional surface. It is the employment of this technique which separates Metzker's space from that of Cézanne's. The juxtapositioning of these two aspects emphasizes their characteristics, while at once opposing and uniting them. Metzker's attempts to break with the rectangularity of the camera's framing device without any actual physical manipulation of the image succeeds through the bleeding effect of the whites in the photographs. Juxtapositioning the hand-held object against the subject, in addition to creating shifting spatial relationships, also changes the illusion of scale, ground-plane relationship, and textures, which are an intrinsic part of the object which they represent.

It would be a mistake to call these images photographic collages, semi-abstractions, or abstractions since the photographer has clearly moved beyond those classifications. *Fissured Foto* has become part of a group which refuses to be given a classification and remains free.

The hand-held object which interrupts the subject and partly obliterates it is used as a device to destroy and reconstruct ordinary perceptions of the photograph, ordinary perceptions of physical reality, and ordinary conceptions of the inherent quality of photography in and outside the circle of art, while at the same time remaining a part of the pictorial form. What is surprising about *Fissured Foto* and the other photographs in this series is that the photographer is able to accomplish all this while maintaining formal properties of the photographic tradition.

Metzker's work asks and challenges us to reconsider the significance and value of our tightly held perceptions of society and nature, of all that we can see and not see. He acknowledges that we are endowed with the intelligence to perceive his challenge through the formal aspects of his photographs. Indeed, we are urged to the next higher level of content and asked to consider another challenge: are the norms, structures, and actions with which we identify ourselves and our environment depriving us of a richer and fuller existence through our reluctance to let go of them and the security they provide? Are we willing to take the risk he has taken as an artist in questioning what we perceive in order to understand? If this is what Metzker's work offers us directly and honestly, how can we not accept his questions and his challenges?

On a purely visual level, *Fissured Foto*, and this entire series are graceful, radiant, and pure in their efforts to organize the physical materials in order to dematerialize them. The shifting, kaleidoscopic shapes and textures shimmering in light and atmospheric effects are transcendent in relation to their actual position in the physical environment. The complexities created by the interconnectedness of all the formal visual elements offers rewards which cannot be gleaned without time and effort. Metzker's dual offering of visual delights and content through photography has without a doubt placed his work in an axial position in the history of photography.

Photography today is a many-faceted medium, and its diversity of expressions, concepts, and approaches may be seen in both commerical and industrial photography. It is this multiformity which characterizes photography today as an art form that is continually growing and redefining itself. Typifying this richness are the photographs of Gary Hallman. His series "construction sites," like the photographs of Ray Metzker, explores the endless possibilities of physical reality and uses it as a metaphor. *New Construction*, 1980 (Figure 8-11) is the Northwestern Communications Center, sublevel number 3, in Minneapolis, Minnesota. Although Hallman also photographs in color, it is his black-and-white photographs which appear to have the necessary strength to carry his

Figure 8-11   GARY HALLMAN, *New Construction* 1980 (Courtesy of the photographer)

series of architectural subjects, especially in the case of *New Construction*. The allover quality of grey in this print functions as a reinforcement of the quality of the concrete blocks and cement he records.

The spareness of the image at first appears to be overextended to the point of blankness, however this first impression is quickly dispelled once the tactile aspects of the image begin to assert themselves. The cool greyness reinforced by the artificial light permeates the image with an allover calm and quietness; it is as if one could feel the stillness within the damp substructure and smell the cement mixed with the scent of fresh pungent earth in the heavy moist air. On a formal level, Hallman works with the visual elements directly and simply. They are manipulated to construct a composition which reflects the power and simplicity of the substructure itself. The picture plane is divided into unequal thirds, and within each third, line, texture, shape, and movement are repeated without being duplicated. The camera is tilted in order to keep the verticals of the structure from aligning with the verticals of the picture plane. Spatial relationships are built by keeping the structure away from a parallel position to the lens at an angle that allows the left side of the concrete block wall to project beyond the two-dimensional surface. By this camera maneuver Hallman has made the observer aware of the actual space occupied by the spectator, the illusionistic space represented in front of the concrete block structure, and the space that the concrete block encloses, which is seen through the opening with a fretlike design on the left and right verticals of the doorway.

Hallman's photograph is a conceptual image in that he has transformed an unfinished architectural substructure into a primary structuralist or minimalist sculpture. This is accomplished by the photographer's ability to isolate an object from its environment and place it in another by association. This requires keen awareness, finesse, intelligence, and understanding of the intrinsic qualities of the object's presence. Donald Judd and Tony Smith are but two sculptors among many who may be called primary structuralists or minimalists. Hallman's work has a certain affinity with theirs in that it possesses unity through repetition, consisting of identical self-contained units. Furthermore, like Hallman's photographs, Judd's work raises some fundamental questions about the nature and validity of the work of art, space, aesthetic experience, and form. Judd employed mathematical systems in his sculpture by choice to arrange and proportion forms, but Hallman's photograph records those aspects which preexisted and were employed by an architect out of necessity as part of function rather than strict aesthetic concern. But does this difference separate Hallman from Judd? Perhaps not.

Judd's insistence on the nonenvironmental character of his sculpture is unlike Hallman's architectural images, which retain vestiges of the surrounding world. It is the contextual aspect of Hallman's photograph which pulls it away from the minimalists, and in the final analysis to another plane of endeavor. Minimalist sculpture was never intended to invite human interaction, that is, it was detached from the spectator so that he could not enter into it or become part of the structure. Hallman's image not only invites spectator participation, but gives visual clues as a reminder that human participation in fact took place. In the foreground of *New Construction* a wooden ramp roughly put together suggests a temporary human need as well as the communication with the structure itself. Bits of wood and scraps of paper are strewn about on the floor, and a wooden plank rests against the right wall. All of these clues are the residue of human action and participation with the construction site. Minimalist sculpture never allows this sort of evidence to occur; all surfaces are highly finished and machined, as though never touched by human hands.

Earth art, which employs mechanical equipment in the construction of projects, such as Robert Smithson's colossal *Spiral Jetty*, 1970, located at the Great Salt Lake, Utah, also bears some resemblance to Hallman's work. Many of the earthwork projects are architectural in concept, and some are partly underground. For many earth artists, space manipulation, or the defining of outdoor space, is a major concern, and in Hallman's work the manipulation of space is very much in evidence. No matter how Hallman's photographs are related to the sculptural movements or to particular sculptors, his concerns for architectural form and space appear to be formal expressions, which are vehicles for content.

New Construction is free of embarrassing generalizations and superfluous decorative elements; it represents itself as a maximal state of concept in which rhythmic succession of recurrence, regeneration, and renewal are psychological-physical realities. Rather than the nihilism of cheaply designed architectural expansionism, Hallman records what may be interpreted as the ideal, positive, and essential technical-rational aspects of human behavior. His intellectual approach to the construction site series reflects truths which prevail in his photographic images. His selective process continually determines what is perceived and remembered by the spectator as an elemental and unusual experience of reality.

Many photographers who regard themselves as purists, as well as others outside the profession, consider the manipulated photograph to be something other than photography, and the person who made it not truly a photographer. Often snubbed and relegated to a dark corner in an exhibition space, if accepted at all, the manipulated photograph has had a difficult time until recently. John Reuter, like Lucas Samaras, is a rare breed among photographers. His work with the Polaroid SX-70 is extraordinary. His method is painstaking and complicated. The layers of an SX-70 photograph are peeled apart, and then lifting off sections that he does not wish to use, he replaces them with odd bits of materials or sections taken from other photographs. At times he paints on the photograph with acrylic paint, but this is done on the back of the picture surface instead of on top of it, and then the finished image is sealed in acrylic gel. There is no negative, and each print is a true original. The result of his process, due largely to his careful craftsmanship, is that the parts seem to have been there all the time, just waiting to be photographed by Reuter.

Reuter says that he was influenced by the work of Max Ernst, Francis Bacon, and René Magritte. There is no doubt that the spirit of the Surrealists is reflected in his work, but there is never any specific resemblance to their creations. Reuter's images are determinedly his own. His photographs are manipulations of the photographic materials, painting, drawing, and montage, resulting in images which have a dreamlike quality, even mythical overtones. "By changing the image-context, I am not looking for a specific, literal result, but rather I hope to enhance, transform, or even dissolve the original claim to reality and have it become a new existence—one created through the manipulation of two-dimensional facts."[2] Reuter's statement, like his photographs, gently asks us to consider the validity of a continuation of photography as it has been defined in Western society, and whether photography can have greater dimensions than those that have been assigned to it. Reuter can be compared to the turn-of-the-century East Indian photographers who refused to accept the Western definitions of photography and ripped it from its Western roots by painting on their photographs, turning them into a version of Indian miniature painting and thus connecting photography with the other arts (painting, drawing, and collage). Reuter has also brought into question the traditional concepts of photography. If for no other reason, his work has been invaluable.

The Wanderer, 1982 (Figure 8-12), a sparkling gem of craftsmanship and imagination, depicts a female who appears to be nude from the waist down, standing in a stream in the foreground. It is not until one looks closely at the feet that it is discovered that the figure is not nude at all, but is in fact wearing tights, which is discernible in that the heel and toe of the foot are free. In the background a landscape opens up to reveal forests, fields, mountains, a small lake, and a bearded male figure standing in a clearing holding a long pole, which he points up into the air. This entire background is a reproduction of one of Bruegel's paintings, although just a small section from the background. It is significant to note that the photographer has selected the work of Bruegel as part of his image since this sixteenth-century genius was also deeply influenced by Bosch's pessimism and fantasy and demonstrates a strong fantastic content in his own work. It is generally believed that Bruegel had an association with Antwerp humanists who maintained that humanity, driven to sin by foolishness, is bound to the inevitable cycle of nature, from which it is folly to attempt escape. This doctrine is referred to in Bruegel's work often, but with peaceful acceptance.

Reuter's art is related to the fantasy and dreamlike quality of Bosch and Bruegel, not because he uses Bruegel's actual painting as part of his own photograph, but because of his conception of the figure's relationship to pictorial space and to the self-constructed environment from the imagination. The photographer's method of uniting the top and bottom of the picture plane by strong verticals placed near the foreground is a compositional device visible in Bruegel's work.

As Reuter says, "I hope to enhance, transform, or even dissolve the original claim to reality and have it become a new existence . . ."[3] reinforced by his photographs. This may be translated as a desire to escape the physical existence to the existence of fantasy, that is, exchanging one reality for another, but this is not completely possible since fantasy has deep roots in physical reality, and from *that* we cannot escape.

The visual pleasure, often sensual at times, combined with his unique fantasy is an unusual combination, not seen very often in photography, from which one may derive endless intellectual and visual satisfaction. *The Wanderer,* like the other images created by this inventive photographer, is an artistry which not only proves the interconnectedness of the arts, but also that no artist creates within a complete vacuum. His intelligent and selective use of other artists' work eliminates the possibility that his success with these images is luck or mere mimicry through tricky manipulations of the photographic process. His images also prove that through creative touch and invention, he can transform the ordinary into the extraordinary while demonstrating restraint, wry wit, unusual juxtapositioning of opposites, and above all, imagination within the framework of Surrealism. If Reuter can dissolve reality and reassemble it in such a way as to induce the spectator to reevaluate it, and to lead him into a world without actuality and without logic, and still prove the actual experience of being, then just one of his images is worth the time required to read it.

Few photographers have emerged as successful and as triumphant over the constrictions imposed on the photographer by the SX-70 as has Reuter. This photographer is to photography as Joseph Cornell is to sculpture. Cornell's glass-fronted boxes (Figure 8-13) are assemblages with surrealist associations, usually consisting of objects, photographs, maps, bits of junk, and are sometimes drawn and painted on. His surreal assemblages are personal, referring to private experiences, family, childhood, and home. But there are also in these boxes strong references to Renaissance perspective in drawing and painting, as well as to the trompe l'oeil paintings of the American nineteenth century, which he translated into the third dimension. And like Reuter, his early work was inspired by such surrealists as Max Ernst.

The manipulated photograph is not new to the history of photography—

Figure 8-12 JOHN REUTER,
The Wanderer 1982
(Courtesy of the photographer)

Figure 8-13 JOSEPH CORNELL,
Untitled c. 1953 (Collection, The
Fort Worth Art Museum)

many photographers at the turn of the century were concerned with this process—but it is Reuter's new approach to the manipulated photograph that has expanded the boundaries for photographer and spectator alike.

Photography's history is remarkable in that photography began as a blend of technology and art and continues as such. This fact is central to photography's very being, and its adaptability is dependent on this dual nature. Its true relationship to other fields is not yet fully investigated or understood. During its short history, photography has produced some artists who have worked out personal visions and styles, while others have concerned themselves more with photographic technology. Even though there have been periods in the history of photography that appeared to exclude it as an art form, it has nevertheless integrated itself into art from the beginning. That integration has not always resulted in visible outward acceptance, but rather an attitude on the part of those who have practiced it, which has not altered but continued into the present. While art has gone through such phases as Modernism, Revisionism, Pluralism, and Post-Modernism, photography has been continuous, binding the nineteenth and twentieth centuries together in an even flow of image making.

The incorporation of photography into art history, a recent development, has led to a greater understanding of representation and the modern period. However, many fundamental issues in the history of photography remain to be investigated in a clear, methodical, sensitive manner, particularly nineteenth-century photography. The inclusion of the history of photography in the history of art can reflect nothing less than a broadening understanding of the complexities of photography, its personalities, stylistic developments, patronage, and dynamic ability to express the spirit of this century.

Currently, a number of artists have returned to representation in an effort to restore it to the respectability it once enjoyed, but that effort has not yet succeeded. If photography is observed in the light of its intellectual power, content, and values, there can be little doubt that those artists who have returned to the more academic modes of representation have been greatly assisted by what photography has to offer.

The advent of photography has awakened in us the desire for a new reality, different from that supplied by painting, sculpture, and drawing. Still photography, television, and cinema have freed our minds from many traditional art values and given us a new way of seeing and looking. Physical reality is presented to us directly, free of the artist's interpretation, free of his will imposed upon that reality. This inherent ability of the camera to outline the external world, as well as the artist's internal one, has opened a gap in art that painting and sculpture have not been able to close or fill. Each scientific advance made, documented, or photographed tends to increase the desire for fact, not fiction. Proofs of what we cannot see or imagine, given to us by the photograph, supported by accurate scientific investigation, has led us to believe that our lives are more comfortable, that we are better informed, that we are people of the twenty-first century.

As our political, economic, and environmental situations grow more complex and science looks as though it is our only hope for the future, painting and sculpture appear less important, unable to supply the needs of contemporary society. Painting and sculpture seem to have lost their impetus and their sense of direction. This attitude may be a reflection of what many feel is their inadequacy to do anything much about the growing threat to existence itself. As we are surrounded by difficult realities now and in the future, and conservation of our natural resources presses in on our consciousness, the traditional art forms appear as something of an extravagance, having little to do with the way in which we now see.

The styles of all periods of art in the past were partly formed by political, economic, social, and technological phenomena, and these forces interacting with one another also affected the way in which each individual perceived and conducted himself within his environment. Furthermore, the fundamental way each person looked at, and saw, art was specific to the period in which it was produced. We cannot in any way see the art produced during the Italian Renaissance as the people of that period did. Still photography, cinema, and television have induced a slow but certain change in our way of seeing. This entirely mechanical method of image production has replaced what painting and sculpture supplied in the past and has been accepted almost without question. But more important, it has effectively changed our concepts and expectations of art. Presently, the entire concept of art, as collectable or not, cannot meet the expectations founded in a society dependent on mechanically produced images. Although there have been efforts by a number of artists to cross over into the production of mechanical images, known as Soft Ware, to meet the obvious growing interest in mechanical images, Soft Ware was quick to rise, fall, and be forgotten. Quite simply for the present, expectations are not so much a desire for representation as for realism, or, more to the point, a symbol of physical reality with meaning to the individual observer. To a degree, "regional art" has touched on this theme lightly and met with great enthusiasm and acceptance by the public. But "regional art" misses slightly by an overemphasis on the handmade look. No doubt these regional artists are beginning to recognize that the public has grown tired of the inaccessibility of formalist art.

Apparent in the variety of photographic approaches at this moment is a noticeable move toward color, some of it on a large scale, such as the more recent work of Lucas Samaras. But for many of these practitioners of color photography, the chromatic harmonies of the external world have been ignored in favor of photographic color technology, which can only obscure the realities so well articulated by earlier photography. Perhaps the current demand for realism will facilitate color prospects with an alignment to the emotional, expressive, symbolic truths already firmly placed in photographic history. Doubtless there are those photographers who have made decisions with materials, exploring color technologies without ignoring the fundamental truths established early in the history of photography.

Photography's past, present, and, quite possibly, its future are joined together by an unconditioned, absolute certainty in the reality of life evidenced in each photograph. This inherent quality of photography is fundamental to the photographic process, from the camera to the photograph. The concrete reality of life is ascertained by photography's quasi-scientific, artistic nexus. Rather than making the observer of photographs a bystander, a spectator of life, excluding him (as has been suggested in critical analyses of photography), the photograph has, in reality, worked the other way around. For the photographer and observer, the photograph is an acknowledgment, a cognition of life, excluding doubts. Photography is the personification of the modern ideal, an absolute affirmation of the successful marriage of science and art, forming a tool of great potential for expressive means in a new age of exactitude, when experimentation, calculation, and method have become part of human experience. It is a medium in which clarity of thought and vision may reveal itself with absolute immediacy as in no other time in the entire history of art.

Rather than existing as an intrusion into our lives, photography has shown that it can be part of the homogeneous, scientifically oriented period as one method by which any artist may expound clearly and unequivocally ideas that are germinal to his work and which may become an integral part of our lives. Ontologically, photography exemplifies the process of bringing idea into existence, perception (including the senses) to physical image (the photograph). It is a tool that can assist in exploring the nature of material things and differentiate between matter and the nature of the human mind guided by human intervention. It is a device that can encourage participation in life by example, through the photographer's reason or intuition.

The turning point for photography now and for the future does not inevitably depend on further technological advances in the medium, nor is it centered on now-existent equipment. Empirically, photography has demonstrated the supremacy of subject over object, ideal over medium, freedom over discipline, and individual consciousness transcendent through personal order. A priority for the future of photography is the specific autonomy it has achieved without separating itself from the other arts, and the unshakable certainty that this medium can substantiate individual will. As an art form specific to our time, it has revealed individual and environmental truths without the necessity for justifications. As a universal language, photography has built from its very beginning a freethinking tradition of action of which individual thought, expression, and viewpoint have always been an integral part. The monolithic history of photography, free of fragmentation by movements, is a realm of revelation in which unlimited freedom of expression and will celebrates humankind. Humanity in all its aspects past, present, and future is the single transcendent goal of this medium.

Let us end our consideration of photography as we began, with an observation by Aristotle, a master of perception and observation, as true today as when it was written over two thousand years ago.

"Of all the wonders of the universe, man is still the greatest of them all."

NOTES TO THE TEXT

Introduction

1. R. H. M. Elwes, *The Chief Works of Benedict De Spinoza* (London: Bell and Hyman, 1889), p. 22. Used by permission.

Chapter 1

1. All quotations are from Nathan Lyons, *Photographers on Photography* (Englewood Cliffs, N.J.: Prentice-Hall, 1966), pp. 15, 22, 96, 40, 168, 106.

Chapter 2

1. Rudolf Arnheim, *Visual Thinking* (Berkeley and Los Angeles: University of California Press, 1971), pp. 20, 21. Used by permission.
2. James Gibson, *The Senses Considered as Perceptual Systems* (New York: Houghton Mifflin, 1950), p. 21. © 1966 by Houghton Mifflin Company. Used by permission.
3. Arnheim, *Visual Thinking*, pp. 21, 22.
4. Gibson, *The Senses Considered as Perceptual Systems*, p. 133.
5. Aaron Scharf, *Art and Photography* (Baltimore: Penguin Press, 1968–69), p. 310.
6. Arnheim, *Visual Thinking*, p. 27.
7. Lyons, *Photographers on Photography*, p. 96.
8. *Ibid.*, p. 81.
9. Gibson, *The Senses Considered as Perceptual Systems*, p. 38.
10. *Ibid.*, p. 82.
11. *Ibid.*, p. 129.
12. Floris Neususs, *Photography as Art: Art as Photography* (Kassel: Fotoforum, 1977), p. 57.
13. Gibson, *The Senses Considered as Perceptual Systems*, p. 130.
14. E. H. Gombrich, *Art and Illusion* (Princeton: Princeton University Press, 1960), p. 86.

Chapter 3

1. Edward MacCurdy, *The Notebooks of Leonardo da Vinci* (New York: Braziller, 1955), p. 947.
2. Lyons, *Photographers on Photography*, p. 37.
3. Andy Grundberg, *New York Times*, February 28, 1982, sec. 2, p. 21, col. 1.
4. John Szarkowski, *Windows and Doors* (New York: Museum of Modern Art, 1978), p. 24.
5. Lyons, *Photographers on Photography*, p. 167.

Chapter 7

1. MacCurdy, *The Notebooks of Leonardo da Vinci*, p. 983.
2. *Ibid.*, p. 949.
3. Siegfried Kracauer, *Theory of Film* (New York: Oxford University Press, 1960), p. 230.
4. Rudolf Arnheim, *Film as Art* (New York: Oxford University Press, 1957), p. 230.
5. Kracauer, *Theory of Film*, pp. 289, 299.
6. Paul Goldberger, *New York Times*, March 28, 1982, sec. 2, p. 59, col. 1. © 1982 by The New York Times Company. Reprinted by permission.
7. Scharf, *Art and Photography*, p. 310.
8. Daniel Mendelowitz, *A History of American Art* (New York: Holt, Rinehart and Winston, 1980), p. 509.
9. Anna Kisselgoff, *New York Times Magazine*, March 28, 1982, p. 13, col. 1.

Chapter 8

1. Frederick Hartt, *Art* (New York: Abrams, 1976), vol. II, p. 424.
2. John Reuter, *"After the Fact"* statement in exhibition at the Clarence Kennedy Gallery, Cambridge, Mass., 1980.
3. *Ibid.*

BIBLIOGRAPHY

ALBERS, JOSEF. *Interaction of Color.* New Haven: Yale University Press, 1963.

ALLOWAY, LAWRENCE. *Photo-Realism.* New York: Serpentine Gallery Catalogue, 1973.

ARANSON, HARVARD H. *History of Modern Art.* New York: Abrams, 1968.

ARNHEIM, RUDOLF. *Art and Visual Perception.* Berkeley: University of California Press, 1974.

_____. *Film as Art.* Berkeley: University of California Press, 1957.

_____. *Toward a Psychology of Art.* Berkeley: University of California Press, 1966.

_____. *Visual Thinking.* Berkeley: University of California Press, 1969.

ATKINSON, THOMAS. *Man Ray.* Milwaukee: Milwaukee Art Center Catalogue, 1973.

BACA, MURTHA. *Man Ray.* Woodbury, N.Y.: Barron's, 1980.

BASSHAM, BEN. *Napoleon Sarony.* Kent, Ohio: Kent State University Press, 1978.

BAZIN, ANDRÉ. *What is Cinema?* Berkeley and Los Angeles: University of California Press, 1967.

BERGER, PAUL L. *A Rumor of Angels.* New York: Doubleday, 1969.

BERNARD, BRUCE. *Photodiscovery.* New York: Abrams, 1980.

BOYLE, ANDREW. *Spinoza's Ethics.* New York, N.J.: Dutton, reprinted 1970.

BROWN, THEODORE M. *The Photographs of Margaret Bourke-White.* Greenwich, Conn.: New York Graphic Society, 1972.

CAMPBELL, BRYN. *Exploring Photography.* New York: Hudson Hills Press, 1979.

CHASE, LINDA. *Hyperrealism.* New York: Rizzoli International, 1975.

CLEMENTS, BEN, AND DAVID ROSENFELD. *Photographic Composition.* New York: Van Nostrand Reinhold, 1974.

COBURN, ALVIN LANGDON. *Coburn.* London: Faber and Faber, 1966.

COKE, VAN DEREN. *The Painter and the Photograph* (Rev. ed.). Albuquerque: University of New Mexico Press, 1972.

COLOMBO, ATTILIO. *Fantastic Photography.* New York: Pantheon, 1979.

CRAVEN, GEORGE M. *Object and Image.* Englewood Cliffs, N.J.: Prentice-Hall, 1975.

CRONE, RAINER. *Andy Warhol.* New York and Washington: Prager, 1970.

CURL, DAVID. *Photocommunication.* New York: Macmillan, 1979.

DAIX, PIERRE. *La Vie De Peintre De Pablo Picasso.* Paris, France: Editions Du Seuil, 1977.

DUNCAN, DAVID DOUGLAS. *Picasso's Picassos.* New York: Harper, Graber, 1961.

EHRENZWEIG, ANTON. *The Psychoanalysis of Artistic Vision and Hearing.* London: Sheldon Press, 1953. Reprinted 1965, 1975.

ELWES, R. H. M. *The Chief Works of Benedict De Spinoza.* London: Bell and Hyman, 1889.

FELDMAN, EDMUND B. *The Artist.* Englewood Cliffs, N.J.: Prentice-Hall, 1982.

FISHER, DENNIS, AND CALVIN F. NODINE. *Perception and Pictorial Representation.* New York: Praeger, 1979.

FLACK, AUDREY. *Photo-Realism.* New York: A. N. Adams, 1981.

FORTINI, F. *Man Ray.* Venice: Alfieri Edizioni D'Arte, La Biennale Di Venezia, 1977.

FRANK, STEVEN. *Diane Arbus.* Millerton, N.Y.: Aperture, 1972.

GIBSON, JAMES J. *The Senses Considered as Perceptual Systems.* New York: Houghton Mifflin, 1966.

_____. *The Perception of the Visual World.* New York: Houghton Mifflin, 1950.

GIEDION, SIGFRIED. *Space, Time and Architecture: The Growth of a New Tradition.* Cambridge, Mass.: Harvard University, 1967.

GIRSBERGER, H. *Le Corbusier.* New York: George Wittenborn, Inc., 1966.

GOETHE, JOHANN WOLFGANG VON. *Theory of Colors.* New York: Van Nostrand Reinhold, 1971.

GOMBRICH, ERNST HANS. *Art and Illusion.* New York: Phaidon Press, 1960.

GOODRICH, LLOYD. *Eakins.* Exhibition Catalogue. National Gallery of Art, The Art Institute of Chicago, The Philadelphia Museum of Art, 1961.

GOSLING, NIGEL. *Nadar.* New York: Knopf, 1976.

GOWING, LAWRENCE T. *Imagination and Reality.* Garden City, N.Y.: Doubleday, 1966.

HAAS, EUGENE. *Reflections.* New York: Holt, Rinehart and Winston, 1978.

HAENLEIN, CARL ALBRECHT. *Dada Photographie Und Photocollage.* Hanover, Germany: Gesellschaft, 1979.

HARTT, FREDERICK. *Art.* New York: Abrams, 1976.

HAUS, ANDREAS. *Moholy-Nagy.* Munich: Schimer/Mosel, 1978.

HENLE, MARY. *Documents of Gestalt Psychology.* Berkeley and Los Angeles: University of California Press, 1961.

HILL, PAUL, AND THOMAS COOPER. *Dialogue with Photographers.* New York: McGraw-Hill Ryerson, 1979.

HILLER, DAVID B. *Victorian Studio Photography.* New York: Godine, 1976.

HOCHBERG, JOSEF HANS ERNST. *Art, Perception, Reality.* Baltimore: Johns Hopkins University Press, 1972.

————. *Perception.* Englewood Cliffs, N.J.: Prentice-Hall, 1964.

ITTEN, JOHANNES. *The Art of Color.* New York: Reinhold, 1961.

JACOBS, LEWIS. *The Emergence of Film Art.* New York: Hopkinson and Blake, 1979.

JACOBUS, LEE A. *Aesthetics and the Arts.* New York: McGraw-Hill, 1968.

JANSON, HORST WOLDMAR. *History of Art.* New York: Abrams, 1969.

JOHNSON, HERBERT. *Photo Synthesis.* Ithaca, N.Y.: Herbert F. Johnson Museum of Art, 1979.

JOHNSON, LINCOLN. *Film.* New York: Holt, Rinehart and Winston, 1973.

JULLIAN, PHILIPPE. *de Meyer.* New York: Knopf, 1976.

JUNG, CARL GUSTAV. *Man and His Symbols.* New York: Doubleday, 1969.

KAHMEN, VOLKER. *Fotografie als Kunst.* Tübingen: Verlag Ernst Wasmuth, 1972.

KARSH, YOUSUF. *Portraits of Greatness.* New York and London: Thomas Nelson and Sons, 1960.

KEPES, GYORGY. *The Visual Arts Today.* Middletown, Conn.: Wesleyan University Press, 1960.

————. *Language of Vision.* Chicago: Paul Theobald and Co., 1944.

KNOBLER, NATHAN. *Sign, Image, Symbol.* New York: Braziller, 1966.

KOFFKA, KURT. *Principles of Gestalt Psychology.* New York: Harcourt Brace, 1935.

KOZLOFF, MAX. *Photography and Fascination.* Danbury, N.H.: Addison House, 1979.

KRACAUER, SIEGFRIED. *Theory of Film.* New York: Oxford University Press, 1960.

KUHNS, WILLIAM, AND ROBERT STANLEY. *Exploring the Film.* Dayton, Ohio: Pflaum, 1968.

LE CORBUSIER. *Towards a New Architecture.* London: John Rodker, 1931.

————. *Le Corbusier.* New York: Wittenborn and Company, 1966.

LIFAR, SERGE. *Ma Vie.* Paris: Rene Julliard, 1965.

LINKSZ, ARTHUR. *An Essay on Color Vision.* New York: Grune and Stratton, 1964.

LISTA, GIOVANNI. *Futurist Photography.* New York: Art Journal, Winter, 1981, pp. 358–364.

LOWENFELD, VIKTOR. *Creative and Mental Growth.* New York: Macmillan, 1970.

LUCE, HENRY. *Alfred Eisenstaedt.* New York: Penguin Books, 1980.

LYONS, NATHAN. *Photographers on Photography.* Englewood Cliffs, N.J.: Prentice-Hall, 1966.

MacCURDY, EDWARD. *The Notebooks of Leonardo da Vinci.* New York: Braziller, 1955.

MADDOW, BEN. *Faces.* Boston: New York Graphic Society, 1977.

MATEJKA, LADISLAV, AND IRWIN TITUNIK. *Semiotics of Art.* Cambridge, Mass.: M.I.T. Press, 1976.

MAURIBER, SAUL. *Portraits: The Photography of Carl Van Vechten.* Indianapolis, Ind.: Bobbs-Merrill, 1978.

MEISS, MILLARD. *The Painter's Choice.* New York: Harper and Row, 1976.

MENDELOWITZ, DANIEL MARCUS. *A History of American Art.* New York: Holt, Rinehart and Winston, 1970.

MERLEAU-PONTY, MAURICE. *Penomenologie De la Perception.* New York: Routledge and Paul, 1970.

MILLER, RICHARD. *Brassai: The Secret Paris of The 30's.* New York: Pantheon, 1976.

MOZLEY, ANITA VENTURA. *American Photography: Past into Present.* Seattle: Washington Press, 1976.

MUNSELL, ALBERT HENRY. *A Grammar of Color.* New York: Munsell Color Co., 1925.

NEUSUSS, FLORIS MICHAEL. *Photography as Art: Art as Photography.* Gesamthoschschule Kassel: Fotoforum, 1977.

NEWHALL, BEAUMONT. *Herbert Bayer.* New York: Museum of Modern Art, 1938.

————. *The History of Photography.* New York: Museum of Modern Art, 1964.

NORI, CLAUDE. *French Photography.* New York: Pantheon, 1979.

PADGETTE, PAUL. *The Dance Photography of Carl Van Vechten.* New York: Schirmer, 1981.

PANOFSKY, ERWIN. *Idea: A Concept in Art Theory.* Columbia, S.C.: University of South Carolina Press, 1968.

PARKER, OLIVIA. *Signs of Life.* Boston: David R. Godine, 1978.

PARKER, WILLIAM E. *On the Recent Photography of Siegfried Halus.* Millerton, N.Y.: Aperture, 1981.

PAROLA, RENE. *Optical Art: Theory and Practice.* New York: Reinhold, 1976.

PENROSE, ROLAND. *Man Ray.* London: Thames and Hudson, 1975.

PFISTER, HAROLD FRANCIS. *Facing the Light.* Washington, D.C.: Portrait Gallery of the Smithsonian Institution Press, 1978.

PLOWDEN, DAVID. *Commonplace.* New York: The Chatham Press, 1974.

POLLACK, PETER. *Picture History of Photography.* New York: Abrams, 1969.

PORTER, FAIRFIELD. *Thomas Eakins.* New York: Braziller, 1959.

PROKOPOFF, S. S. *Against Order.* Philadelphia: Catalogue, Institute of Contemporary Art. University of Pennsylvania, 1970.

RANK, OTTO. *Art and the Artist: Creative Urge and Personality Development.* New York: Tudor, 1932.

READ, HERBERT EDWARD. *Art and Alienation.* New York: Viking Press, 1969.

RHODE, ERIC. *A History of the Cinema.* New York: Hill and Wang, 1976.

ROSENBERG, HAROLD. *Avedon Portraits.* New York: McGraw-Hill Ryerson, 1976.

————. *The De-definition of Art.* New York: Collier Books, Division of Macmillan Publishing Co., 1972.

ROTHBERG, A. *The Unconscious and Creativity.* New York: Columbia University Press, 1978.

SAFF, D., AND SACIOLOTTO, D. *Printmaking History and Process.* New York: Holt, Rinehart and Winston, 1978.

SAMARAS, LUCAS. *Samaras Album.* New York: Whitney Museum of American Art and Pace Editions, 1971.

SCHAPIRO, MEYER. *Modern Art 19th and 20th Centuries.* New York: Braziller, 1978.

————. *Vincent Van Gogh.* New York: Abrams, 1950.

SCHARF, AARON. *Art and Photography.* Baltimore: Penguin Press, 1968–69.

SEYMOUR, CHARLES, JR. *Dark Chamber and Light-Filled Room: Vermeer and the Camera Obscura.* New York: Art Bulletin, 1964, vol. 46, pp. 323–332.

SHEARMAN, JOHN. *Mannerism.* Baltimore: Penguin Press, 1967.

SMEETS, RENE. *Signs, Symbols and Ornaments.* New York: Van Nostrand Reinhold, 1975.

SOMMER, ROBERT. *Personal Space.* Englewood Cliffs, N.J.: Prentice-Hall, 1969.

STRELOW, LISELOTTE. *Portraits.* Bonn, Germany: Rheinisches Landesmuseum, 1977.

SZARKOWSKI, JOHN. *Callahan.* New York: Aperture Books in Association with the Museum of Modern Art, 1975.

————. *Looking at Photographs.* New York: Museum of Modern Art, 1973.

————. *Mirrors and Windows.* New York: Museum of Modern Art, 1978.

VYGOTSKY, L. S. *The Psychology of Art.* Cambridge, England: Trans-Scripts Technica, M.I.T. Publishers.

WEBSTER, J. C. *The Technique of Impressionism.* New York: Art Journal, Nov. 1944, vol. 4, pp. 3–22.

WHITE, JOHN. *The Birth and Rebirth of Pictorial Space.* Boston: Boston Book and Art Shop, 1967.

WITTKOWER, RUDOLF. *Architectural Principles in the Age of Humanism.* New York: Random House, 1965.

INDEX